Imperialism and the National Question

This title is one of a series published to commemorate the centenary of V. I. Lenin's death. The others are as follows:

The State and Revolution, V. I. Lenin

The Lenin Scenario, Tariq Ali
Lenin's Childhood, Isaac Deutscher
Not by Politics Alone: The Other Lenin, edited by Tamara Deutscher

Imperialism and the National Question

V. I. Lenin

Introduction by
Ruth Wilson Gilmore

VERSO
London • New York

The text we have used in this edition is from the
Marxist Internet Archive, available at marxists.org.

This paperback edition first published by Verso 2024
© Verso 2024
Introduction © Ruth Wilson Gilmore 2024
All rights reserved
The moral rights of the author have been asserted
1 3 5 7 9 10 8 6 4 2

Verso
UK: 6 Meard Street, London W1F 0EG
US: 388 Atlantic Avenue, Brooklyn, NY 11217
versobooks.com

Verso is the imprint of New Left Books

ISBN-13: 978-1-80429-271-6
ISBN-13: 978-1-80429-273-0 (US EBK)
ISBN-13: 978-1-80429-272-3 (UK EBK)

British Library Cataloguing in Publication Data
A catalogue record for this book is available from the British Library

Library of Congress Cataloging-in-Publication Data
A catalog record for this book is available from the Library of Congress

Typeset in Minion Pro by MJ & N Gavan, Truro, Cornwall
Printed and bound by CPI Group (UK) Ltd, Croydon CR0 4YY

Contents

Introduction: The Soviets and Abolition

Ruth Wilson Gilmore

1. Looks Like Lenin

Lenin was present in my early consciousness of politics and communism: the Soviets and 'us'. In this instance, 'us' was some combination of Negro peoples – soon to become Black in the US – who were involved in the post–WWII round of emancipation. Universalist and internationalist in ambition, this movement linked up and shared inspiration and analysis with global anti-imperial liberation movements. The weapon of theory, as we understood it, was meant to both guide and to respond to action. We had to repeatedly assess our own resources. Was anything consistently reliable? We were constantly debating and acting on our insights about how to fight, which included making decisions about what we were fighting. In other words, the struggles, and the people who fought them, developed constantly – driven by the ongoing effort to know the dynamic objects of our antagonism. We wanted to win.

In order to evade being absorbed – formally emancipated – into a social reality that would perpetuate the domination that generations had organised to undo, we had to not only 'resist' culturally and politically but also build our awareness of organised violence as an ensemble of activities impeding abolition in general. This ensemble of activities turns every 'what' into a 'where' because violence is always a spatial practice that produces and defines territories, peoples, mobility, possibility.

If capitalism reached its highest stage at the beginning of the twentieth century, it surely hasn't run out of energy. Capitalism saving capitalism from capitalism is a way to think about the mode of production's necessary dynamic through which it realises its inherent imperative. Whatever problem production or accumulation runs up against, innovation appears to resolve. Technological and financial barriers to entry enable capitals that innovate with particular time-space felicity to dominate and eventually monopolise. What Lenin noticed in thinking about finance, monopoly, and imperialism is akin to what many kinds of intellectuals throughout modernity keep noticing too: tools for innovation comprise technologies of many kinds – productive but also political, military, murderous. There is no singular rationality of power, as Herman Bennett reminds us.

When Rosie Warren asked me if I'd like to write something to recognise the centenary of Lenin's death, I thought it would be a great opportunity to share what thinking with Lenin might help us see as we make our way in this unrolling present. This introduction offers a meditation on why we should read this collection of Lenin's writing today. What do these writings show us about theory breaking into practice, and how might the politics explained or implied in these writings inform our analytical and practical grasp of what is to be done now? How are the two key concepts – imperialism and self-determination – explored here by Lenin relevant? The organised violence of imperialism continues to stalk the earth in the form of its fleshly and ghostly remnants – accumulated underdevelopment – and viscerally in contemporary unequal relations of power that rush value upward, by way of elites, to the 'economic north', wherever the owners might reside. But in its muscular liveliness, self-determination hasn't disappeared from the earth's surface, nor wholly been absorbed into the system of nation-states mostly disciplined by debt and developmentalism.

We should read as though we are thinking with Lenin in his time while also thinking about the struggle at hand, so that Marxism's contemporary practicality doesn't get lost. This practicality cannot be overstated, even if the frenzy of many debates obscures underlying necessity. As an organiser active during the 1930s in New York City explained, 'We went out every night after supper to knock on strangers' doors. I'd say "I am from the Communist Party and I am here to help you solve your problems."'

In contrast to such theoretically guided practicality, a good deal of mainstream Western Marxism seems culturally shaped by a quest for truth revealed on the page. That might be because so many of its adherents are themselves born-again historical materialists. Their fundamentalism is barely Methodist (though method plays a big role in the confusion), but rather more Calvinist. The sober assessment of how the world works casts a shadow dividing the elect from the rest in austere dismissal of politically meaningful conditions of existence and analytically powerful categories of analysis. More than communism, it would seem, the specter of Weber haunts the West.

There was always something about Lenin, to my youthfully vigorous mind, that was other than the West. This was due in part to reassuring if woeful presumptions about physique – eyelids, cheekbones, and other aftermaths of the racist 'science' of humanity that raged as Ulyanov came of age. But something else, too – less easy to confess but viscerally there – a peculiarly not-liberal universalism that offered theoretical muscle for the struggle at hand as something we all could and should exercise. One night in the late 1960s, during the point-counterpoint of assassinations and riots, I wandered through town looking for my father in hope of a ride home. He'd been invited to speak at a teach-in, one of those noisy aftermaths to the din of police and fire and sirens and bullets and protest, in which people try to craft sentences out of crisis and churn. He had street cred. Whatever he said, though most certainly in the style of harangue, would have tightly followed the locally fatal contours of power and difference. He would have insisted on how they at once originated from *and* radiated in dynamic connection to liberation struggle in general. Skipping that talk, I found my father's car with the event flyer stuck under the windshield wiper – his name circled, annotated: 'Looks like Lenin.'

2. 'That's Life'

What a fine thing our Congress is. Opportunities for open fighting and opinions expressed. Tendencies revealed. Groups defined. Hands raised. A decision taken. A stage passed through. That's what I like. That's life. It's something different from the endless wearying intellectual discussions

which finish not because people have solved the problem, but simply because
they have got tired of talking.

                                                                  – Lenin 1903

Two major themes unfold in these texts. In the *Imperialism* pamphlet, Lenin proposes a broad understanding of why and how capitalist competition, rather than developing the productive forces for humanity to flourish, degenerates into monopoly and war. The argument turns on a key phrase summarising the ongoing result: 'partition and repartition'. In the various debates on self-determination, Lenin is at pains to specify how imperialism's inbred contradiction – materialised in the form of oppressed nations themselves – might emerge and align as social forces capable of interrupting imperialism's tendency towards war and extraction, and thereby set human history onto a different, though not final, path. Much has been made of the co-constitutive interdependencies – the fundamental contradiction, if you will – between 'imperialism' on the one hand and 'self-determination' on the other. In this introduction we'll meditate on how Lenin's analysis helps us reflect on specifically grounded examples, not as remnants of what might have been but as energetic possibilities arising from refreshed struggle today.

The twentieth-century liberation movements remain unfinished although not thoroughly vanquished. Through organised intensity in the broader context of anti-colonial revolution, the Marxism of the Third World reconfigured a good deal of the planet's social reality. These revolutionaries never lacked Lenin even as they frequently and deliberately reworked the thinking proposed from capitalism's rapidly industrialising imperial periphery – Russia. They did so to address problems of how to make and sustain freedom elsewhere. The Third World's emancipatory interregnum wasn't peaceful, serially sliced open by assassinations and coups intended to turn even moderate attempts at socialism back towards a capitalist track.

And yet with all the suffering, for a few decades, broadly speaking, humanity flourished. The planet's human population has grown from about 1.4 billion in 1870, the year Lenin was born, to about 8 billion today. The most dramatic year-on-year increases were during the interregnum, tapering off since the counter-revolution cumulatively took hold. Are people tired of making more people? Some countries appear to have this issue. Are people lacking adequate nutrition again as they were before and during the two great imperial wars? Yes, although not everywhere. We see here basic features of today's predicaments, elaborated through globalisation on the one hand and ecological disaster on the other.

More than a century's dust has settled since Lenin conceived and wrote these texts. The world as we find it has not resolved the contradictions that hold these writings together – domination confronts self-determination, while economic territory is key to our understanding of the social realities in and through which struggle occurs. A contemporary, spirited, frequently ill-tempered debate asks whether the concept of imperialism – Lenin's or a fresher version of it – offers necessary insight into today's dynamics of domination. I lean towards 'yes': the combination of institutional tools for transferring surplus from the 'economic south' (wherever it is) to the 'north' (whoever they are) has become more elaborate, yes, but is still tied together by the effective control of military, technology (productive and financial), money, property, and most people's ability to move about or stay put. The 'no' side insists that contemporary firefights should be against national bourgeoisies that were never disempowered, either in a peaceful transition to socialism or by other means. Given how frequently such national bourgeoisies have depended on overt and covert support to interrupt redistribution, restricting interpretive energy to the nation-state scale obscures wider forces articulating through those bourgeoisies, whose agency is not in doubt even if their autonomy is, like all autonomy, only ever relative.

But relative to what? Here is where Lenin's impressive exploration of 'self-determination' helps us to think hard about what now contours economic territory as it stretches across borders and nestles within them. If self-determination a century ago appeared to communism's most successful strategist as an urgent social energy confronting imperialism within and across regions, his care in specifying context strongly militates against the notion of any narrowly identitarian 'nation' as miraculously poised to do battle. Here many raise M. N. Roy's 1920 Comintern debate with Lenin as transformative for Lenin's understanding. And yet political analysis concerning the possible participants in revolutionary formation characterise Lenin's pieces that predate that debate; the doubt that shaped those pieces helped make the Comintern debate possible. Consider a wider context: Lenin, Roy, and the toilers of the East (who actually hailed from many directions of the planet) were talking about self-determination while apologists and hacks, alongside the occasional serious scholar, were writing for organs like the *Journal of Race Development* and otherwise figuring out how to make the world safe for capitalism. Stated differently, the analytical preconditions for the 1920 revision were already present because the one abiding characteristic of Lenin's thought was that it was open – in rehearsal rather than reprint. This is a brief for Roy and for Lenin, and a lesson for all of us now. The purpose here is not to hold Lenin up as immune to error – that would be plain stupid – but rather to ask ourselves how better to think systematically and strategically and collectively, in part by listening carefully, to accomplish what we came to do.

If we can imagine that the struggle is over economic territory, including what happens to and on the land, our imaginative capacity demands we understand that it's a beginning, not the end. We also know – whether thinking about self-determination or the exposition of consolidated, competing forces presented in the *Imperialism* pamphlet – that any territory has natural, cultural, political, and other interdependent characteristics. These characteristics, or 'endowments', include water and land and other tangible and intangible resources, as well as the presence of institutions through which people organise, derive meaning from, and improve their lives. This isn't a romantic point. 'Self-determination' from the communist perspective is shorthand for imagining these endowments marshalled by history's protagonists, and then finding that work as it actually happens to revise social reality. Therefore, part of the struggle is defining – becoming – history's protagonists, repeatedly. Relations of power, accumulated and expressed through social processes, determine the possibility, scope, and urgency of emancipatory struggle.

It is also the case that self-determination is vulnerable to capture by liberalism – especially liberalism's paternalistic embrace of group individualism, which itself is partly motivated out of fear of fascism and the absurd but sturdy belief that fascism can be domesticated. Stated differently, self-determination compels us to confront analytically and practically the actual substantive and formal initiatives through which it can, but hardly must, move towards openness. We will explore some examples shortly. But for now what's important is to contrast radical self-determination with liberalism's seduction, because the latter *at best* promises to enlarge already-existing social reality to accommodate a slight variation of what already exists, with predictably brutal effects for everyone abandoned at the margin of that reality.

Lenin proposed a century ago that the highest stage of capitalism took formal and substantive shape through imperialism, as competing polities, in the hunt to control economic territory, arrayed themselves for war on behalf of their domestic monopolies, with finance in the lead. The subsequent explosive backwash of Axis and Allied industrialised killing – colonialism's long-suffered genocide and environmental destruction inundating the core – may have signalled the end of twentieth-century wars among late modernity's last-standing imperialists. But this was by no means the end of imperialism or of powerful warmakers. Philosophers get cranky when concepts degenerate into metaphor, even if that's where concepts originate in the first place as energising capacities to think relationally about the world. Imperialism here is not a metaphor. The partition and repartition of the earth never ground to a halt, even if the great pressures that are externally determined cooperate and conflict differently to produce territories ripe for exploitation. The national bourgeoisies act on their own institutional behalf – becoming fabulously wealthy in the process – and meet demands that drain resources. Militaries lurk around the planet poised to enforce or interrupt value transfer, which is another way of saying that claims on resources do not redound without friction to those who live with or work them.

The expansive forces of organised violence, also perfected in public and private policing bodies, meet up alongside less apparently warlike yet still murderously destructive forces of international financial institutions, trade agreements, intellectual property, and NGOs. Together these forces insinuate the concertina wire of 'civil society' into fraying political fabric – 'abetted decline' – while pundits, as well as peoples who experience organised abandonment, decry failed or captured states. Such a constellation of forces appears to constitute 'imperialism' – neither more nor less naked than at the turn of the previous century, or the century before that or before that or before that. Monopolies matter, whether chartered or otherwise consolidated through protected competition. Monopolies have military and fiduciary seconds everywhere, even as extraction, appropriation, and the transfer of value to the coffers of the rich continue apace. They don't always win, but they rarely lose.

Who or what constitutes self-determination in these contexts? If the goal of creating or seizing a state is what 'self-determination' has meant, conceptually, what mediating movements headed in such a direction matter? In other words, does learning about discrete cases where the armature of sovereignty isn't a near goal distract from or build towards the need for big things? Might such learning show us ways of seeing, as it were, what 'the soviets plus electrification' might mean, in practice, today? Lenin noticed during the St Petersburg general strike something that surprised him: that the St Petersburg soviet would keep society going. This surprise shows there wasn't a set revolutionary blueprint. But something happened in the realm of becoming: profoundly social conviviality determined the political-subjective means for realising interim goals. This in turn showed how revolution is a fundamentally practical program even if the steps cannot all be plotted out in advance. 'We are from the Communist Party and we are here to help you solve your problems.' Let's leap.

The capacity to leap into an unknown that promises both terror and salvation is the foundation of Christian evangelical conversion. In the first decades of the twentieth century, while Lenin was writing these pieces and fomenting revolution, evangelism spread as it had a century earlier, and in the century before that. This indicates a general puzzle that interests me. Scholars of religion, historical-geographical materialists, and others who seek to grasp the complexities of subjectivity wonder what compels people to reinterpret abstract principles and reinvent themselves through that reinterpretation. Beyond the urgent need to assuage suffering (including Marx's inactivity and loneliness), evangelical millenarianism (again, as an example) features news of certain change. Adherents devote great subjective effort to imagining and embodying change in preparation for change, while hurtling towards the brink of an objectively irresistible unknown.

From time to time evangelical eruptions have, through organised activity and polemic, connected with various emancipatory movements that might fall under the aegis not narrowly of wage-worker class politics but also, expansively, abolitionism: they have worked towards embracing everybody in a territory of need. Now, it is true that throughout modernity the disciplining forces of religious hierarchy enabled capture, exploitation, subjugation, and transfer to realise value. And yet, the dialectics of moral value have also meant that even if explicitly faith-schooled to displace or pacify oppositional energy, people have socially fashioned something they could use for their own purpose from the symbolic and material resources at hand. And further, while this self-fashioning did not necessarily instigate capacities for creative aggression, it did, amidst immense spiritual diversity and syncretism, broaden and strengthen those capacities. Awareness brings examples to our attention. For instance, in 1906, when labor actions erupted across South Africa, Jehovah's Witnesses appeared ready to proselytise alongside secular agitators, and those who took up their pamphlets had, among other things, literacy in their collective arsenal. In other words – perhaps a central lesson from Lenin – learning is never an indifferent antithesis even if the dominant pedagogy intends conformity not rebellion.

And further, as we reflect on today's evangelical enthusiasm for harvesting souls – especially across the wide swathe of tropical landmass on either side of the equator – we are reminded that these terrains form part of the economic territory besieged by domestic, international, and transnational monopolies and their political, non-governmental, police, and militarised enablers. Social structures that enhance belonging make evangelism's appeal sensible when converts do not otherwise feel they can fulfill their purpose. This is because conversion elegantly becomes its own purpose. I put my finger on evangelism here to make a point that evangelism illustrates but does not remotely exhaust: purpose, rather than characteristics or interest, initiates and determines so much of political and social life. While religion, through dense systems of signification, appeals abstractly as few other social forces do, its felt practicality in relation to subjectivity – to becoming – suggests clues one might look for in building formations that are this-worldly in their orientation to relieve suffering and produce joy. Such this-worldly-ness, perhaps, is what radical self-determination always was making its way through, with 'nation' sometimes ascriptively real but also, importantly, a loose stand-in for a wide range of collectivities combined in excess of oppression yet undeniably consolidated by it. 'We are from the Communist Party and we are here to help you solve your problems.'

3. Economic Territory

Territory signifies political, social, cultural, and economic space in and through which activities comprising social reality unfold. Territories vary depending on what people do, as we shall see later. Extra-market as well as non-market activities are crucial. Anything in territories is vulnerable to becoming commodified, though not all relations are determined by commercial or labor processes. This vulnerability, potential or ongoing, makes territory 'economic' although it's never only that. Political and other forms of action constantly assert and test the boundedness and the dynamic content of territories. We are all participants in multiple territories while at the same time we embody, whatever our philosophical understanding of 'the individual' might be, 8 billion territories of selves. Schools and faith communities and labor processes and households and governments and sporting clubs and so many other institutions offer narrative coherence – or the theoretical and practical wherewithal to de-cohere. When an IFI or a monopoly agribusiness or brand drops in to sell debt or grab land, to license seeds or establish an 'offshore' factory, or to buy or sell primary, producer, or consumer goods, its capacity to realise the value it is organised to accumulate isn't a result of its monopoly-ness no matter how gargantuan its thirst for cash. Every capitalist relation has political and social characteristics. What forms do these take, and what capacities determine value's flow or stickiness? One thing is for sure: there's always got to be some mediating sovereign (somebody with the authority to dispense with life) somewhere to guarantee, for capitalism, private property as the primary value that shapes human activity. Stated differently, humans' creative energy isn't passively surrendered – not without the intervention of terror or love or some kind of 'moral espionage that restrains the very enthusiasm that sets it in motion'. And the energy is never wholly depleted, though people do get very tired.

Put this way, Lenin's analyses encourage us to approach the *multiplicity* of co-constitutive interdependencies that enliven the dynamics of social reality. This is the takeaway lesson of all social reproduction theory, and what underlies abolition as an ideology, system, and outcome. If the struggle for domination under capitalism consists of the struggle over territory *as economic* territory, then self-determination is *both* in dialectical antagonism to control from outside or above *and* replete with its own internal struggles, none of which has an automatic outcome, anti-capitalist or otherwise.

A century on, where does struggle to emancipate economic territory, by transforming it into something else, arise from or lead to? How might we recognise the social characteristics of such struggle today? There are still oppressed nations and national minorities; there are also the many lineaments of political-economic inequality that fall under the useful rubric of 'racial capitalism', although 'race' does not exhaust social differentiations so much as gesture emphatically in their absurdly heritable direction. We can all name efforts of old, new, and refreshed polities to establish self-governing states of their own – whether by seceding from former empires such as the UK or Spain or Turkey, or by carving pieces from already-existing postcolonial states from Bangladesh to Eritrea and beyond, plus the insistence by indigenous peoples throughout the Fourth World for Land Back, or Palestine's one- or two-state solution. Pulses of self-determining counter-partition haven't evaporated but rather continue to assert territorially-defined rights in the context of varied relative sovereignty. This is true whether the intention is to make value flow or stick, and the intention is heightened by symbolic no less than material determinations of authorised belonging.

4. Partition and Repartition

The three huge eruptions of capitalist modernity – colonialism, settler colonialism, and chattel slavery – threw people and places into motion characterised by intense friction that goes by different names: de-industrialisation, underdevelopment, genocide, racism. All these forces are part of imperialism rather than extra-imperial activities, because they are resolved through partition, repartition, war, and sorting and stacking people, places, and things.

Like any other border, partitions can be invisible and depthless – even if they are fortified with soldiers, landmines, towers, walls, and floodlights, or visible from space because practices of tillage or irrigation leave evidence that shows up as though defined by a cartographer's paintbox. Partition is definitive and transformative and can include (re)divisions of labor, changes in household regimes, gender relations and land use, conscriptions and expulsions, and movement of what is produced, how, and to what end. The workers in this story can be wage workers or direct producers or all the available labor that makes the productive labor possible. Local and regional power regimes, through inherited, seized, or comprador entailments, connect across space, enabling and disabling matter in motion. In other words, the division of people from control of the means of their own reproduction, and the division of space among capitals for the purpose of realising money, commodity, and productive good circulation, are aspects of partition and repartition.

Partitions distort and sometimes obliterate social reality. Emplotment gives definition and meaning to partition as the geometrical and narrative ordering of space. As a result of the multiple complexities inhering in any social reality, forces of domination renovate and make critical already-existing activity from without and within in order to assert symbolic as well as material order through the exercise of power and difference. When the purpose is to drain resources, power and difference couple to define and enforce through partition legal, cultural, bureaucratic, and discursive regimes – notably including discourses that materialise through differentiating humanity in biological or cultural terms. The reality is held together by the direct or indirect threat of organised violence, which acts both on behalf of whichever elites are in command and on its own behalf insofar as organized violence produces self-realising and self-aggrandising relatively autonomous institutions.

We can concentrate our attention on big things and global processes by considering two centuries of capital mobility and banking crises. They show a very peculiar thing: the few decades in which mobility and crises were low (around 1945–80) correspond to the decades during which, in fits and starts, people were making a decolonised future (the emancipatory interregnum we've already touched on). The brief period suggests, therefore, what incited counter-revolution, stated most generally as the thirst for cash. The assembled forces of counter-revolution – from outside and within the economic territories in question – figured out, through trial and error, how to use combinations of extra-economic as well as economic pressure to realise cash from property entitlements. The goal is always the same even if the means are organised differently – the capture of surplus as profit or interest, transfer, or rent. The unsteady process of capture, accumulated over time, sets the stage for where we are today: both how things are and how they might become different. The relations of power and difference have, over time, become more, not less, shadowed and herded by the forces of organised violence. A century on we cannot emphasise enough that the forces of austerity and its related enterprises of abandonment and depoliticisation have broadened and deepened inequality on a global scale.

In such a context, surpluses that drip or gush from matter in motion require barriers – we can still call them partitions – that determine the speed and direction of those flows; not only guardrails but also armed guards keep people from changing those flows. Here we encounter sites for contemporary struggles over economic territory that also reveal themselves as the never settled production of scale. As we shall see in the next section, power and difference do not automatically signal exploitation, precisely because solidarity arises to repurpose relations. In the process they become radically interdependent and thereby change the social reality of territory, slicing through the economic to produce life in battle against, while at the same time in excess of, capitalism, rehearsing what *becoming after* will be like.

The universal openness towards which Third World internationalism urged itself, in a contradiction that comes as no surprise, tended both to oppose and strengthen the power of partitions. In turn, partitions can be as likely to revive as to remedy the antagonisms history's protagonists keep slugging away at. But to repeat, in the brief period following the end of the old imperial order – punctuated as it relentlessly was by assassination and coup, and the steady imposition of structural adjustment – relatively encalmed economies enabled small-d development, delinked or not, that resulted in (among other things) the greatest year-over-year increases in the number of human lives. This suggests but does not prove that struggles over the territorial entailments of hierarchical relationships – many predating colonialism, and others emerging from the profound social distortions of colonialism and slavery – usefully put into question what self-determination should become as a project of universalising emancipation.

In other words, if the point of Marxism lies in anything it's figuring out communist philanthropy – the antagonistic contradiction to all other forms of philanthropy. There's no private allocation of the stolen social wage nor is there competitive application or status-restricted eligibility for public social wage reserves. Imagine abundance as an entitlement that binds us in radical interdependence. Mutual aid is a modest form of communist philanthropy, while the challenge is to imagine meeting needs and desires of strangers one can't touch or of despised people one might prefer not to be around. Here's where the otherworldly commitments of evangelism, as experiments in reinterpretation towards an inevitable future, come back to mind. The human capacity to imagine life otherwise inspired Marx and kept him pushing pen across paper as much as figuring out the mystifying contortions of capitalism. In fact, this imagining and analysis are one thing. And just as piecing together the globalising, shapeshifting forces of capitalism – of matter in motion – is important, so too is seeing how the concrete struggles, whether or not they actually recognise each other at any given time, articulate concrete points of possible solidarity. Think communist philanthropy as conviviality – a social goal as well as politically-subjective means to that goal. I'm thinking here of a story I read long ago about an eighteenth-century enslaved person who ran towards freedom. Her story reminds us that emancipation is more than a change of status, and that we frequently must try a different path even if it heightens the difficulty of arriving. The advertisement offering a bounty for her recovery noted that she knew river navigation. For that reason, and because she had friends in nearby farms or villages, her hunters warned she might 'bend her route' – not taking the shortest path across the partition between slavery and freedom, but rather following the route more likely to build her cadre.

5. Communist Philanthropy, or Scenes from Abolition's Soviets

The struggle to build cadres is real. We've noted that all territories have endowments, which only become 'economic' through social processes. Lots of forces combine in creating any given economic territory, while the grind of capitalist competition and consolidation recombines in, for example, gargantuan firms. Big things have big needs, including juridical and discursive partitions, death-fences labeled 'earned initiative' that surround the power difference of private property. They send out their militaries, their diplomats, their salesforces, their guards, to transform territories into reliably economic fonts of value. Foundations and NGOs participate in abandonment, to lessen the sting or hasten resistance's demise by shuttling energies off into 'female empowerment' or technical training – two examples of not bad things that become warped by organisations shielded from and sheltered by monopolies' imperial force. Brutally creative, capitalism makes and unmakes realities. The differentiated presence of people – who grow, move, make, care for or guard or kill people and things – highlights multiple aspects of social reality foregone or set aside in the process: home family, recreation, pleasure, beauty, belonging, conscription, exclusion, life. In other words, what Lenin outlined hasn't gone away, but rather propagated through a variety of institutional types that, guaranteed by organised violence, continue in collaboration and conflict to govern the world.

If the substantial features of the global economy have changed in order for capitalism to continue to flourish, what Lenin outlined in the debates on self-determination hasn't disappeared either but rather both diversified and strengthened, relying in shifting configurations, ever hardened on the anvil of war. War, like other forms of organised abandonment, insists that territories are full of historical protagonists rather than victims who fill undifferentiated spaces of extraction. The social grind of valorisation produces consciousness for direct producers, wage workers, wageless workers, long-distance migrants; those who journey and those who wait. And, as embodied territories of selves, humans reconfigure space-time through practicalities of self-determination, interrupting partitions while provisionally setting up new ones. There are reasons guards and military, no less than courts and police and international trade and patent agreements, saturate the social world with organised violence. In other words, economic territory is always ripe for picking – but by whom?

Contemporary abolition arose in creative antagonism to the widening scope of militarism, police, prisons, and punishment as all-purpose solutions to social problems. Wherever inequality is deepest, incarceration – and all the relations necessary to hold people against their will for part or all of their lives – is most prevalent. Inequality here isn't measured by income alone. Rather it indicates the capacity for people to use, creatively, the territorial endowments which form their social realities. Most modestly, the goal of social reproduction promises, as Gargi Bhattacharyya puts it, 'learning early in life and rest towards the end'. The organised abandonment that signifies repartitioned territory produces geographies where it takes more and more human and not human energy to keep lives and households together. Wherever organised abandonment occurs on the planet's surface, the composition of communities – not identical to labor forces – weighs heavily on a land that does not house or feed or employ or care for them. (It's useful to remember that the economic south is a condition of existence rather than a set of coordinates.) Political elites and those who line up with them agree that more police are the appropriate response to whatever social challenges arise. Police state socialists agree with this appraisal, confusing organised violence with the capacity to minimise vulnerability to harm – the latter abolitionist goal in stark contrast to a rush to punish harm more swiftly after it happens. The forces of organised violence frequently employ people who come from communities not altogether unlike those destined for brutal control. In fact, when the US Supreme Court recently outlawed affirmative action, turning back decades of minimal expansion of a liberal social reality to absorb difference into itself, the judges explicitly exempted the military from the prohibition. These complexities demand analytical fluency to sort them out.

Let's think through an example. The politics of policing are actually obvious. Take a truncheon. For a cop to be paid to use a truncheon to bust your head open means the truncheon maker had a contract to produce truncheons – not luncheons – which means a whole series of political decisions about the allocation of material and symbolic resources already steadied the cop's hand before she raised it. But also, in bringing it down she applied violence to create power for herself, for cops, for truncheon makers, for the process of resource allocation, for the government that runs on a platform of criminalisation to justify taxes to use the social wage for that purpose. And there's more: your head was there, beneath the falling truncheon, because an entire series of decisions or defeats over where your head might be or whether your life might be – the sum of organised abandonment – put the territory of your self beneath that truncheon. The weapon of theory doesn't neutralise the truncheon, but it shows how it got there, to your head, and therefore gives some clues about making the world otherwise.

Liberal economic nostrums such as 'sound finance' paper over the international financial institutions' structural adjustment of postcolonial and industrialising economies. Meanwhile, the intellectual authors and social agents of debt, special economic zones, transnational production establishments, and changes in land use, depend on policing – layers and layers, public and private – to discipline and get payment from denizens of territories wracked by the destructive tendencies of contemporary globalisation. Put differently, all the assassinations and coups and structural adjustment happened not despite anti-colonialism but in response to it. In other words, the contemporary power of, say, finance capital, isn't a distortion of good capitalism but rather a form the thirst for cash takes, successfully, to suck more cash out of the hands and pockets and accumulated value and collective futures of workers and their land and water and communities and time. Today's national mega-capitals, much discussed in recent years, arose thanks to neoliberalism as well as anti-anti-colonialism. They devour energy at home and abroad, but contrary to what some wish to argue, they are not getting in the way of 'good capitalism'; they are what 'good capitalism' has become. Lenin, like Marx, was careful to avoid attributing systemic imperatives to individual preferences. Combining the ongoing transfer of value from the economic south to the global north, and the explosion of multicultural billionaires based in many polities, gives us a big picture of today's imperialism, still held together by the machinery of war, the proliferation of police, and the size of firms able to determine the fate of myriad small producers as well as industrial workers. Where and how then might one fight?

A decade ago, Aijaz Ahmad was trying to make sense out of recent events, noting the ongoing imaginative and practical energies of what he described as 'a massive experimentation with diverse ways and means of popular uprising until a revolutionary form is found that will be adequate to revolutions of the twenty-first century'. These movements, some already dispersed since he wrote, have been finding their way through a variety of structures that reverberate with Bolshevism, antifascism, and the mid-twentieth century emancipatory struggles across Asia, Africa, and Latin America.

Below are three examples that show us what internationalist emancipatory struggle looks like in territorial terms, suggesting how rescaled territory is an imperative for emancipatory struggle today. Emancipatory struggle tends towards realisation of communist philanthropy, demanding practical abolition for its achievement. The idea here is to think about these examples as resonant with Lenin's reflections on self-determination. Conceptual continuity moves through purpose, not characteristics, as Ahmad pointed out. In other words, our purpose is to consider how these movements constitute, with varying degrees of mutual awareness, political consciousness. How are collectivity and strategy built? Who travels in movements with constantly revised vision in order to share and connect strategy-deepening values?

First, in South Africa, houseless people occupy land and buildings that not only provide shelter but are the basis for self-governing communities. Ranging in size and complexity, from the Cissie Gool house in Cape Town where one thousand people live cooperatively in a former hospital, to the many self-built neighborhoods established by Abahlali baseMjondolo members in several provinces, these struggles over land use in urban and less urban situations underscore the politics of territory and the possibility of transforming territory from narrowly economic to fully social space. Interestingly enough, the people who initiated the Cissie Gool occupation were the hospital security guards who, laid off when the hospital closed, knew how to get inside. For people in Abahlali communities (which are particular expressions of the generally extensive self-built neighborhoods shaping peripheries of cities throughout the economic south today), the fight to be able to stay in the first place has evolved, over time, into struggles over how to compel municipal, provincial, and federal agencies to guarantee utilities and other infrastructure. These same governmental bodies have added specialised police, both public and private, to the forces of organised violence assigned to partition land from those who need it on behalf of those, including governments, who own it.

Second, in Brazil, the Movimento dos Trabalhadores Rurais Sem Terra (MST) (Landless Workers' Movement) has initiated building and land occupations with an expansive rural presence. The villages established at land occupations have generally become agriculturally productive, facing off against organised violence (vigilante, military) while growing organic food in the discontinuous places that in sum comprise the MST territory – surprisingly protected by the constitution's requirement that land fulfill its social purpose. The biggest producer of organic rice in Latin America, the MST shares knowledge with organisations and comrades from around the economic south – including indigenous unceded territory and Black farmers' small parcels in the US. Their green abolition differs markedly from green capitalism. The latter characterises land grabs across continents, in order to grow inputs for biofuels to power vehicles in the economic north. In an eerie echo of early twentieth-century notions of a labor aristocracy in the economic north, pension funds for North American public employees, teachers, and other nonprofit workers have been 'invested' in green capitalism under the rubric of 'social responsibility'. This in turn has provoked organising a now decade-long campaign for solidarity across the geometrically discontinuous but economically conjoined terrain of deferred compensation and debauched farmland, which builds internationally with others who are fighting against land grabs. Most of the world's agrarian workers (numbering around 2 billion according to the ILO) work as or for small producers, yet it is also true that in addition to international finance capitalism grabbing land under various pretexts, a small number of gargantuan firms buy and process agricultural inputs. The MST has figured out how to circumvent the imperial forces of agribusiness, although every day presents a fresh challenge to individuals, villages, and the logistics required for commercial routes.

Third, stretching in another way across the north and beyond, nurses in the US organised by the National Nurses United (NNU), many of whom are the descendants of or are themselves long-distance migrants, have been organising tirelessly to interrupt the stranglehold of transnational medical firms on themselves as workers, on the patients they care for, and on the communities where they live. By extension then, also included are the communities to which many long-distance migrants send remittances and also strategy-sharing solidarity with nurses who organise in distinct contexts to achieve similar goals elsewhere. In other words, this economic territory is dynamic and multifaceted. The hospitals spread around the planet, seeding establishments where the mix of organised abandonment and discretionary income means there's the possibility to transform a place into an economic territory selling exclusive healthcare. Meanwhile, in the US context, the NNU fights to secure free healthcare as a public good, so they don't have to put patients out on the street. While the NNU is not a political party, and there is great diversity of opinion and affiliation among the rank and file, some general features of the NNU's public asssertions are notable. First, their resolutions take on global issues including challenging militarism, police budgets, deportation, and the ongoing struggles for decolonisation in Palestine and elsewhere.

Further, the NNU is part of an organisation it helped to form called Global Nurses United (GNU) that includes unions in Brazil, India, and elsewhere. Their internationalism encourages the same sorts of coordinated direct action that characterises nurses' workplace and state-philanthropy-based militancy. For example, while US labor law requires labor actions to be directed against a particular establishment (the site where you work), nurses have brilliantly timed actions to stretch not only between different establishments, but also across different employers in a particular city or region. When it comes to internationalism, the NNU has featured as a plenary presenter a medical organiser from the economic south who described direct action to fight vaccine apartheid in terms of manufacturing doses without going through the labyrinthine and costly procedures of intellectual property rights or waivers. Interestingly, US-based big pharma has long outsourced manufacturing to lower wage areas, meaning the factories are or could become available for different purposes. Here we are reminded that it is possible for a union to be 'a school of communism and administration'.

The economic territory in which the nurses – like the MST or the Abahlali baseMjondolo – agitate coheres not just descriptively but also through their concerted energy to make and hold it for purposes other than those it was meant for when they initiated their practical political tasks. These are three examples of self-determination in action, not as metaphor but as urgent reality. We can think of each of these organisations as individual soviets or as soviets of soviets given their size and locational diversity.

All three of these examples face off against organised violence as the condition of possibility for political action. The military and police and guards and vigilantes that suppress their radicalism is typical in the heightened context of deepening inequality on a global scale. There are more cops and guards, and every labor action, in the old-fashioned sense, is only one degree separated from the application or experience of violence, whether or not the forces invoke criminalisation (yet another partition) to individualise social abandonment and exclusion. One example stands in for many: the public police murder of striking miners at Marikana in South Africa occurred the same year (2012) as ten thousand other police actions against labor, student, and other demonstrations. Indeed, there's a connection to that country's proliferation and aggrandisement of policing that ties to public pension funds in the economic north. A Pennsylvania (US) company called Allied Universal recently acquired G4S – the world's largest private security firm – using Canadian public sector pension funds to buy it.

Just think: laying down an enormous chunk of deferred compensation to build global capacity for organised violence means the Canada workers' pensions go to inhibit demands for just wages or access to safe lodging or movement or health care. These examples illustrate the supple, transnational modalities that articulate the economic north to the rest of the world, through violence, large firms, and partitions. The complexity of police forces, along with militaries public and private, give some keen sense of the global wars, proxy or not, that brings the urgency of abolition persuasion to the fore as central to the various, ongoing fights that morph into contemporary soviets and provisionally emancipate territories of struggle.

6. Big Things

Read the winners. Read Lenin!
        – John Bracey

In the late 1990s, a piously gleeful group gathered at Berkeley to celebrate the establishment of a new PhD in African American Studies. Speaker after speaker laid out an understanding of how we'd gotten to where we were, citing key texts and categories and concepts, most of which turned on culture. The great John Bracey (who passed in 2022), a lifelong, laser-sharp stalwart of Africana studies, shrugged off a lot of what had been claimed as the intellectual lineages for a doctoral program devoted to the study of the ongoing struggle for emancipation. 'Read the winners!', he said. 'Read Lenin!'

There are many well-documented, big examples we could consider, as the agrarian south network and others try to figure out how to regulate the private sector, build independent united fronts, and practice something that both proponents and detractors call 'resource nationalism'. Land redistribution and access to adequate calories are two aspects of a single process. The contemporary vulnerability of states that have elected left-leaning governments lies in the contest over resources that, while in the short run are destined for capitalist innovation, would be different if differently owned (see the vaccine case above). This is more reason, not less, to consider the learning condensed in these few cases.

Lenin showed how we reveal the new world through criticism of the old. These examples, brought into focus by thinking with his writing on imperialism and self-determination, encourage us to see possibilities arising through old and new(er) institutional forms. By way of abolition, the contemporary soviets move urgently towards rehearsing life-affirming social reproduction as it coheres through but isn't reducible to the multi-dimensional intrigues of class formation. Capitalism is never not a central contradiction.

This raises some questions. If the soviets are diversified, what helps them connect? Does there need to be a party, or a constellation of parties, that enable some participants at least to move through and with movements according to a sturdy, if not fixed, sense of orientation? The fact we read books like this one strongly suggests the answer is yes, but then where do we see realisation that doesn't become weighed down by blueprints and bureaucratisation? The answer seems to be to look at large-scale organisations – the MST, Abahlali, the NNU – and pay attention to how they refresh and strengthen their ongoing work, shaped by constant political education and debate. Are these proto-parties? They're certainly political, and parties need not be parliamentary. There are some potentially useful lessons as we think about forming and deepening soviets in their diversity. One is to look at a state like Kerala and take seriously the effort it has required, over time, to make and remake itself while expanding participation (the word 'democratising' comes to mind but it might not be adequate to the descriptive task). Another is to take Kerala's relative sovereignty seriously and consider other territorial political formations, with the new municipalism raising some invigorating expectation that it might be possible, at least provisionally, to secure public goods that aspire to communist philanthropy.

Not everything is externally imposed. This much we know, and so did Lenin. In fact, not very long ago, as I was thinking about what to write for these pages, I gathered with comrades at Cape Town's Bertha House to discuss, in great detail, how movement organisers concentrated their intellectual energies to figure out as abolitionists the details of power/ difference (the political economy of a truncheon, as it were) in order to build better soviets. Under the same roof, Surplus Books presented many titles old and new to entice readers to learn more as part of the analytical labor. And there it was, face up on a table, almost pristine from 1977: *Lenin for Beginners*. The book, produced by a collective in Brixton, UK, reflects the arguments in this introduction and those that follow: if the purpose is to make big things – electrification to power the power of the soviets – then that means figuring things out and patiently explaining them. To do that requires listening. Listening enhances learning. Expect surprise. Stay true to purpose. Be creatively aggressive.

Bibliography

A & Z. 1977. *Lenin for Beginners*. London: Writers and Readers.

Abahlali baseMjondolo.abahlali.org.

Adler-Bolton, Beatrice & Artie Vierkant. 2022. *Health Communism*. London: Verso.

Ahmad, Aijaz. 2011. 'The Progressive Movement in its International Setting.' *Social Scientist* 39(11/12). Nov–Dec: 26–32.

Al-Bulushi, Yousuf. 2024 (forthcoming). *Ruptures in the Afterlife of the Apartheid City*. London and New York: Palgrave Macmillan.

Alexander, Neville. 2023. *Against Racial Capitalism*. London: Pluto.

Amel, Mahdi. 2021. *Arab Marxism*. Leiden & Boston: Brill.

Bagchi, Amiya. 1983. 'Towards a Correct Reading of Lenin's Theory of Imperialism.' *Economic and Political Weekly* 18(31): 2–12.

Banaji, Jairus. 1977. 'The Comintern and Indian Nationalism.' *International* 3: 4: 25–41.

Bennett, Herman. 2018. *African Kings and Black Slaves*. Philadelphia: University of Pennsylvania Press.

Bhandar, Brenna. 2018. *The Colonial Lives of Property*. Durham: Duke University Press.

Bhattacharya, Tithi, ed. 2017. *Social Reproduction Theory: Remapping Class and Oppression*. London: Pluto.

Bhattacharyya, Gargi. 2018. *Rethinking Racial Capitalism*. Lanham, MD: Rowman and Littlefield.

Bonner, Philip, J. Hyslop, and L. van der Walt. 2007. 'Rethinking Worlds of Labor.' *African Studies* 66(1–2): 137–68.

Borges, Sónia Vaz. 2019. *Militant Education, Liberation Struggle, Consciousness*. Berlin: Peter Lang

Cabral, Amílcar. 1979. *Unity and Struggle*. New York: Monthly Review.

Camp, Jordan T. and Christina Heatherton, eds. 2016. *Policing the Planet*. London: Verso.

Conforti, Joseph. 1991. 'The Invention of the Great Awakening: 1795–1842.'

Early American Literature 26/27: 99–118.

Costa, Daniel. 2021. Farmworker Wage Gap Continued in 2020. Economic Policy Institute Working Economics Blog. epi.org.

Davis, Angela. *Freedom Is a Constant Struggle*. Chicago: Haymarket.

Dussel, Enrique and Anibal Yanez. 1990. 'Marx's Economic Manuscripts of 1861–63 and the "Concept" of Dependency.' *Latin American Perspectives* 17(2): 62–101.

Estes, Nick. 2019. *Our History is the Future*. London: Verso.

First, Ruth. 1970. *The Barrel of a Gun: Political Power and the Coup d'état*. London: Allen Lane.

Gilmore, Ruth Wilson. 2022. *Abolition Geography*. London: Verso.

Gilroy, Paul. 1993. *The Black Atlantic*. Cambridge: Harvard University Press.

Gilroy, Paul. 2010. *Darker than Blue*. Cambridge: Harvard University Press.

Hall, Stuart. 2021. *Race and Difference*. Durham: Duke University Press.

Hall, Stuart, Chas Critcher, Tony Jefferson, John Clarke, and Brian Roberts. 1978. *Policing the Crisis: Mugging, the State, and Law and Order*. New York: Holmes & Meier.

Heatherton, Christina. 2022. *Arise!* Oakland: University of California Press.

Ho Chi Minh. 1960. 'The Path Which Led me to Leninism.' *Selected Works of Ho Chi Minh, Vol 4*. marxists.org.

Idrissa, Rahmane. 2021. 'Mapping the Sahel.' *New Left Review* 132: 1–42.

James, C. L. R. 1960 (1973 ed.). *Modern Politic: A Series of Lectures on the Subject Given at the Trinidad Public Library in its Adult Education Program*. Detroit: be wick/ed.

Jones, Claudia. 2011. *Beyond Containment*. London: Ayebia Clark.

Kundnani, Arun. 2023. *What Is Anti-Racism? And Why Must it be Anti-Capitalist?* London: Verso.

MacIntyre, Alasdair. 1984. *Marxism and Christianity*. Notre Dame: Notre Dame University Press.

Mannathukkaren, Nissim. 2021. *Communism, Subaltern Studies, and Postcolonial Theory: The Left in South India*. New Delhi: Routledge India.

Marx, Karl. Nd. 'Private Property and Communism.' In *Economic and Social Manuscripts of 1844*. marxists.org.

McAuliffe, M. and A. Triandafyllidou, eds. 2022. *World Migration Report 2022*. Geneva: International Office for Migration.

Mendonça, María Luísa. 2023. *Political Economy of Agribusiness*. Toronto: Fernwood.

Moyo, Sam. 2011. 'Primitive Accumulation and the Destruction of African Peasantries.' In *The Agrarian Question in the Neoliberal Era* by Utsa Patnaik and Sam Moyo. Cape Town: Pambazuka Press: 61–84.

Movimento dos trabalhadores rurais sem terra (MST). mst.org.br.

Naidu, Sirisha. 2022. 'Circuits of Social Reproduction: Nature, Labor, and Capitalism.' *Review of Radical Political Economics* 55(1): 93–111.

National Nurses United. nationalnursesunited.org.

Negri, Antonio. 2004. *Factory of Strategy: 33 Lessons on Lenin*. New York: Columbia University Press.

Nkrumah, Kwame. 1966. *Neo-colonialism: The Last Stage of Imperialism*. New York: International Publishers.

Norton, Jack and Cindi Katz. 2017. 'Social Reproduction.' In Douglas Richardson et al., eds. *The International Encyclopedia of Geography*. New York: Wiley: 1–11.

Patnaik, Utsa and Patnaik, Prabhat. 2021. *Capital and Imperialism*. New York: Monthly Review.

Patterson, William. 1951. *We Charge Genocide*. New York: Civil Rights Congress.

Phyllis, Yvonne. 2022. *This Land is the Land of Our Ancestors*. Johannesburg: Tricontinental.

Pithouse, Richard. 2006. 'Struggle is a School.' *Monthly Review* 57(9).

Prasad-Aleyemma, Mythri. 2017. 'Resisting Aadhaar, Resisting Islamophobia.' *GenderIt*. file:///Users/rgilmore/Downloads/genderit-gn-apc-org.pdf.

Prashad, Vijay. 2014. *The Poorer Nations*. London: Verso.

Prashad, Vijay. 2020. *Red Star over the Third World*. New Delhi: Leftword.

Raj, Rekha. 2013. 'Dalit Women as Political Agents.' *Economic and Political Weekly* 48(18): 56–63.

Raman, Bhuvaneswari, Mythri Prasad-Aleyamma, Rémi de Bercegol, Eric Denis and Marie-Hélène Zerah. 2015. *Selected Readings on Small Town Dynamics in India*. USR3330 'Savoirs et Mondes Indiens'. Working papers series number 7; SUBURBIN Working papers series number 2. 114 pages.

Reinhart, Carmen M. & Kenneth S. Rogoff. 2009. *This Time is Different*. Princeton: Princeton University Press.

Robinson, Cedric. 1983. *Black Marxism*. London: Zed.

Rodney, Walter. 1981. *How Europe Underdeveloped Africa*. Washington, DC: Howard University Press.

Rodney, Walter. 2018. *The Russian Revolution*. London: Verso.

Santos, Milton. 1977. 'Society and Space as Theory and Method.' *Antipode* 9(1): 3–13.

Thompson, Edward F. 1963 (1968 ed.). *The Making of the English Working Class*. London: Pelican.

Torvikey, Gertrude Dzifa. 2021. 'Reclaiming our Land and Labor.' *Feminist Africa* 2(1): 49–70.

Toscano, Alberto. 2023. *Terms of Disorder*. Kolkata: Seagull Books.

Toscano, Alberto. 2023. *Late Fascism*. London: Verso.

Vergès, Françoise. 2022. *A Feminist Theory of Violence*. London: Pluto.

Ware, Vron. 2014. *Military Migrants*. London: Palgrave.

Ware, Vron. 2022. *Return of a Native*. London: Repeater.

Yaro, Joseph Awetori, J. K. Teye, and G. D. Torvikey. 2017. 'Agricultural Commercialization Models, Agrarian Dynamics, and Local Development in Ghana.' *Journal of Peasant Studies* 44(3): 538–54.

Zedong, Mao. 1940 (1965 ed.). *On New Democracy*. Peking: Lang: 1–34.

Critical Remarks on the National Question[1]

It is obvious that the national question has now become prominent among the problems of Russian public life. The aggressive nationalism of the reactionaries, the transition of counter-revolutionary bourgeois liberalism to nationalism (particularly Great-Russian, but also Polish, Jewish, Ukrainian, etc.), and lastly, the increase of nationalist vacillations among the different 'national' (i.e., non-Great-Russian) Social-Democrats, who have gone to the length of violating the Party Programme – all these make it incumbent on us to give more attention to the national question than we have done so far.

This article pursues a special object, namely, to examine, in their general bearing, precisely these programmatic vacillations of Marxists and would-be Marxists, on the national question. In *Severnaya Pravda*[2] No. 29 (for 5 September 1913, 'Liberals and Democrats on the Language Question'[3]) I had occasion to speak of the opportunism of the liberals on the national question; this article of mine was attacked by the opportunist Jewish newspaper *Zeit*,[4] in an article by Mr. F. Liebman. From the other side, the programme of the Russian Marxists on the national question has been criticised by the Ukrainian opportunist Mr. Lev Yurkevich (*Dzvin*,[5] 1913, Nos. 7–8). Both these writers touched upon so many questions that to reply to them we are obliged to deal with the most diverse aspects of the subject. I think the most convenient thing would be to start with a reprint of the article from *Severnaya Pravda*.

1. Liberals and Democrats on the Language Question

On several occasions, the newspapers have mentioned the report of the Governor of the Caucasus, a report that is noteworthy, not for its Black-Hundred spirit but for its timid 'liberalism'. Among other things, the Governor objects to artificial Russification of non-Russian nationalities. Representatives of non-Russian nationalities in the Caucasus are *themselves* striving to teach their children Russian, as, for example, in the Armenian church schools, in which the teaching of Russian is not obligatory.

Russkoye Slovo (No. 198), one of the most widely circulating liberal newspapers in Russia, points to this fact and draws the correct conclusion that the hostility towards the Russian language in Russia 'stems exclusively' from the 'artificial' (the right word would have been 'forced') implanting of that language.

'There is no reason to worry about the fate of the Russian language. It will itself win recognition throughout Russia,' says the newspaper. This is perfectly true, because the requirements of economic exchange will always compel the nationalities living in one state (as long as they wish to live together) to study the language of the majority. The more democratic the political system in Russia becomes, the more powerfully, rapidly and extensively capitalism will develop, the more urgently will the requirements of economic exchange impel various nationalities to study the language most convenient for general commercial relations.

The liberal newspaper, however, hastens to slap itself in the face and demonstrate its liberal inconsistency.

'Even those who oppose Russification', it says, 'would hardly be likely to deny that in a country as huge as Russia there must be one single official language, and that this language can be only Russian.'

Logic turned inside out! Tiny Switzerland has not lost anything, but has gained from having not *one single* official language, but three – German, French and Italian. In Switzerland 70 per cent of the population are Germans (in Russia 43 per cent are Great Russians), 22 per cent French (in Russia 17 per cent are Ukrainians) and 7 per cent Italians (in Russia 6 per cent are Poles and 4.5 per cent Byelorussians). If Italians in Switzerland often speak French in the common parliament, they do not do so because they are compelled by some savage police law (there are none such in Switzerland), but because the civilised citizens of a democratic state themselves prefer a language that is understood by a majority. The French language does not excite hatred in Italians because it is the language of a free civilised nation, a language that is not imposed by disgusting police measures.

Why should 'huge' Russia, a much more varied and terribly backward country, *inhibit* her development by the retention of any kind of privilege for any one language? Should not the contrary be true, liberal gentlemen? Should not Russia, if she wants to overtake Europe, put an end to every kind of privilege as quickly as possible, as completely as possible and as vigorously as possible?

If all privileges disappear, if the imposition of any one language ceases, all Slavs will easily and rapidly learn to understand each other and will not be frightened, by the 'horrible' thought that speeches in different languages will be heard in the common parliament. The requirements of economic exchange will themselves *decide* which language of the given country it is to the *advantage* of the majority to know in the interests of commercial relations. This decision will be all the firmer because it will be adopted voluntarily by a population of various nationalities, and its adoption will be the more rapid and extensive the more consistent the democracy and, as a consequence, the more rapid will be the development of capitalism.

The liberals approach the language question in the same way as they approach all political questions – like hypocritical hucksters, holding out one hand (openly) to democracy and the other (behind their backs) to the serf-owners and police. We are against privileges, shout the liberals, and under cover they haggle with the serf-owners for first one, then another, privilege.

Such is the nature of *all* liberal-bourgeois nationalism – not only Great-Russian (it is the worst of them all because of its violent character and its kinship with the Purishkeviches) but Polish, Jewish, Ukrainian, Georgian and every other nationalism. Under the slogan of 'national culture', the bourgeoisie of *all* nations, both in Austria and in Russia, are *in fact* pursuing the policy of splitting the workers, emasculating democracy and haggling with the serf-owners over the sale of the people's rights and the people's liberty.

The slogan of working-class democracy is not 'national culture' but the international culture of democracy and the world-wide working-class movement. Let the bourgeoisie deceive the people with various 'positive' national programmes. The class-conscious worker will answer the bourgeoisie – there is only one solution to the national problem (insofar as it can, in general, be solved in the capitalist world, the world of profit, squabbling and exploitation), and that solution is consistent democracy.

The proof – Switzerland in Western Europe, a country with an old culture, and Finland in Eastern Europe, a country with a young culture.

The national programme of working-class democracy is: absolutely no privilege for any one nation or any one language; the solution of the problem of the political self-determination of nations, that is, their separation as states by completely free, democratic methods; the promulgation of a law for the whole state by virtue of which any measure (Zemstvo, urban or communal, etc., etc.) introducing any privilege of any kind for one of the nations and militating against the equality of nations or the rights of a national minority, shall be declared illegal and ineffective, and any citizen of the state shall have the right to demand that such a measure be annulled as unconstitutional, and that those who attempt to put it into effect be punished.

Working-class democracy counterposes to the nationalist wrangling of the various bourgeois parties over questions of language, etc., the demand for the unconditional unity and complete solidarity of workers of *all* nationalities in *all* working-class organisations – trade union, co-operative, consumers', educational and all others – in contradistinction to any kind of bourgeois nationalism. Only this type of unity and solidarity can uphold democracy and defend the interests of the workers against capital – which is already international and is becoming more so – and promote the development of mankind towards a new way of life that is alien to all privileges and all exploitation.

2. 'National Culture'

As the reader will see, the article in *Severnaya Pravda*, made use of a particular example, i.e., the problem of the offic al language, to illustrate the inconsistency and opportunism of the liberal bourgeoisie, which, in the national question, extends a hand to the feudalists and the police. Everybody will understand that, apart from the problem of an official language, the liberal bourgeoisie behaves just as treacherously, hypocritically and stupidly (even from the standpoint of the interests of liberalism) in a number of other related issues.

The conclusion to be drawn from this? It is that *all* liberal-bourgeois nationalism sows the greatest corruption among the workers and does immense harm to the cause of freedom and the proletarian class struggle. This bourgeois (and bourgeois-feudalist) tendency is all the more dangerous for its *being concealed* behind the slogan of 'national culture'. It is under the guise of national culture – Great-Russian, Polish, Jewish, Ukrainian, and so forth – that the Black-Hundreds and the clericals, and also the bourgeoisie of *all* nations, are doing their dirty and reactionary work.

Such are the facts of the national life of today, if viewed from the Marxist angle, i.e., from the standpoint of the class struggle, and if the slogans are compared with the interests and policies of classes, and not with meaningless 'general principles', declamations and phrases.

The slogan of national culture is a bourgeois (and often also a Black-Hundred, and clerical) fraud. Our slogan is: the international culture of democracy and of the world working-class movement.

Here the Bundist Mr. Liebman rushes into the fray and annihilates me with the following deadly tirade:

> Anyone in the least familiar with the national question knows that international culture is not non-national culture (culture without a national form); non-national culture, which must not be Russian, Jewish, or Polish, but only pure culture, is nonsense; international ideas can appeal to the working class only when they are adapted to the language spoken by the worker, and to the concrete national conditions under

which he lives; the worker should not be indifferent to the condition and development of his national culture, because it is through it, and only through it, that he is able to participate in the 'international culture of democracy and of the world working-class movement'. This is well known, but V. I. turns a deaf ear to it all …

Ponder over this typically Bundist argument, designed, if you please, to demolish the Marxist thesis that I advanced. With the air of supreme self-confidence of one who is 'familiar with the national question', this Bundist passes off ordinary bourgeois views as 'well-known' axioms.

It is true, my dear Bundist, that international culture is not non-national. Nobody said that it was. Nobody has proclaimed a 'pure' culture, either Polish, Jewish, or Russian, etc., and your jumble of empty words is simply an attempt to distract the reader's attention and to obscure the issue with tinkling words.

The *elements* of democratic and socialist culture are present, if only in rudimentary form, in *every* national culture, since in *every* nation there are toiling and exploited masses, whose conditions of life inevitably give rise to the ideology of democracy and socialism. But *every* nation also possesses a bourgeois culture (and most nations a reactionary and clerical culture as well) in the form, not merely of 'elements', but of the *dominant* culture. Therefore, the general 'national culture' is the culture of the landlords, the clergy, and the bourgeoisie. This fundamental and, for a Marxist, elementary truth, was kept in the background by the Bundist, who 'drowned' it in his jumble of words, i.e., *instead* of revealing and clarifying the class gulf to the reader, he in fact obscured it. *In fact*, the Bundist acted like a bourgeois, whose every interest requires the spreading of a belief in a non-class national culture.

In advancing the slogan of 'the international culture of democracy and of the world working-class movement', we take *from each* national culture *only* its democratic and socialist elements; we take them *only* and *absolutely* in opposition to the bourgeois culture and the bourgeois nationalism of *each* nation. No democrat, and certainly no Marxist, denies that all languages should have equal status, or that it is necessary to polemise with one's 'native' bourgeoisie in one's native language and to advocate anti-clerical or anti-bourgeois ideas among one's 'native' peasantry and petty bourgeoisie. That goes without saying, but the Bundist uses these indisputable truths to obscure the point in dispute, i.e., the real issue.

The question is whether it is permissible for a Marxist, directly or indirectly, to advance the slogan of national culture, or whether he should *oppose* it by advocating, in all languages, the slogan of workers' *internationalism* while 'adapting' himself to all local and national features.

The significance of the 'national culture' slogan is not determined by some petty intellectual's promise, or good intention, to 'interpret' it as 'meaning the development through it of an international culture'. It would be puerile subjectivism to look at it in that way. The significance of the slogan of national culture is determined by the objective alignment of all classes in a given country, and in all countries of the world. The national culture of the bourgeoisie is a *fact* (and, I repeat, the bourgeoisie everywhere enters into deals with the landed proprietors and the clergy). Aggressive bourgeois nationalism, which drugs the minds of the workers, stultifies and disunites them in order that the bourgeoisie may lead them by the halter – such is the fundamental fact of the times.

Those who seek to serve the proletariat must unite the workers of all nations, and unswervingly fight bourgeois nationalism, *domestic* and foreign. The place of those who advocate the slogan of national culture is among the nationalist petty bourgeois, not among the Marxists.

Take a concrete example. Can a Great-Russian Marxist accept the slogan of national, Great-Russian, culture? No, he cannot. Anyone who does that should stand in the ranks of the nationalists, not of the Marxists. Our task is to fight the dominant, Black-Hundred and bourgeois national culture of the Great Russians, and to develop, exclusively in the internationalist spirit and in the closest alliance with the workers of other countries, the rudiments also existing in the history of our democratic and working-class movement. Fight your own Great-Russian landlords and bourgeoisie, fight their 'culture' in the name of internationalism, and, in so fighting, 'adapt' yourself to the special features of the Purishkeviches and Struves – that is your task, not preaching or tolerating the Slogan of national culture.

The same applies to the most oppressed and persecuted nation –
the Jews. Jewish national culture is the slogan of the rabbis and the
bourgeoisie, the slogan of our enemies. But there are other elements
in Jewish culture and in Jewish history as a whole. Of the ten and a
half million Jews in the world, somewhat over a half live in Galicia and
Russia, backward and semi-barbarous countries, where the Jews are
forcibly kept in the status of a caste. The other half lives in the civilised
world, and there the Jews do not live as a segregated caste. There the
great world-progressive features of Jewish culture stand clearly revealed:
its internationalism, its identification with the advanced movements of
the epoch (the percentage of Jews in the democratic and proletarian
movements is everywhere higher than the percentage of Jews among
the population).

Whoever, directly or indirectly, puts forward the slogan of Jewish
'national culture' is (whatever his good intentions may be) an enemy
of the proletariat, a supporter of all that is *outmoded* and connected
with *caste* among the Jewish people; he is an accomplice of the rabbis
and the bourgeoisie. On the other hand, those Jewish Marxists who
mingle with the Russian, Lithuanian, Ukrainian and other workers
in international Marxist organisations, and make their contribution
(both in Russian and in Yiddish) towards creating the international
culture of the working-class movement – those Jews, despite the separatism of the Bund, uphold the best traditions of Jewry by fighting
the slogan of 'national culture'.

Bourgeois nationalism and proletarian internationalism – these are
the two irreconcilably hostile slogans that correspond to the two great
class camps throughout the capitalist world, and express the two policies
(nay, the two world outlooks) in the national question. In advocating
the slogan of national culture and building up on it an entire plan and
practical programme of what they call 'cultural-national autonomy',
the Bundists are *in effect* instruments of bourgeois nationalism among
the workers.

3. The Nationalist Bogey of 'Assimilation'

The question of assimilation, i.e., of the shedding of national features, and absorption by another nation, strikingly illustrates the consequences of the nationalist vacillations of the Bundists and their fellow-thinkers.

Mr. Liebman, who faithfully conveys and repeats the stock arguments, or rather, tricks, of the Bundists, has qualified as 'the *old assimilation story*' the demand for the unity and amalgamation of the workers of all nationalities in a given country in united workers' organisations (see the concluding part of the article in *Severnaya Pravda*).

'Consequently,' says Mr. F. Liebman, commenting on the concluding part of the article in *Severnaya Pravda*, 'if asked what nationality he belongs to, the worker must answer: I am a Social-Democrat.'

Our Bundist considers this the acme of wit. As a matter of fact, he gives himself away completely by *such* witticisms and outcries about 'assimilation', *levelled against* a consistently democratic and *Marxist* slogan.

Developing capitalism knows two historical tendencies in the national question. The first is the awakening of national life and national movements, the struggle against all national oppression, and the creation of national states. The second is the development and growing frequency of international intercourse in every form, the break-down of national barriers, the creation of the international unity of capital, of economic life in general, of politics, science, etc.

Both tendencies are a universal law of capitalism. The former predominates in the beginning of its development, the latter characterises a mature capitalism that is moving towards its transformation into socialist society. The Marxists' national programme takes both tendencies into account, and advocates, firstly, the equality of nations and languages and the impermissibility of all *privileges* in this respect (and also the right of nations to self-determination with which we shall deal separately later); secondly, the principle of internationalism and uncompromising struggle against contamination of the proletariat with bourgeois nationalism, even of the most refined kind.

The question arises: what does our Bundist mean when he cries out to heaven against 'assimilation'? He *could not* have meant the oppression of nations, or the *privileges* enjoyed by a particular nation, because the word 'assimilation' here does not fit at all, because all Marxists, individually, and as an official, united whole, have quite definitely and unambiguously condemned the slightest violence against and oppression and inequality of nations, and finally because this general Marxist idea, which the Bundist has attacked, is expressed in the *Severnaya Pravda* article in the most emphatic manner.

No, evasion is impossible here. In condemning 'assimilation' Mr. Liebman had in mind, *not* violence, *not* inequality, and *not* privileges. Is there anything real left in the concept of assimilation, after all violence and all inequality have been eliminated?

Yes, there undoubtedly is. What is left is capitalism's world-historical tendency, to break down national barriers, obliterate national distinctions, and to *assimilate* nations – a tendency which manifests itself more and more powerfully with every passing decade, and is one of the greatest driving forces transforming capitalism into socialism.

Whoever does not recognise and champion the equality of nations and languages, and does not fight against all national oppression or inequality, is not a Marxist; he is not even a democrat. That is beyond doubt. But it is also beyond doubt that the pseudo-Marxist who heaps abuse upon a Marxist of another nation for being an 'assimilator' is simply a *nationalist philistine*. In this unhandsome category of people are all the Bundists and (as we shall shortly see) Ukrainian nationalist-socialists such as L. Yurkevich, Dontsov and Co.

To show concretely how reactionary the views held by these nationalist philistines are, we shall cite facts of three kinds.

It is the Jewish nationalists in Russia in general, and the Bundists in particular, who vociferate most about Russian orthodox Marxists being 'assimilators'. And, yet, as the aforementioned figures show, out of the ten and a half million Jews all over the world, *about half* that number live in the *civilised* world, where conditions favouring 'assimilation' are *strongest*, whereas the unhappy, downtrodden, disfranchised Jews in Russia and Galicia, who are crushed under the heel of the Purishkeviches (Russian and Polish), live where conditions for 'assimilation' *least* prevail, where there is most segregation, and even a 'Pale of Settlement',[6] a *numerus clausus*[7] and other charming features of the Purishkevich regime.

The Jews in the civilised world are not a nation, they have, in the main, become assimilated, say Karl Kautsky and Otto Bauer. The Jews in Galicia and in Russia are not a nation; unfortunately (through *no* fault of their own but through that of the Purishkeviches), they are still a *caste* here. Such is the incontrovertible judgement of people who are undoubtedly familiar with the history of Jewry and take the above-cited facts into consideration.

What do these facts prove? It is that only Jewish reactionary philistines, who want to turn back the wheel of history, and make it proceed, not from the conditions prevailing in Russia and Galicia to those prevailing in Paris and New York, but in the reverse direction – only they can clamour against 'assimilation'.

The best Jews, those who are celebrated in world history, and have given the world foremost leaders of democracy and socialism, have never clamoured against assimilation. It is only those who contemplate the 'rear aspect' of Jewry with reverential awe that clamour against assimilation.

A rough idea of the scale which the general process of assimilation of nations is assuming under the present conditions of advanced capitalism may be obtained, for example, from the immigration statistics of the United States of America. During the decade between 1891–1900, Europe sent 3,700,000 people there, and during the nine years between 1901 and 1909, 7,200,000. The 1900 census in the United States recorded over 10,000,000 foreigners. New York State, in which, according to the same census, there were over 78,000 Austrians, 136,000 Englishmen, 20,000 Frenchmen, 480,000 Germans, 37,000 Hungarians, 425,000 Irish, 182,000 Italians, 70,000 Poles, 166,000 people from Russia (mostly Jews), 43,000 Swedes, etc., grinds down national distinctions. And what is taking place on a grand, international scale in New York is also to be seen in *every* big city and industrial township.

No one unobsessed by nationalist prejudices can fail to perceive that this process of assimilation of nations by capitalism means the greatest historical progress, the breakdown of hidebound national conservatism in the various backwoods, especially in backward countries like Russia.

Take Russia and the attitude of Great Russians towards the Ukrainians. Naturally, every democrat, not to mention Marxists, will strongly oppose the incredible humiliation of Ukrainians, and demand complete equality for them. But it would be a downright betrayal of socialism and a silly policy *even* from the standpoint of the bourgeois 'national aims' of the Ukrainians to *weaken* the ties and the alliance between the Ukrainian and Great-Russian proletariat that now exist within the confines of a single state.

Mr. Lev Yurkevich, who calls himself a 'Marxist' (poor Marx!), is an example of that silly policy. In 1906, Sokolovsky (Basok) and Lukashevich (Tuchapsky) asserted, Mr. Yurkevich writes, that the Ukrainian proletariat had become completely Russified and needed no separate organisation. Without quoting a single fact *bearing on the direct issue*, Mr. Yurkevich falls upon both for saying this and cries out hysterically – quite in the spirit of the basest, most stupid and most reactionary nationalism – that this is 'national passivity', 'national renunciation', that these men have 'split [!!] the Ukrainian Marxists', and so forth. Today, despite the 'growth of Ukrainian national consciousness among the workers', the *minority* of the workers are 'nationally conscious', while the majority, Mr. Yurkevich assures us, 'are still under the influence of Russian culture'. And it is our duty, this nationalist philistine exclaims, 'not to follow the masses, but to lead them, to explain to them their national aims (*natsionalna sprava*)' (*Dzvin*, p. 89).

This argument of Mr. Yurkevich's is wholly bourgeois-nationalistic. But, even from the point of view of the bourgeois nationalists, some of whom stand for complete equality and autonomy for the Ukraine, while others stand for an independent Ukrainian state, this argument will not wash. The Ukrainians' striving for liberation is opposed by the Great-Russian and Polish landlord class and by the bourgeoisie of these two nations. What social force is capable of standing up to these classes? The first decade of the twentieth century provided an actual reply to this question: that force is none other than the working class, which rallies the democratic peasantry behind it. By striving to divide, and thereby weaken, the genuinely democratic force, whose victory would make national oppression impossible, Mr. Yurkevich is betraying, not only the interests of democracy in general, but also the interests of his own country, the Ukraine. Given united action by the Great-Russian and Ukrainian proletarians, a free Ukraine *is possible*; without such unity, it is out of the question.

But Marxists do not confine themselves to the bourgeois-national standpoint. For several decades, a well-defined process of accelerated economic development has been going on in the South, i.e., the Ukraine, attracting hundreds of thousands of peasants and workers from Great Russia to the capitalist farms, mines and cities. The 'assimilation' – within these limits – of the Great-Russian and Ukrainian proletariat is an indisputable fact. *And this* fact is *undoubtedly* progressive. Capitalism is replacing the ignorant, conservative, settled muzhik of the Great-Russian or Ukrainian backwoods with a mobile proletarian whose conditions of life break down specifically national narrow-mindedness, both Great-Russian and Ukrainian. Even if we assume that, in time, there will be a state frontier between Great Russia and the Ukraine, the historically progressive nature of the 'assimilation' of the Great-Russian and Ukrainian workers will be as undoubted as the progressive nature of the grinding down of nations in America. The freer the Ukraine and Great Russia become, the *more extensive and more rapid* will be the development of capitalism, which will still more powerfully attract the workers, the working masses of *all* nations from all regions of the state and from all the neighbouring states (should Russia become a neighbouring state in relation to the Ukraine) to the cities, the mines, and the factories.

Mr. Lev Yurkevich acts like a real bourgeois, and a short-sighted, narrow-minded, obtuse bourgeois at that, i.e., like a philistine, when he dismisses the benefits to be gained from, the intercourse, amalgamation and assimilation of the *proletariat* of the two nations, for the sake of the momentary success of the Ukrainian national cause (*sprava*). The national cause comes first and the proletarian cause second, the bourgeois nationalists say, with the Yurkeviches, Dontsovs and similar would-be Marxists repeating it after them. The proletarian cause must come first, we say, because it not only protects the lasting and fundamental interests of labour and of humanity, but also those of democracy; and without democracy neither an autonomous nor an independent Ukraine is conceivable.

Another point to be noted in Mr. Yurkevich's argument, which is so extraordinarily rich in nationalist gems, is this: the minority of Ukrainian workers are nationally conscious, he says; 'the majority are still under the influence of Russian culture' (*bilshist perebuvaye shche pid vplyvom rosiiskoi kultury*).

Contraposing Ukrainian culture as a whole to Great-Russian culture as a whole, when speaking of the proletariat, is a gross betrayal of the proletariat's interests for the benefit of bourgeois nationalism.

There are two nations in every modern nation – we say to all nationalist-socialists. There are two national cultures in every national culture. There is the Great-Russian culture of the Purishkeviches, Guchkovs and Struves – but there is also the Great-Russian culture typified in the names of Chernyshevsky and Plekhanov. There are *the same two* cultures in the Ukraine as there are in Germany, in France, in England, among the Jews, and so forth. If the majority of the Ukrainian workers are under the influence of Great-Russian culture, we also know definitely that the ideas of Great-Russian democracy and Social-Democracy operate parallel with the Great-Russian clerical and bourgeois culture. In fighting the latter kind of 'culture', the Ukrainian *Marxist* will always bring the former into focus and say to his workers: 'We must snatch at, make use of, and develop to the utmost every opportunity for intercourse with the Great-Russian class-conscious workers, with their literature and with their range of ideas; the fundamental interests of *both* the Ukrainian and the Great-Russian working-class movements demand it.'

If a Ukrainian Marxist allows himself to be swayed by his *quite legitimate and natural* hatred of the Great-Russian oppressors to *such a degree* that he transfers even a particle of this hatred, even if it be only estrangement, to the proletarian culture and proletarian cause of the Great-Russian workers, then such a Marxist will get bogged down in bourgeois nationalism. Similarly, the Great-Russian Marxist will be bogged down, not only in bourgeois, but also in Black-Hundred nationalism, if he loses sight, even for a moment, of the demand for complete equality for the Ukrainians, or of their *right* to form an independent state.

The Great-Russian and Ukrainian workers must work together, and, as long as they live in a single state, act in the closest organisational unity and concert, towards a common or international culture of the proletarian movement, displaying absolute tolerance in the question of the language in which propaganda is conducted, and in the purely local or purely national *details* of that propaganda. This is the imperative demand of Marxism. All advocacy of the segregation of the workers of one nation from those of another, all attacks upon Marxist 'assimilation', or attempts, where the proletariat is concerned, to contrapose one national culture as a whole to another allegedly integral national culture, and so forth, is *bourgeois* nationalism, against which it is essential to wage a ruthless struggle.

4. 'Cultural-National Autonomy'

The question of the 'national culture' slogan is of enormous importance to Marxists, not only because it determines the ideological content of all our propaganda and agitation on the national question, as distinct from bourgeois propaganda, but also because the entire programme of the much-discussed cultural-national autonomy is based on this slogan.

The main and fundamental flaw in this programme is that it aims at introducing the most refined, most absolute and most extreme nationalism. The gist of this programme is that every citizen registers as belonging to a particular nation, and every nation constitutes a legal entity with the right to impose compulsory taxation on its members, with national parliaments (Diets) and national secretaries of state (ministers).

Such an idea, applied to the national question, resembles Proudhon's idea, as applied to capitalism. Not abolishing capitalism and its basis – commodity production – but *purging* that basis of abuses, of excrescences, and so forth; not abolishing exchange and exchange value, but, on the contrary, making it 'constitutional', universal, absolute, '*fair*', and free of fluctuations, crises and abuses – such was Proudhon's idea.

Just as Proudhon was petty-bourgeois, and his theory converted exchange and commodity production into an absolute category and exalted them as the acme of perfection, so is the theory and programme of 'cultural-national autonomy' petty bourgeois, for it converts bourgeois nationalism into an absolute category, exalts it as the acme of perfection, and purges it of violence, injustice, etc.

Marxism cannot be reconciled with nationalism, be it even of the 'most just', 'purest', most refined and civilised brand. In place of all forms of nationalism Marxism advances internationalism, the amalgamation of all nations in the higher unity, a unity that is growing before our eyes with every mile of railway line that is built, with every international trust, and every workers' association that is formed (an association that is international in its economic activities as well as in its ideas and aims).

The principle of nationality is historically inevitable in bourgeois society and, taking this society into due account, the Marxist fully recognises the historical legitimacy of national movements. But, to prevent this recognition from becoming an apologia of nationalism, it must be strictly limited to what is progressive in such movements, in order that this recognition may not lead to bourgeois ideology obscuring proletarian consciousness.

The awakening of the masses from feudal lethargy, and their struggle against all national oppression, for the sovereignty of the people, of the nation, are progressive. Hence, it is the Marxist's *bounden* duty to stand for the most resolute and consistent democratism on all aspects of the national question. This task is largely a negative one. But this is the limit the proletariat can go to in supporting nationalism, for beyond that begins the 'positive' activity of the *bourgeoisie* striving to *fortify* nationalism.

To throw off the feudal yoke, all national oppression, and all privileges enjoyed by any particular nation or language, is the imperative duty of the proletariat as a democratic force, and is certainly in the interests of the proletarian class struggle, which is obscured and retarded by bickering on the national question. But to go *beyond* these strictly limited and definite historical limits in helping bourgeois nationalism means betraying the proletariat and siding with the bourgeoisie. There is a borderline here, which is often very slight and which the Bundists and Ukrainian nationalist-socialists completely lose sight of.

Combat all national oppression? Yes, of course! Fight *for* any kind of national development, *for* 'national culture' in general? – Of course not. The economic development of capitalist society presents us with examples of immature national movements all over the world, examples of the formation of big nations out of a number of small ones, or to the detriment of some of the small ones, and also examples of the assimilation of nations. The development of nationality in general is the principle of bourgeois nationalism; hence the exclusiveness of bourgeois nationalism, hence the endless national bickering. The proletariat, however, far from undertaking to uphold the national development of every nation, on the contrary, warns the masses against such illusions, stands for the fullest freedom of capitalist intercourse and welcomes every kind of assimilation of nations, except that which is founded on force or privilege.

Consolidating nationalism within a certain 'justly' delimited sphere, 'constitutionalising' nationalism, and securing the separation of all nations from one another by means of a special state institution – such is the ideological foundation and content of cultural-national autonomy. This idea is thoroughly bourgeois and thoroughly false. The proletariat cannot support any consecration of nationalism; on the contrary, it supports everything that helps to obliterate national distinctions and remove national barriers; it supports everything that makes the ties between nationalities closer and closer, or tends to merge nations. To act differently means siding with reactionary nationalist philistinism.

When, at their Congress in Brünn (in 1899), the Austrian Social-Democrats discussed the plan for cultural-national autonomy, practically no attention was paid to a theoretical appraisal of that plan. It is, however, noteworthy that the following two arguments were levelled against this programme: (1) it would tend to strengthen clericalism; (2) 'its result would be the perpetuation of chauvinism, its introduction into every small community, into every small group' (p. 92 of the official report of the Brünn Congress, in German. A Russian translation was published by the Jewish nationalist party, the JSLP).[8]

There can be no doubt that 'national culture', in the ordinary sense of the term, i.e., schools, etc., is at present under the predominant influence of the clergy and the bourgeois chauvinists in all countries in the world. When the Bundists, in advocating 'cultural-national' autonomy, say that the constituting of nations will keep the class struggle within them *clean* of all extraneous considerations, then that is manifest and ridiculous sophistry. It is primarily in the economic and political sphere that a serious class struggle is waged in any capitalist society. To separate the sphere of education *from this* is, firstly, absurdly utopian, because schools (like 'national culture' in general) cannot be separated from economics and politics; secondly, it is the economic and political life of a capitalist country that *necessitates* at every step the smashing of the absurd and outmoded national barriers and prejudices, whereas separation of the school system and the like, would only perpetuate, intensify and strengthen 'pure' clericalism and 'pure' bourgeois chauvinism.

On the boards of joint-stock companies we find capitalists of different nations sitting together in complete harmony. At the factories workers of different nations work side by side. In any really serious and profound political issue, sides are taken according to classes, not nations. Withdrawing school education and the like from state control and placing it under the control of the nations is in effect an attempt to *separate* from economics, which unites the nations, the most highly, so to speak, ideological sphere of social life, the sphere in which 'pure' national culture or the national cultivation of clericalism and chauvinism has the freest play.

In practice, the plan for 'extra-territorial' or 'cultural national' autonomy could mean only one thing: *the division of educational affairs according to nationality*, i.e., the introduction of national curias in school affairs. Sufficient thought to the *real* significance of the famous Bund plan will enable one to realise how utterly reactionary it is even from the standpoint of democracy, let alone from that of the proletarian class struggle for socialism.

A single instance and a single scheme for the 'nationalisation' of the school system will make this point abundantly clear. In the United States of America, the division of the States into Northern and Southern holds to this day in all departments of life; the former possess the greatest traditions of freedom and of struggle against the slave-owners;

the latter possess the greatest traditions of slave ownership, survivals of persecution of the Negroes, who are economically oppressed and culturally backward (44 per cent of Negroes are illiterate, and 6 per cent of whites), and so forth. In the Northern States, Negro children attend the same schools as white children do. In the South, there are separate 'national', or racial, whichever you please, schools for Negro children. I think that this is the sole instance of actual 'nationalisation' of schools.

In Eastern Europe, there exists a country where things like the Beilis case are still possible, and Jews are condemned by the Purishkeviches to a condition worse than that of the Negroes.[9] In that country, a scheme for *nationalising Jewish schools* was recently mooted in the Ministry. Happily, this reactionary utopia is no more likely to be realised than the utopia of the Austrian petty bourgeoisie, who have despaired of achieving consistent democracy or of putting an end to national bickering, and have invented for the nations school-education *compartments* to keep them from bickering *over the distribution* of schools . . . but have 'constituted' themselves for an *eternal* bickering of one 'national culture' with another.

In Austria, the idea of cultural-national autonomy has remained largely a flight of literary fancy, which the Austrian Social-Democrats themselves have not taken seriously. In Russia, however, it has been incorporated in the programmes of all the Jewish bourgeois parties, and of several petty-bourgeois, opportunist elements in the different nations – for example, the Bundists, the liquidators in the Caucasus, and the conference of Russian national parties of the Left-Narodnik trend. (This conference, we will mention parenthetically, took place in 1907, its decision being adopted *with abstention* on the part of the Russian Socialist-Revolutionaries and the PSP, the Polish social-patriots. Abstention from voting is a method surprisingly characteristic of the Socialist-Revolutionaries and PSP, when they want to show their attitude towards a most important question of principle in the sphere of the national programme!)

In Austria it was Otto Bauer, the principal theoretician of 'cultural-national autonomy', who devoted a special chapter of his book to prove that such a programme cannot possibly be proposed for the Jews. In Russia, however, it is precisely among the Jews that all the bourgeois parties – and the Bund which echoes them – have adopted this programme.[10] What does this go to show? It goes to show that history, through the political practice of another state, has exposed the absurdity of Bauer's invention, in exactly the same way as the Russian Bernsteinians (Struve, Tugan-Baranovsky, Berdayev and Co.), through their rapid evolution from Marxism to liberalism, have exposed the real ideological content of the German Bernsteinism.[11]

Neither the Austrian nor the Russian Social-Democrats have incorporated 'cultural-national' autonomy in their programme. However, the Jewish bourgeois parties in a most backward country, and a number of petty-bourgeois, so-called socialist groups *have adopted it* in order to spread ideas of bourgeois nationalism among the working class in a refined form. This fact speaks for itself.

Since we have bad to touch upon the Austrian programme on the national question, we must reassert a truth which is often distorted by the Bundists. At the Brünn Congress, a *pure* programme of 'cultural-national autonomy' *was* presented. This was the programme of the South-Slav Social Democrats, § 2 of which reads: 'Every nation living in Austria, irrespective of the territory occupied by its members, constitutes an autonomous group which manages all its national (language and cultural) affairs quite independently.' This programme was supported, not only by Kristan but by the influential Ellenbogen. But it was withdrawn; not a single vote was cast for it. A *territorialist* programme was adopted, i.e., one that did not create *any* national groups 'irrespective of the territory occupied by the members of the nation'.

Clause 3 of the adopted programme reads: 'The self governing *regions* of one and the same nation shall jointly form a nationally united association, which shall manage its national affairs on an absolutely autonomous basis' (cf. *Prosveshcheniye*, 1913, No. 4, p. 28).[12] Clearly, this compromise programme is wrong too. An example will illustrate this. The German colonists' community in Saratov Gubernia, plus the German working-class suburb of Riga or Lodz, plus the German housing estate near St. Petersburg, etc., would constitute a 'nationally united association' of Germans in Russia. Obviously the Social-Democrats cannot *demand* such a thing or *enforce* such an association, although of course they do not in the least deny *freedom* of every kind of association, including associations of any communities of any nationality in a given state. The segregation, by a law of the state, of Germans, etc., in different localities and of different classes in Russia into a single German-national association may be practised by anybody – priests, bourgeois or philistines, but not by Social-Democrats.

5. The Equality of Nations and the Rights of National Minorities

When they discuss the national question, opportunists in Russia are given to citing the example of Austria. In my article in *Severnaya Pravda* (No. 10, *Prosveshcheniye*, pp. 96–98), which the opportunists have attacked (Mr. Semkovsky in *Novaya Rabochaya Gazeta*,[13] and Mr. Liebman in *Zeit*), I asserted that, insofar as that is at all possible under capitalism, there was only one solution of the national question, viz., through consistent democracy. In proof of this, I referred, among other things, to Switzerland.

This has not been to the liking of the two opportunists mentioned above, who are trying to refute it or belittle its significance. Kautsky, we are told, said that Switzerland is an exception; Switzerland, if you please, has a special kind of decentralisation, a special history, special geographical conditions, unique distribution of a population that speak different languages, etc., etc.

All these are nothing more than attempts to *evade* the issue. To be sure, Switzerland is an exception in that she is not a single-nation state. But Austria and Russia are also exceptions (or are backward, as Kautsky adds). To be sure, it was only her special, unique historical and social conditions that ensured Switzerland *greater* democracy than most of her European neighbours.

But where does all this come in, if we are speaking of the *model* to be adopted? In the whole world, under present-day conditions, countries in which any particular institution has been founded on *consistent* democratic principles are the exception. Does this prevent us, in our programme, from upholding consistent democracy in all institutions?

Switzerland's special features lie in her history, her geographical and other conditions. Russia's special features lie in the strength of her proletariat, which has no precedent in the epoch of bourgeois revolutions, and in her shocking general backwardness, which objectively necessitates an exceptionally rapid and resolute advance, under the threat of all sorts of drawbacks and reverses.

We are evolving a national programme from the proletarian standpoint; since when has it been recommended that the worst examples, rather than the best, be taken as a model?

At all events, does it not remain an indisputable and undisputed fact that national peace under capitalism has been achieved (insofar as it is achievable) *exclusively* in countries where consistent democracy prevails?

Since this is indisputable, the opportunists' persistent references to Austria instead of Switzerland are nothing but a typical Cadet device, for the Cadets always copy the worst European constitutions rather than the best.

In Switzerland, there are *three* official languages, but bills submitted to a referendum are printed in *five* languages, that is to say, in two Romansh dialects, in addition to the three official languages. According to the 1900 census, these two dialects are spoken by 38,651 out of the 3,315,443 inhabitants of Switzerland, i.e., by a little over *one per cent*. In the army, commissioned and non-commissioned officers 'are given the fullest freedom to speak to the men in their native language'. In the cantons of Graubünden and Wallis (each with a population of a little over a hundred thousand) both dialects enjoy complete equality.[14]

The question is: should we advocate and support this, the living *experience* of an advanced country, or borrow from the Austrians *inventions* like 'extra-territorial autonomy', which have not yet been tried out anywhere in the world (and not yet been adopted by the Austrians themselves)?

To advocate this invention is to advocate the division of school education according to nationality, and that is a downright harmful idea. The experience of Switzerland proves, however, that the greatest (relative) degree of national peace *can be, and has been, ensured in practice* where you have, a consistent (again relative) democracy throughout the state.

'In Switzerland', say people who have studied this question, 'there is *no national question* in the East-European sense of the term. The very phrase (national question) is unknown there ...' 'Switzerland left the struggle between nationalities a long way behind, in 1797–1803.'[15]

This means that the epoch of the great French Revolution, which provided the most democratic solution of the current problems of the transition from feudalism to capitalism, *succeeded* incidentally, *en passant*, in '*solving*' the national question.

Let the Semkovskys, Liebmans, and other opportunists now try to assert that this 'exclusively Swiss' solution is *ir applicable* to any uyezd or even part of an uyezd in Russia, where out of a population of only two hundred thousand, forty thousand speak *two dialects* and want to have *complete equality* of language in their area!

Advocacy of complete equality of nations and languages distinguishes only the consistently democratic elements in each nation (i.e., only the proletarians), and *unites* them, not according to nationality, but in a profound and earnest desire to improve the entire system of state. On the contrary, advocacy of 'cultural-national autonomy', despite the pious wishes of individuals and groups, *divides the nations* and in fact draws the workers and the bourgeoisie of any one nation closer together (the adoption of this 'cultural-national autonomy' by all the Jewish bourgeois parties).

Guaranteeing the rights of a national minority is inseparably linked up with the principle of complete equality. In my article in *Severnaya Pravda* this principle was expressed in almost the same terms as in the later, official and more accurate decision of the conference of Marxists. That decision demands 'the incorporation in the constitution of a fundamental law which shall declare null and void all privileges enjoyed by any one nation and all infringements of the rights of a national minority'.

Mr. Liebman tries to ridicule this formula and asks: 'Who knows what the rights of a national minority are?' Do these rights, he wants to know, include the right of the minority to have 'its own programme' for the national schools? How large must the national minority be to have the right to have its own judges, officials, and schools with instruction in its own language? Mr. Liebman wants it to be inferred from these questions that a '*positive*' national programme is essential.

Actually, these questions clearly show what reactionary ideas our Bundist tries to smuggle through under cover of a dispute on supposedly minor details and particulars.

'Its own programme' in its national schools! ... Marxists, my dear nationalist-socialist, have a *general* school programme which demands, for example, an absolutely secular school. As far as Marxists are concerned, no *departure* from this general programme is anywhere or at any time permissible in a democratic state (the question of introducing any 'local' subjects, languages, and so forth into it being decided by the local inhabitants). However, from the principle of 'taking educational affairs out of the hands of the state' and placing them under the control of the nations, it ensues that we, the workers, must allow the 'nations' in our democratic state to spend the people's money on clerical schools! Without being aware of the fact, Mr. Liebman has clearly demonstrated the reactionary nature of 'cultural-national autonomy'!

'How large must a national minority be?' This is not defined even in the Austrian programme, of which the Bundists are enamoured. It says (more briefly and less clearly than our programme does): 'The rights of the national minorities are protected by a special law to be passed by the Imperial Parliament' (§ 4 of the Brünn programme).

Why has nobody asked the Austrian Social-Democrats the question: what exactly is that law, and exactly which rights and of which minority is it to protect?

That is because all sensible people understand that it is inappropriate and impossible to define particulars in a programme. A programme lays down only fundamental principles. In this case, the fundamental principle is implied with the Austrians, and directly expressed in the decision of the latest conference of Russian Marxists. That principle is: no national privileges and no national inequality.

Let us take a concrete example to make the point clear to the Bundist. According to the school census of 18 January 1911, St. Petersburg elementary schools under the Ministry of Public 'Education' were attended by 48,076 pupils. Of these, 396, i.e., less than one per cent, were Jews. The other figures are: Romanian pupils – 2, Georgians – 1, Armenians – 3, etc.[16] Is it possible to draw up a 'positive' national programme that will cover this diversity of relationships and conditions? (And St. Petersburg is, of course, far from being the city with the most mixed population in Russia.) Even such specialists in national 'subtleties' as the Bundists would hardly be able to draw up such a programme.

And yet, if the constitution of the country contained a fundamental law rendering null and void every measure that infringed the rights of a minority, any citizen would be able to demand the rescinding of orders prohibiting, for example, the hiring, at state expense, of special teachers of Hebrew, Jewish history, and the like, or the provision of state-owned premises for lectures for Jewish, Armenian or Romanian children, or even for the one Georgian child. At all events, it is by no means impossible to meet, on the basis of equality, all the reasonable and just wishes of the national minorities, and nobody will say that advocacy of equality is harmful. On the other hand, it would certainly be harmful to advocate division of schools according to nationality, to advocate, for example, special schools for Jewish children in St. Petersburg, and it would be utterly impossible to set up national schools for *every* national minority, for one, two or three children.

Furthermore, it is impossible, in any country-wide law, to define how large a national minority must be to be entitled to special schools, or to special teachers for supplementary subjects, etc.

On the other hand, a country-wide law establishing equality can be worked out in detail and developed through special regulations and the decisions of regional Diets, and town, Zemstvo, village commune and other authorities.

6. Centralisation and Autonomy

In his rejoinder, Mr. Liebman writes:

Take our Lithuania, the Baltic province, Poland, Volhynia, South Russia, etc. – everywhere you will find a *mixed* population; there is not a single city that does not have a large national minority. However far decentralisation is carried out, different nationalities will always be found living together in different places (chiefly in urban communities); and it is democratism that surrenders a national minority to the national

majority. But, as we know, V. I. is opposed to the federal state structure
and the boundless decentralisation that exist in the Swiss Federation.
The question is: what was his point in citing the example of Switzerland?

My object in citing the example of Switzerland has already been
explained above. I have also explained that the problem of protecting
the rights of a national minority can be solved *only* by a country-
wide law promulgated in a consistently democratic state that does
not depart from the principle of equality. But in the passage quoted
above, Mr. Liebman repeats still another of the most common (and
most fallacious) arguments (or sceptical remarks) which are usually
made against the Marxist national programme, and which, therefore,
deserve examination.

Marxists are, of course, opposed to federation and decentralisation,
for the simple reason that capitalism requires for its development the
largest and most centralised possible states. *Other conditions being
equal*, the class-conscious proletariat will always stand for the larger
state. It will always fight against medieval particularism, and will
always welcome the closest possible economic amalgamation of large
territories in which the proletariat's struggle against the bourgeoisie
can develop on a broad basis.

Capitalism's broad and rapid development of the productive forces
calls for large, politically compact and united territories, since only
here can the bourgeois class – together with its inevitable antipode, the
proletarian class – unite and sweep away all the old, medieval, caste,
parochial, petty-national, religious and other barriers.

The right of nations to self-determination, i.e., the right to secede
and form independent national states, will be dealt with elsewhere.[17]
But while, and insofar as, different nations constitute a single state,
Marxists will never, under any circumstances, advocate either the
federal principle or decentralisation. The great centralised state is a
tremendous historical step forward from medieval disunity to the future
socialist unity of the whole world, and only *via* such a state (*inseparably*
connected with capitalism), can there be any road to socialism.

It would, however, be inexcusable to forget that in advocating centralism we advocate exclusively *democratic* centralism. On this point all

the philistines in general, and the nationalist philistines in particular (including the late Dragomanov), have so confused the issue that we are obliged again and again to spend time clarifying it.[18]

Far from precluding local self-government, with *autonomy* for regions having special economic and social conditions, a distinct national composition of the population, and so forth, democratic centralism necessarily demands *both*. In Russia centralism is constantly confused with tyranny and bureaucracy. This confusion has naturally arisen from the history of Russia, but even so it is quite inexcusable for a Marxist to yield to it.

This can best be explained by a concrete example.

In her lengthy article 'The National Question and Autonomy', Rosa Luxemburg, among many other curious errors (which we shall deal with below), commits the exceptionally curious one of trying to *restrict* the demand for autonomy to Poland alone.[19]

But first let us see *how* she defines autonomy

Rosa Luxemburg admits – and, being a Marxist, she is, of course, bound to admit – that all the major and important economic and political questions of capitalist society must be dealt with exclusively by the central parliament of the whole country concerned, not by the autonomous Diets of the individual regions. These questions include tariff policy, laws governing commerce and industry, transport and means of communication (railways, post, telegraph, telephone, etc.), the army, the taxation system, civil[20] and criminal law, the general principles of education (for example, the law on purely secular schools, on universal education, on the minimum programme, on democratic school management, etc.), the labour protection laws and political liberties (right of association), etc., etc.

The autonomous Diets – on the basis of the general laws of the country – should deal with questions of purely local, regional or national significance. Amplifying this idea in great – not to say excessive – detail, Rosa Luxemburg mentions, for example, the construction of local railways (No. 12, p. 149) and local highways (No. 14–15, p. 376), etc.

Obviously, one cannot conceive of a modern, truly democratic state that did not grant such autonomy to every region having any appreciably distinct economic and social features, populations of a specific national composition, etc. The principle of centralism, which is essential for the development of capitalism, is not violated by this (local and regional) autonomy, but on the contrary is applied by it *democratically*, not bureaucratically. The broad, free and rapid development of capitalism would be impossible, or at least greatly impeded, by the *absence* of such autonomy, which *facilitates* the concentration of capital, the development of the productive forces, the unity of the bourgeoisie and the unity of the proletariat on a *country-wide* scale; for bureaucratic interference in *purely* local (regional, national, and other) questions is one of the greatest obstacles to economic and political development in general, and an obstacle to *centralism* in serious, important and fundamental matters in particular.

One cannot help smiling, therefore, when reading how our magnificent Rosa Luxemburg tries to prove, with a very serious air and 'purely Marxist' phrases, that the demand for autonomy is applicable *only* to Poland and *only* by way of exception! Of course, there is not a grain of 'parochial' patriotism in this; we have here only 'practical' considerations ... in the case of Lithuania, for example.

Rosa Luxemburg takes four gubernias – Vilna, Kovno, Grodno and Suvalki – assuring her readers (and herself) that these are inhabited 'mainly' by Lithuanians; and by adding the inhabitants of these gubernias together she finds that Lithuanians constitute 23 per cent of the total population, and if Zhmuds are added, they constitute 31 per cent – less than a third. The natural inference is that the idea of autonomy for Lithuania is 'arbitrary and artificial' (No. 10, p. 807).

The reader who is familiar with the commonly known defects of our Russian official statistics will quickly see Rosa Luxemburg's mistake. Why take Grodno Gubernia where the Lithuanians constitute only 0.2 per cent, *one-fifth of one per cent*, of the population? Why take the whole Vilna Gubernia and not its Troki Uyezd alone, where the Lithuanians constitute the *majority* of the population? Why take the whole Suvalki Gubernia and put the number of Lithuanians at 52 per cent of the population, and not the Lithuanian uyezds of that gubernia, i.e., five out of the seven, in which Lithuanians constitute *72* per cent of the population?

It is ridiculous to talk about the conditions and demands of modern capitalism while at the same time taking not the 'modern', not the 'capitalist', but the medieval, feudal and official-bureaucratic administrative divisions of Russia, and in their crudest form at that (gubernias instead of uyezds). Plainly, there can be no question of any serious local reform in Russia until these divisions are abolished and superseded by a *really* 'modern' division that really meets the requirements, *not* of the Treasury, *not* of the bureaucracy, *not* of routine, *not* of the landlords, *not* of the priests, but of capitalism; and one of the modern requirements of capitalism is undoubtedly the greatest possible national uniformity of the population, for nationality and language identity are an important factor making for the complete conquest of the home market and for complete freedom of economic intercourse.

Oddly enough, this obvious mistake of Rosa Luxemburg's is repeated by the Bundist Medem, who sets out to prove, not that Poland's specific features are 'exceptional', but that the principle of national-territorial autonomy is unsuitable (the Bundists stand for national extra-territorial autonomy!). Our Bundists and liquidators collect from all over the world all the errors and all the opportunist vacillations of Social-Democrats of different countries and different nations and appropriate to themselves the *worst* they can find in world Social-Democracy. A scrapbook of Bundist and liquidator writings could, taken together, serve as a model Social-Democratic *museum of bad taste*.

Regional autonomy, Medem tells us didactically, is good for a region or a 'territory', but not for Lettish, Estonian, or other areas (*okrugs*), which have populations ranging from half a million to two million and areas equal to a gubernia. '*That would not be autonomy, but simply a Zemstvo* ... Over this Zemstvo it would be necessary to establish real autonomy' ... and the author goes on to condemn the 'break-up' of the old gubernias and uyezds.[21]

As a matter of fact, the preservation of the medieval, feudal, official administrative divisions means the 'break up' and mutilation of the conditions of modern capitalism. Only people imbued with the spirit of these divisions can, with the learned air of the expert, speculate on the contra-position of 'Zemstvo' and 'autonomy', calling for the stereotyped application of 'autonomy' to large regions and of the Zemstvo to small ones. Modern capitalism does not demand these bureaucratic stereotypes at all. Why national areas with populations, not only of half a million, but even of fifty thousand, should not be able to enjoy autonomy; why such areas should not be able to unite in the most diverse ways with neighbouring areas of different dimensions into a single autonomous 'territory' if that is convenient or necessary for economic intercourse – these things remain the secret of the Bundist Medem.

We would mention that the Brünn Social-Democratic national programme is based entirely on national-territorial autonomy; it proposes that Austria should be divided into 'nationally distinct' areas 'instead of the historical crown lands' (Clause 2 of the Brünn programme). We would not go as far as that. A uniform national population is undoubtedly one of the most reliable factors making for free, broad and really modern commercial intercourse. It is beyond doubt that not a single Marxist, and not even a single firm democrat, will stand up for the Austrian crown lands and the Russian gubernias and uyezds (the latter are not as bad as the Austrian crown lands, but they are very bad nevertheless), or challenge the necessity of replacing these obsolete divisions by others that will conform as far as possible with the national composition of the population, Lastly, it is beyond doubt that in order to eliminate all national oppression it is very important to create autonomous areas, however small, with entirely homogeneous populations, towards which members of the respective nationalities scattered all over the country, or even all over the world, could gravitate, and with which they could enter into relations and free associations of every kind. All this is indisputable, and can be argued against only from the hidebound, bureaucratic point of view.

The national composition of the population, however, is *one* of the very important economic factors, *but not the sole and not* the most important factor. Towns, for example, play an *extremely important* economic role under capitalism, and everywhere, in Poland, in Lithuania, in the Ukraine, in Great Russia, and elsewhere, the towns are marked by mixed populations. To cut the towns off from the villages and areas that economically gravitate towards them, for the sake of the 'national' factor, would be absurd and impossible. That is why Marxists must not take their stand entirely and exclusively on the 'national-territorial' principle.

The solution of the problem proposed by the last conference of Russian Marxists is far more correct than the Austrian. On this question, the conference advanced the following proposition:

> … must provide for wide regional autonomy [not for Poland alone, of course, but for all the regions of Russia][22] and fully democratic local self-government, and the boundaries of the self-governing and autonomous regions must be determined [not by the boundaries of the present gubernias, uyezds, etc., but] by the local inhabitants themselves on the basis of their economic and social conditions, national make-up of the population, etc.

Here the national composition of the population is placed on *the same level* as the other conditions (economic first, then social, etc.) which must serve as a basis for determining the new boundaries that will meet the needs of modern capitalism, not of bureaucracy and Asiatic barbarism. The local population alone can 'assess' those conditions with full precision, and on that basis the central parliament of the country will determine the boundaries of the autonomous regions and the powers of autonomous Diets.

∽

We have still to examine the question of the right of nations to self-determination. On this question a whole collection of opportunists of all nationalities – the liquidator Semkovsky, the Bundist Liebman and the Ukrainian nationalist-socialist Lev Yurkevich – have set to work to 'popularise' the errors of Rosa Luxemburg. This question, which has been so utterly confused by this whole 'collection', will be dealt with in our next article.[23]

The Right of Nations to Self-Determination

Clause 9 of the Russian Marxists' Programme, which deals with the right of nations to self-determination, has (as we have already pointed out in *Prosveshcheniye*) given rise lately to a crusade on the part of the opportunists. The Russian liquidator Semkovsky, in the St. Petersburg liquidationist newspaper, and the Bundist Liebman and the Ukrainian nationalist-socialist Yurkevich in their respective periodicals have violently attacked this clause and treated it with supreme contempt. There is no doubt that this campaign of a motley array of opportunists against our Marxist Programme is closely connected with present-day nationalist vacillations in general. Hence, we consider a detailed examination of this question timely. We would mention, in passing, that none of the opportunists named above has offered a single argument of his own; they all merely repeat what Rosa Luxemburg said in her lengthy Polish article of 1908–09, 'The National Question and Autonomy'. In our exposition we shall deal mainly with the 'original' arguments of this last-named author.

1. What Is Meant by the Self-Determination of Nations?

Naturally, this is the first question that arises when any attempt is made at a Marxist examination of what is known as self-determination. What should be understood by that term? Should the answer be sought in legal definitions deduced from all sorts of 'general concepts' of law? Or is it rather to be sought in a historico-economic study of the national movements?

It is not surprising that the Semkovskys, Liebmans and Yurkevi-ches did not even think of raising this question, and shrugged it off by scoffing at the 'obscurity' of the Marxist Programme, apparently unaware, in their simplicity, that the self-determination of nations is dealt with, not only in the Russian Programme of 1903, but in the resolution of the London International Congress of 1896 (with which I shall deal in detail in the proper place). Far more surprising is the fact that Rosa Luxemburg, who declaims a great deal about the supposedly abstract and metaphysical nature of the clause in question, should herself succumb to the sin of abstraction and metaphysics. It is Rosa Luxemburg herself who is continually lapsing into generalities about self-determination (to the extent even of philosophising amusingly on the question of how the will of the nation is to be ascertained), without anywhere clearly and precisely asking herself whether the gist of the matter lies in legal definitions or in the experience of the national movements throughout the world.

A precise formulation of this question, which no Marxist can avoid, would at once destroy nine-tenths of Rosa Luxemburg's arguments. This is not the first time that national movements have arisen in Russia, nor are they peculiar to that country alone. Throughout the world, the period of the final victory of capitalism over feudalism has been linked up with national movements. For the complete victory of commodity production, the bourgeoisie must capture the home market, and there must be politically united territories whose population speak a single language, with all obstacles to the development of that language and to its consolidation in literature eliminated. Therein is the economic foun-dation of national movements. Language is the most important means of human intercourse. Unity and unimpeded development of language are the most important conditions for genuinely free and extensive commerce on a scale commensurate with modern capitalism, for a free and broad grouping of the population in all its various classes and, lastly, for the establishment of a close connection between the market and each and every proprietor, big or little, and between seller and buyer.

Therefore, the tendency of every national movement is towards the formation of *national states*, under which these requirements of modern capitalism are best satisfied. The most profound economic factors drive towards this goal, and, therefore, for the whole of Western Europe, nay, for the entire civilised world, the national state is *typical* and normal for the capitalist period.

Consequently, if we want to grasp the meaning of self-determination of nations, not by juggling with legal definitions, or 'inventing' abstract definitions, but by examining the historico-economic conditions of the national movements, we must inevitably reach the conclusion that the self-determination of nations means the political separation of these nations from alien national bodies, and the formation of an independent national state.

Later on, we shall see still other reasons why it would be wrong to interpret the right to self-determination as meaning anything but the right to existence as a separate state. At present, we must deal with Rosa Luxemburg's efforts to 'dismiss' the inescapable conclusion that profound economic factors underlie the urge towards a national state.

Rosa Luxemburg is quite familiar with Kautsky's pamphlet *Nationality and Internationality*. (Supplement to *Die Neue Zeit*[1] No.11, 1907–08; Russian translation in the journal *Nauchnaya Mysl*,[2] Riga, 1908.) She is aware that, after carefully analysing the question of the national state in § 4 of that pamphlet, Kautsky arrived at the conclusion that Otto Bauer '*underestimates* the strength of the urge towards a national state' (p. 23 of the pamphlet). Rosa Luxemburg herself quotes the following words of Kautsky's:

> The national state is the form *most suited* to present-day conditions, [i.e., capitalist, civilised, economically progressive conditions, as distinguished from medieval, pre-capitalist, etc.]; it is the form in which the state can best fulfil its tasks' (i.e., the tasks of securing the freest, widest and speediest development of capitalism). To this we must add Kautsky's still more precise concluding remark that states of mixed national composition (known as multinational states, as distinct from national states) are 'always those whose internal constitution has for some reason or other remained abnormal or underdeveloped' (backward). Needless to say, Kautsky speaks of abnormality exclusively in the sense of lack of conformity with what is best adapted to the requirements of a developing capitalism.

The question now is: How did Rosa Luxemburg treat these historico-economic conclusions of Kautsky's? Are they right or wrong? Is Kautsky right in his historico-economic theory, or is Bauer, whose theory is basically psychological? What is the connection between Bauer's undoubted 'national opportunism', his defence of cultural-national autonomy, his nationalistic infatuation ('an occasional emphasis on the national aspect', as Kautsky put it), his 'enormous exaggeration of the national aspect and complete neglect of the international aspect' (Kautsky) – and his underestimation of the strength of the urge to create a national state?

Rosa Luxemburg has not even raised this question. She has not noticed the connection. She has not considered the *sum total* of Bauer's theoretical views. She has not even drawn a line between the historico-economic and the psychological theories of the national question. She confines herself to the following remarks in criticism of Kautsky: 'This "best" national state is only an abstraction, which can easily be developed and defended theoretically, but which does not correspond to reality.' (*Przeglad Socjaldemokratyczny*, 1908, No. 6, p. 499.)

And, in corroboration of this emphatic statement, there follow arguments to the effect that the 'right to self-determination' of small nations is made illusory by the development of the great capitalist powers and by imperialism. 'Can one seriously speak', Rosa Luxemburg exclaims, 'about the "self-determination" of the formally independent Montenegrins, Bulgarians, Romanians, Serbs, Greeks, partly even the Swiss, whose independence is itself a result of the political struggle and the diplomatic game of the "concert of Europe"?!' (p. 500) The state that best suits these conditions is 'not a national state, as Kautsky believes, but a predatory one'. Some dozens of figures are quoted relating to the size of British, French and other colonial possessions.

After reading such arguments, one cannot help marvelling at the author's ability to misunderstand *the how and the why of things*. To teach Kautsky, with a serious mien, that small states are economically dependent on big ones, that a struggle is raging among the bourgeois states for the predatory suppression of other nations, and that imperialism and colonies exist – all this is a ridiculous and puerile attempt to be clever, for none of this has the slightest bearing on the subject.

Not only small states, but even Russia, for example, is entirely dependent, economically, on the power of the imperialist finance capital of the 'rich' bourgeois countries. Not only the miniature Balkan states, but even nineteenth-century America was, economically, a colony of Europe, as Marx pointed out in *Capital*.[2] Kautsky, like any Marxist, is, of course, well aware of this, but that has nothing whatever to do with the question of national movements and the national state.

For the question of the political self-determination of nations and their independence as states in bourgeois society, Rosa Luxemburg has substituted the question of their economic independence. This is just as intelligent as if someone, in discussing the programmatic demand for the supremacy of parliament, i.e., the assembly of people's representatives, in a bourgeois state, were to expound the perfectly correct conviction that big capital dominates in a bourgeois country, whatever the regime in it.

There is no doubt that the greater part of Asia, the most densely populated continent, consists either of colonies of the 'Great Powers', or of states that are extremely dependent and oppressed as nations. But does this commonly known circumstance in any way shake the undoubted fact that, in Asia itself, the conditions for the most complete development of commodity production and the freest, widest and speediest growth of capitalism have been created only in Japan, i.e., only in an independent national state? The latter is a bourgeois state, and for that reason has itself begun to oppress other nations and to enslave colonies. We cannot say whether Asia will have had time to develop into a system of independent national states, like Europe, before the collapse of capitalism, but it remains an undisputed fact that capitalism, having awakened Asia, has called forth national movements everywhere in that continent, too; that the tendency of these movements is towards the creation of national states in Asia; that it is such states that ensure, the best conditions for the development of capitalism. The example of Asia speaks *in favour* of Kautsky and *against* Rosa Luxemburg.

The example of the Balkan states likewise contradicts her, for anyone can now see that the best conditions for the development of capitalism in the Balkans are created precisely in proportion to the creation of independent national states in that peninsula.

Therefore, Rosa Luxemburg notwithstanding, the example of the whole of progressive and civilised mankind, the example of the Balkans and that of Asia prove that Kautsky's proposition is absolutely correct: the national state is the rule and the 'norm' of capitalism; the multi-national state represents backwardness, or is an exception. From the standpoint of national relations, the best conditions for the development of capitalism are undoubtedly provided by the national state. This does not mean, of course, that such a state, which is based on bourgeois relations, can eliminate the exploitation and oppression of nations. It only means that Marxists cannot lose sight of the powerful *economic* factors that give rise to the urge to create national states. It means that 'self-determination of nations' in the Marxists' Programme *cannot*, from a historico-economic point of view, have any other meaning than political self-determination, state independence, and the formation of a national state.

The conditions under which the bourgeois-democratic demand for a 'national state' should be supported from a Marxist, i.e., class-proletarian, point of view will be dealt with in detail below. For the present, we shall confine ourselves to the definition of the *concept* of 'self-determination', and only note that Rosa Luxemburg *knows* what this concept means ('national state'), whereas her opportunist partisans, the Liebmans, the Semkovskys, the Yurkeviches, *do not even know that!*

2. The Historically Concrete Presentation of the Question

The categorical requirement of Marxist theory in investigating any social question is that it be examined within *definite* historical limits, and, if it refers to a particular country (e.g., the national programme for a given country), that account be taken of the specific features distinguishing that country from others in the same historical epoch.

What does this categorical requirement of Marxism imply in its application to the question under discussion?

First, it implies that a clear distinction must be drawn between the two periods of capitalism, which differ radically from each other as far as the national movement is concerned. On the one hand, there is the period of the collapse of feudalism and absolutism, the period of the formation of the bourgeois-democratic society and state, when the national movements for the first time become mass movements and in one way or another draw *all* classes of the population into politics through the press, participation in representative institutions, etc. On the other hand, there is the period of fully formed capitalist states with a long-established constitutional regime and a highly developed antagonism between the proletariat and the bourgeoisie – a period that may be called the eve of capitalism's downfall.

The typical features of the first period are: the awakening of national movements and the drawing of the peasants, the most numerous and the most sluggish section of the population, into these movements, in connection with the struggle for political liberty in general, and for the rights of the nation in particular. Typical features of the second period are: the absence of mass bourgeois-democratic movements and the fact that developed capitalism, in bringing closer together nations that have already been fully drawn into commercial intercourse, and causing them to intermingle to an increasing degree, brings the antagonism between internationally united capital and the international working-class movement into the forefront.

Of course, the two periods are not walled off from each other; they are connected by numerous transitional links, the various countries differing from each other in the rapidity of their national development, in the national make up and distribution of their population, and so on. There can be no question of the Marxists of any country drawing up their national programme without taking into account all these general historical and concrete state conditions.

It is here that we come up against the weakest point in Rosa Luxemburg's arguments. With extraordinary zeal, she embellishes her article with a collection of hard words directed against § 9 of our Programme, which she declares to be 'sweeping', 'a platitude', 'a metaphysical phrase', and so on without end. It would be natural to expect an author who so admirably condemns metaphysics (in the Marxist sense, i.e., anti-dialectics) and empty abstractions to set us an example of how to make a concrete historical analysis of the question. The question at issue is the national programme of the Marxists of a definite country – Russia, in a definite period – the beginning of the twentieth century. But does Rosa Luxemburg raise the question as to *what historical* period Russia is passing through, or *what are the concrete* features of the national question and the national movements of that *particular* country in that *particular* period?

No, she does not! *She says absolutely nothing about it!* In her work you will not find even the shadow of an analysis of how the national question stands in *Russia* in the present historical period, or of the specific features of *Russia* in this particular respect!

We are told that the national question in the Balkans is presented differently from that in Ireland; that Marx appraised the Polish and Czech national movements in the concrete conditions of 1848 in such and such a way (a page of excerpts from Marx); that Engels appraised the struggle of the forest cantons of Switzerland against Austria and the Battle of Morgarten which took place in 1315 in such and such a way (a page of quotations from Engels with the appropriate comments from Kautsky); that Lassalle regarded the peasant war in Germany of the sixteenth century as reactionary, etc.

It cannot be said that these remarks and quotations have any novelty about them, but at all events it is interesting for the reader to be occasionally reminded just how Marx, Engels and Lassalle approached the analysis of concrete historical problems in individual countries. And a perusal of these instructive quotations from Marx and Engels reveals most strikingly the ridiculous position Rosa Luxemburg has placed herself in, she preaches eloquently and angrily the need for a concrete historical analysis of the national question in different countries at different times, but she *does not make the least* attempt to determine *what* historical stage in the development of capitalism *Russia* is passing through at the beginning of the twentieth century, or what the *specific features* of the national question in this country are. Rosa Luxemburg gives examples of how *others* have treated the question in a Marxist fashion, as if deliberately stressing how often the road to hell is paved with good intentions and how often good counsel covers up unwillingness or inability to follow such advice in practice.

Here is one of her edifying comparisons. In protesting against the demand for the independence of Poland, Rosa Luxemburg refers to a pamphlet she wrote in 1898, proving the rapid 'industrial development of Poland', with the latter's manufactured goods being marketed in Russia. Needless to say, no conclusion whatever can be drawn from this on the question of the *right* to self-determination; it only proves the disappearance of the old Poland of the landed gentry, etc. But Rosa Luxemburg always passes on imperceptibly to the conclusion that, among the factors that unite Russia and Poland, the purely economic factors of modern capitalist relations now predominate.

Then our Rosa proceeds to the question of autonomy, and though her article is entitled 'The National Question and Autonomy' *in general*, she begins to argue that the Kingdom of Poland has an *exclusive* right to autonomy (see *Prosveshcheniye*, 1913, No. 12). To support Poland's right to autonomy, Rosa Luxemburg evidently judges the state system of Russia by her economic, political and sociological characteristics and everyday life – a totality of features which, taken together, produce the concept of 'Asiatic despotism'. (*Przeglad* No. 12, p. 137.)

It is generally known that this kind of state system possesses great stability whenever completely patriarchal and precapitalist features predominate in the economic system and where commodity production and class differentiation are scarcely developed. However, if in a country whose state system is distinctly *precapitalist* in character there exists a nationally demarcated region where capitalism is *rapidly* developing, then the more rapidly that capitalism develops, the greater will be the antagonism between it and the precapitalist state system, and the more likely will be the separation of the progressive region from the whole – with which it is connected, not by 'modern capitalistic', but by 'Asiatically despotic' ties.

Thus, Rosa Luxemburg does not get her arguments to hang together even on the question of the social structure of the government in Russia with regard to bourgeois Poland; as for the concrete, historical, specific features of the national movements in Russia – she does not even raise that question.

That is a point with which we must now deal.

3. The Concrete Features of the National Question in Russia, and Russia's Bourgeois-Democratic Reformation

'Despite the elasticity of the principle of "the right of nations to self-determination", which is a mere platitude, and, obviously, equally applicable, not only to the nations inhabiting Russia, but also to the nations inhabiting Germany and Austria, Switzerland and Sweden, America and Australia, we do not find it in the programmes of any of the present-day socialist parties …' (*Przeglad* No. 6, p. 483.)

This is how Rosa Luxemburg opens her attack upon § 9 of the Marxist programme. In trying to foist on us the conception that this clause in the programme is a 'mere platitude', Rosa Luxemburg herself falls victim to this error, alleging with amusing boldness that this point is, 'obviously, equally applicable' to Russia, Germany, etc.

Obviously, we shall reply, Rosa Luxemburg has decided to make her article a collection, of errors in logic that could be used for schoolboy exercises. For Rosa Luxemburg's tirade is sheer nonsense and a mockery of the historically concrete presentation of the question.

If one interprets the Marxist programme in Marxist fashion, not in a childish way, one will, without difficulty, grasp the fact that it refers to bourgeois-democratic national movements. That being the case, it is 'obvious' that this programme 'sweepingly', and as a 'mere platitude', etc., covers *all* instances of bourgeois-democratic national movements. No less obvious to Rosa Luxemburg, if she gave the slightest thought to it, is the conclusion that our programme refers *only* to cases where such a movement is actually in existence.

Had she given thought to these obvious considerations, Rosa Luxemburg would have easily perceived what nonsense she was talking. In accusing *us* of uttering a 'platitude' she has used *against us* the argument that no mention is made of the right to self-determination in the programmes of countries where there are no bourgeois-democratic national movements. A remarkably clever argument!

A comparison of the political and economic development of various countries, as well as of their Marxist programmes, is of tremendous importance from the standpoint of Marxism, for there can be no doubt

that all modern states are of a common capitalist nature and are therefore subject to a common law of development. But such a comparison
must be drawn in a sensible way. The elementary condition for comparison is to find out whether the historical periods of development
of the countries concerned are at all *comparable*. For instance, only
absolute ignoramuses (such as Prince Y. Trubetskoi in *Russkaya Mysl*)
are capable of 'comparing' the Russian Marxists' agrarian programme
with the programmes of Western Europe, since our programme replies
to questions that concern the *bourgeois-democratic* agrarian reform,
whereas, in the Western countries, no such question arises.

The same applies to the national question. In most Western countries,
it was settled long ago. It is ridiculous to seek an answer to non-existent
questions in the programmes of Western Europe. In this respect, Rosa
Luxemburg has lost sight of the most important thing – the difference
between countries, where bourgeois-democratic reforms have long
been completed, and those where they have not.

The crux of the matter lies in this difference. Rosa Luxemburg's
complete disregard of it transforms her verbose article into a collection
of empty and meaningless platitudes.

The epoch of bourgeois-democratic revolutions in Western, conti-
nental Europe embraces a fairly definite period, approximately between
1789 and 1871. This was precisely the period of national movements
and the creation of national states. When this period drew to a close,
Western Europe had been transformed into a settled system of bourgeois states, which, as a general rule, were nationally uniform states.
Therefore, to seek the right to self-determination in the programmes of
West-European socialists at this time of day is to betray one's ignorance
of the ABCs of Marxism.

In Eastern Europe and Asia the period of bourgeois-democratic
revolutions did not begin until 1905. The revolutions in Russia, Persia,
Turkey and China, the Balkan wars – such is the chain of world events
of *our* period in our 'Orient'. And only a blind man could fail to see
in this chain of events the awakening of a *whole series* of bourgeois-
democratic national movements which strive to create nationally
independent and nationally uniform states. It is precisely and solely
because Russia and the neighbouring countries are passing through

this period that we must have a clause in our programme on the right of nations to self-determination.

But let us continue the quotation from Rosa Luxemburg's article a little more. She writes:

> In particular, the programme of a party which is operating in a state with an extremely varied national composition, and for which the national question is a matter of first-rate importance – the programme of the Austrian Social-Democratic Party – does not contain the principle of the right of nations to self-determination. (Ibid.)

Thus, an attempt is made to convince the reader by the example of Austria 'in particular'. Let us examine this example in the light of concrete historical facts and see just how sound it is.

In the first place, let us pose the fundamental question of the completion of the bourgeois-democratic revolution. In Austria, this revolution began in 1848 and was over in 1867. Since then, a more or less fully established bourgeois constitution has dominated, for nearly half a century, and on its basis a legal workers' party is legally functioning.

Therefore, in the internal conditions of Austria's development (i.e., from the standpoint of the development of capitalism in Austria in general, and among its various nations in particular), there are *no* factors that produce leaps and bounds, a concomitant of which might be the formation of nationally independent states. In assuming, by her comparison, that Russia is in an analogous position in this respect, Rosa Luxemburg not only makes a fundamentally erroneous and antihistorical assumption, but also involuntarily slips into liquidationism.

Secondly, the profound difference in the relations between the nationalities in Austria and those in Russia is particularly important for the question we are concerned with. Not only was Austria for a long time a state in which the Germans preponderated, but the Austrian Germans laid claim to hegemony in the German nation as a whole. This 'claim', as Rosa Luxemburg (who is seemingly so averse to commonplaces, platitudes, abstractions …) will perhaps be kind enough to remember, was shattered in the war of 1866. The German nation predominating in Austria found itself *outside the pale* of the independent

German state which finally took shape in 1871. On the other hand, the Hungarians' attempt to create an independent national state collapsed under the blows of the Russian serf army as far back as 1849.

A very peculiar situation was thus created – a striving on the part of the Hungarians and then of the Czechs, not for separation from Austria, but, on the contrary, for the preservation of Austria's integrity, precisely in order to preserve national independence, which might have been completely crushed by more rapacious and powerful neighbours! Owing to this peculiar situation, Austria assumed the form of a dual state, and she is now being transformed into a triple state (Germans, Hungarians, Slavs).

Is there anything like this in Russia? Is there in our country a striving of the 'subject peoples' for unity with the Great Russians in face of the danger of *worse* national oppression?

One need only pose this question in order to see that the comparison between Russia and Austria on the question of self-determination of nations is meaningless, platitudinous and ignorant.

The peculiar conditions in Russia with regard to the national question are just the reverse of those we see in Austria. Russia is a state with a single national centre – Great Russia. The Great Russians occupy a vast, unbroken stretch of territory, and number about seventy million. The specific features of this national state are: first, that 'subject peoples' (which, on the whole, comprise the majority of the entire population – 57 per cent) inhabit the border regions; secondly, the oppression of these subject peoples is much stronger here than in the neighbouring states (and not even in the European states alone); thirdly, in a number of cases the oppressed nationalities inhabiting the border regions have compatriots across the border, who enjoy greater national independence (suffice it to mention the Finns, the Swedes, the Poles, the Ukrainians and the Romanians along the western and southern frontiers of the state); fourthly, the development of capitalism and the general level of culture are often higher in the non-Russian border regions than in the centre. Lastly, it is in the neighbouring Asian states that we see the beginning of a phase of bourgeois revolutions and national movements which are spreading to some of the kindred nationalities within the borders of Russia.

Thus, it is precisely the special concrete, historical features of the national question in Russia that make the recognition of the right of nations to self-determination in the present period a matter of special urgency in our country.

Incidentally, even from the purely factual angle, Rosa Luxemburg's assertion that the Austrian Social-Democrats' programme does not contain any recognition of the right of nations to self-determination is incorrect. We need only open the Minutes of the Brünn Congress, which adopted the national programme, to find the statements by the Ruthenian Social-Democrat Hankiewicz on behalf of the entire Ukrainian (Ruthenian) delegation (p. 85 of the Minutes), and by the Polish Social-Democrat Reger on behalf of the entire Polish delegation (p. 108), to the effect that one of the aspirations of the Austrian Social-Democrats of both the above-mentioned nations is to secure national unity, and the freedom and independence of their nations. Hence, while the Austrian Social-Democrats did not include the right of nations to self-determination directly in their programme, they did nevertheless allow the demand for national independence to be advanced by *sections* of the party. In effect, this means, of course, the recognition of the right of nations to self-determination! Thus, Rosa Luxemburg's reference to Austria speaks *against* Rosa Luxemburg in *all* respects.

4. 'Practicality' in the National Question

Rosa Luxemburg's argument that § 9 of our Programme contains nothing 'practical' has been seized upon by the opportunists. Rosa Luxemburg is so delighted with this argument that in some parts of her article this 'slogan' is repeated eight times on a single page.

She writes: § 9 'gives no practical lead on the day-by-day policy of the proletariat, no practical solution of national problems'.

Let us examine this argument, which elsewhere is formulated in such a way that it makes § 9 look quite meaningless, or else commits us to support all national aspirations.

What does the demand for 'practicality' in the national question mean?

It means one of three things: support for all national aspirations; the answer 'yes' or 'no' to the question of secession by any nation; or that national demands are in general immediately 'practicable'.

Let us examine all three possible meanings of the demand for 'practicality'.

The bourgeoisie, which naturally assumes the leadership at the start of every national movement, says that support for all national aspirations is practical. However, the proletariat's policy in the national question (as in all others) supports the bourgeoisie only in a certain direction, but it never coincides with the bourgeoisie's policy. The working class supports the bourgeoisie only in order to secure national peace (which the bourgeoisie cannot bring about completely and which can be achieved only with *complete* democracy), in order to secure equal rights and to create the best conditions for the class struggle. Therefore, it is *in opposition to the practicality* of the bourgeoisie that the proletarians advance their *principles* in the national question; they always give the bourgeoisie *only conditional* support. What every bourgeoisie is out for in the national question is either privileges for its *own* nation, or exceptional advantages for it; this is called being 'practical'. The proletariat is opposed to all privileges, to all exclusiveness. To demand that it should be 'practical' means following the lead of the bourgeoisie, falling into opportunism.

The demand for a 'yes' or 'no' reply to the question of secession in the case of every nation may seem a very 'practical' one. In reality it is absurd; it is metaphysical in theory, while in practice it leads to subordinating the proletariat to the bourgeoisie's policy. The bourgeoisie always places its national demands in the forefront, and does so in categorical fashion. With the proletariat, however, these demands are subordinated to the interests of the class struggle. Theoretically, you cannot say in advance whether the bourgeois-democratic revolution will end in a given nation seceding from another nation, or in its equality with the latter; *in either case*, the important thing for the proletariat is to ensure the development of its class. For the bourgeoisie it is important to hamper this development by pushing the aims of its 'own' nation before those of the proletariat. That is why the proletariat confines itself, so to speak, to the negative demand for recognition of the *right* to self-determination, without giving guarantees to any nation, and without undertaking to give *anything at the expense* of another nation.

This may not be 'practical', but it is in effect the best guarantee for the achievement of the most democratic of all possible solutions. The proletariat needs *only* such guarantees, whereas the bourgeoisie of every nation requires guarantees for *its own* interest, regardless of the position of (or the possible disadvantages to) other nations.

The bourgeoisie is most of all interested in the 'feasibility' of a given demand – hence the invariable policy of coming to terms with the bourgeoisie of other nations, to the detriment of the proletariat. For the proletariat, however, the important thing is to strengthen its class against the bourgeoisie and to educate the masses in the spirit of consistent democracy and socialism.

This may not be 'practical' as far as the opportunists are concerned, but it is the only real guarantee, the guarantee of the greater national equality and peace, despite the feudal landlords and the *nationalist* bourgeoisie.

The whole task of the proletarians in the national question is 'unpractical' from the standpoint of the *nationalist* bourgeoisie of every nation, because the proletarians, opposed as they are to nationalism of every kind, demand 'abstract' equality; they demand, as a matter of principle, that there should be no privileges, however slight. Failing to grasp this, Rosa Luxemburg, by her misguided eulogy of practicality, has opened the door wide for the opportunists, and especially for opportunist concessions to Great-Russian nationalism.

Why Great-Russian? Because the Great Russians in Russia are an oppressor nation, and opportunism in the national question will of course find expression among oppressed nations otherwise than among oppressor nations.

On the plea that its demands are 'practical', the bourgeoisie of the oppressed nations will call upon the proletariat to support its aspirations unconditionally. The most practical procedure is to say a plain 'yes' in favour of the secession of a *particular* nation rather than in favour of all nations having the *right* to secede!

The proletariat is opposed to such practicality. While recognising equality and equal rights to a national state, it values above all and places foremost the alliance of the proletarians of all nations, and assesses any national demand, any national separation, *from the angle* of the workers' class struggle. This call for practicality is in fact merely a call for uncritical acceptance of bourgeois aspirations.

By supporting the right to secession, we are told, you are supporting the bourgeois nationalism of the oppressed nations. This is what Rosa Luxemburg says, and she is echoed by Semkovsky, the opportunist, who incidentally is the only representative of liquidationist ideas on this question, in the liquidationist newspaper!

Our reply to this is: no, it is to the bourgeoisie that a 'practical' solution of this question is important. To the workers the important thing is to distinguish the *principles* of the two trends. *Insofar as* the bourgeoisie of the oppressed nation fights the oppressor, we are always, in every case, and more strongly than anyone else, *in favour*, for we are the staunchest and the most consistent enemies of oppression. But insofar as the bourgeoisie of the oppressed nation stands for *its own* bourgeois nationalism, we stand against. We fight against the privileges and violence of the oppressor nation, and do not in any way condone strivings for privileges on the part of the oppressed nation.

If, in our political agitation, we fail to advance and advocate the slogan of the *right* to secession, we shall play into the hands, not only of the bourgeoisie, but also of the feudal landlords and the absolutism of the *oppressor* nation. Kautsky long ago used this argument against Rosa Luxemburg, and the argument is indisputable. When, in her anxiety not to 'assist' the nationalist bourgeoisie of Poland, Rosa Luxemburg rejects the *right* to secession in the programme of the Marxists *in Russia*, she is *in fact* assisting the Great-Russian Black Hundreds. She is in fact assisting opportunist tolerance of the privileges (and worse than privileges) of the Great Russians.

Carried away by the struggle against nationalism in Poland, Rosa Luxemburg has forgotten the nationalism of the Great Russians, although it is *this* nationalism that is the most formidable at the present time. It is a nationalism that is more feudal than bourgeois, and is the principal obstacle to democracy and to the proletarian struggle. The bourgeois nationalism of *any* oppressed nation has a general democratic content that is directed *against* oppression, and it is this content that we *unconditionally* support, At the same time we strictly distinguish it from the tendency towards national exclusiveness; we fight against the tendency of the Polish bourgeois to oppress the Jews, etc., etc.

This is 'unpractical' from the standpoint of the bourgeois and the philistine, but it is the only policy in the national question that is practical, based on principles, and really promotes democracy, liberty and proletarian unity.

The recognition of the right to secession for all; the appraisal of each concrete question of secession from the point of view of removing all inequality, all privileges, and all exclusiveness.

Let us consider the position of an oppressor nation. Can a nation be free if it oppresses other nations? It cannot. The interests of the freedom of the Great-Russian population[4] require a struggle against such oppression. The long, centuries-old history of the suppression of the movements of the oppressed nations, and the systematic propaganda in favour of such suppression coming from the 'upper' classes have created enormous obstacles to the cause of freedom of the Great-Russian people itself, in the form of prejudices, etc.

The Great-Russian Black Hundreds deliberately foster these prejudices and encourage them. The Great-Russian bourgeoisie tolerates or condones them. The Great-Russian proletariat cannot achieve *its own* aims or clear the road to its freedom without systematically countering these prejudices.

In Russia, the creation of an independent national state remains, for the time being, the privilege of the Great-Russian nation alone. We, the Great-Russian proletarians, who defend no privileges whatever, do not defend this privilege either. We are fighting on the ground of a definite state; we unite the workers of all nations living in this state; we cannot vouch for any particular path of national development, for we are marching to our class goal along *all* possible paths.

However, we cannot move towards that goal unless we combat all nationalism, and uphold the equality of the various nations. Whether the Ukraine, for example, is destined to form an independent state is a matter that will be determined by a thousand unpredictable factors. Without attempting idle '*guesses*', we firmly uphold something that is beyond doubt: the right of the Ukraine to form such a state. We respect this right; we do not uphold the privileges of Great Russians with regard to Ukrainians; we *educate* the masses in the spirit of recognition of that right, in the spirit of rejecting *state* privileges for any nation.

In the leaps which all nations have made in the period of bourgeois revolutions, clashes and struggles over the right to a national state are possible and probable. We proletarians declare in advance that we are *opposed* to Great-Russian privileges, and this is what guides our entire propaganda and agitation.

In her quest for 'practicality' Rosa Luxemburg has lost sight of the *principal* practical task both of the Great-Russian proletariat and of the proletariat of other nationalities: that of day-by-day agitation and propaganda against all state and national privileges, and for the right, the equal right of all nations, to their national state. This (at present) is our principal task in the national question, for only in this way can we defend the interests of democracy and the alliance of all proletarians of all nations on an equal footing.

This propaganda may be 'unpractical' from the point of view of the Great-Russian oppressors, as well as from the point of view of the bourgeoisie of the oppressed nations (both demand a *definite* 'yes' or 'no', and accuse the Social-Democrats of being 'vague'). In reality it is this propaganda, and this propaganda alone, that ensures the genuinely democratic, the genuinely socialist education of the masses. This is the only propaganda to ensure the greatest chances of national peace in Russia, should she remain a multi-national state, and the most peaceful (and for the proletarian class struggle, harmless) division into separate national states, should the question of such a division arise.

To explain this policy – the only proletarian policy – in the national question more concretely, we shall examine the attitude of Great-Russian liberalism towards the 'self-determination of nations', and the example of Norway's secession from Sweden.

5. The Liberal Bourgeoisie and the Socialist
Opportunists in the National Question

We have seen that the following argument is one of Rosa Luxemburg's 'trump cards' in her struggle against the programme of the Marxists in Russia: recognition of the right to self-determination is tantamount to supporting the bourgeois nationalism of the oppressed nations. On the other hand, she says, if we take this right to mean no more than combating all violence against other nations, there is no need for a special clause in the programme, for Social-Democrats are, in general, opposed to all national oppression and inequality.

The first argument, as Kautsky irrefutably proved nearly twenty years ago, is a case of blaming other people for one's own nationalism; in her fear of the nationalism of the bourgeoisie of oppressed nations, Rosa Luxemburg is *actually* playing into the hands of the Black-Hundred nationalism of the Great Russians! Her second argument is actually a timid evasion of the question whether or not recognition of national equality includes recognition of the right to secession. If it does, then Rosa Luxemburg admits that, in principle, § 9 of our Programme is correct. If it does not, then she does not recognise national equality. Shuffling and evasions will not help matters here!

However, the best way to test these and all similar arguments is to study the attitude of the *various classes* of society towards this question. For the Marxist this test is obligatory. We must proceed from what is objective; we must examine the relations between the classes on this point. In failing to do so, Rosa Luxemburg is guilty of those very sins of metaphysics, abstractions, platitudes, and sweeping statements, etc., of which she vainly tries to accuse her opponents.

We are discussing the Programme of the Marxists *in Russia*, i.e., of the Marxists of all the nationalities in Russia. Should we not examine the position of the *ruling* classes of Russia?

The position of the 'bureaucracy' (we beg pardon for this inaccurate term) and of the feudal landlords of our united-nobility type is well known. They definitely reject both the equality of nationalities and the right to self-determination. Theirs is the old motto of the days of serfdom: autocracy, orthodoxy, and the national essence – the last term applying only to the Great-Russian nation. Even the Ukrainians are declared to be an 'alien' people and their very language is being suppressed.

Let us glance at the Russian bourgeoisie, which was 'called upon' to take part – a very modest part, it is true, but nevertheless some part – in the government, under the 'June Third' legislative and administrative system. It will not need many words to prove that the Octobrists are following the Rights in this question. Unfortunately, some Marxists pay much less attention to the stand of the Great-Russian liberal bourgeoisie, the Progressists and the Cadets. Yet he who fails to study that stand and give it careful thought will inevitably flounder in abstractions and groundless statements in discussing the question of the right of nations to self-determination.

Skilled though it is in the art of diplomatically evading direct answers to 'unpleasant' questions, *Rech*, the principal organ of the Constitutional-Democratic Party, was compelled, in its controversy with *Pravda* last year, to make certain valuable admissions. The trouble started over the All-Ukraine Students' Congress held in Lvov in the summer of 1913.[5] Mr. Mogilyansky, the 'Ukrainian expert' or Ukrainian correspondent of *Rech*, wrote an article in which he poured vitriolic abuse ('ravings', 'adventurism', etc.) on the idea that the Ukraine should secede, an idea which Dontsov, a nationalist-socialist, had advocated and the above-mentioned congress approved.

While in no way identifying itself with Mr. Dontsov, and declaring explicitly that he was a nationalist-socialist and that many Ukrainian Marxists did not agree with him, *Rabochaya Pravda* stated that the *tone* of *Rech*, or, rather, the *way it formulated the question in principle*, was improper and reprehensible for a Great-Russian democrat, or for anyone desiring to pass as a democrat. Let *Rech* repudiate the Dontsovs if it likes, but, *from the standpoint of principle*, a Great-Russian organ of democracy, which it claims to be, cannot be oblivious of the *freedom* to secede, the *right* to secede.

A few months later, *Rech*, No. 331, published an 'explanation' from Mr. Mogilyansky, who had learned from the Ukrainian news-paper *Shlyakhi*,[6] published in Lvov, of Mr. Dontsov's reply, in which, incidentally, Dontsov stated that 'the chauvinist attacks in *Rech* have been properly sullied [branded?] only in the Russian Social-Democratic press'. This 'explanation' consisted of the thrice-repeated statement that 'criticism of Mr. Dontsov's recipes' 'has nothing in common with the repudiation of the right of nations to self-determination'.

'It must be said', wrote Mr. Mogilyansky, 'that even "the right of nations to self-determination" is not a fetish [mark this!] beyond criticism: unwholesome conditions in the life of nations may give rise to unwholesome tendencies in national self-determination, and the fact that these are brought to light does not mean that the right of nations to self-determination has been rejected.'

As you see, this liberal's talk of a 'fetish' was quite in keeping with Rosa Luxemburg's. It was obvious that Mr. Mogilyansky was trying to evade a direct reply to the question whether or not he recognised the right to political self-determination, i.e., to secession.

The newspaper *Proletarskaya Pravda*, issue No. 4, for 11 December 1913, also put this question *point-blank* to Mr. Mogilyansky and to the Constitutional-Democratic *Party*.

Thereupon *Rech* (No. 340) published an unsigned, i.e., official, editorial statement replying to this question. This reply boils down to the following three points:

1) § 11 of the Constitutional-Democratic Party's programme speaks bluntly, precisely and clearly of the 'right of nations to free *cultural* self-determination'.

2) *Rech* affirms that *Proletarskaya Pravda* 'hopelessly confuses' self-determination with separatism, with the secession of a given nation.

3) '*Actually, the Cadets have never pledged themselves to advocate the right of 'nations to secede' from the Russian state*' (See the article 'National-Liberalism and the Right of Nations to Self-Determination', in *Proletarskaya Pravda* No. 12, December 20, 1913.)

Let us first consider the second point in the *Rech* statement. How strikingly it shows to the Semkovskys, Liebmans, Yurkeviches and other opportunists that the hue and cry they have raised about the alleged 'vagueness', or 'indefiniteness', of the term 'self-determination' is *in fact*, i.e., from the standpoint of objective class relationships and the class struggle in Russia, *simply a rehash* of the liberal-monarchist bourgeoisie's utterances!

Proletarskaya Pravda put the following *three* questions to the enlightened 'Constitutional-Democratic' gentlemen of *Rech*: (1) do they deny that, throughout the entire history of international democracy, and especially since the middle of the nineteenth century, self-determination of nations has been understood to mean precisely political self-determination, the right to form an independent national state? (2) do they deny that the well-known resolution adopted by the International Socialist Congress in London in 1896 has the same meaning? and (3) do they deny that Plekhanov, in writing about self-determination as far back as 1902, meant precisely political self-determination? When *Proletarskaya Pravda* posed these three questions, *the Cadets fell silent*!

Not a word did they utter in reply, for they had nothing to say. They had to admit tacitly that *Proletarskaya Pravda* was absolutely right.

The liberals' outcries that the term 'self-determination' is vague and that the Social-Democrats 'hopelessly confuse' it with separatism are nothing more than attempts to *confuse* the issue, and evade recognition of a universally established democratic principle. If the Semkovskys, Liebmans and Yurkeviches were not so ignorant, they would be ashamed to address the Workers in a *liberal* vein.

But to proceed. *Proletarskaya Pravda* compelled *Rech* to admit that, in the programme of the Constitutional-Democrats, the term 'cultural' self-determination means in effect the *repudiation of political* self-determination.

'Actually, the Cadets have never pledged themselves to advocate the right of 'nations to secede' from the Russian state' – it was not without reason that *Proletarskaya Pravda* recommended to *Novoye Vremya* and *Zemshchina* these words from *Rech* as an example of our Cadets' 'loyalty'. In its issue No. 13563, *Novoye Vremya*, which never, of course, misses an opportunity of mentioning 'the Yids' and taking digs at the Cadets, nevertheless stated: 'What, to the Social-Democrats, is an axiom of political wisdom [i.e., recognition of the right of nations to self-determination, to secede], is today beginning to cause disagreement even among the Cadets.'

By declaring that they 'have never pledged themselves to advocate the right of nations to secede from the Russian state', the Cadets have, in principle, taken exactly the same stand as *Novoye Vremya*. This is precisely one of the fundamentals of Cadet *national-liberalism*, of their kinship with the Purishkeviches, and of their dependence, political, ideological and practical, on the latter. *Proletarskaya Pravda* wrote: 'The Cadets have studied history and know only too well what – to put it mildly – pogrom-like actions the practice of the ancient right of the Purishkeviches to 'grab 'em and hold 'em' has often led to.' Although perfectly aware of the feudalist source and nature of the Purishkeviches' omnipotence; the Cadets are, nevertheless, taking their stand *on the basis* of the relationships and frontiers created by that very class. Knowing full well that there is much in the relationships and frontiers created or fixed by this class that is un-European and anti-European (we would say Asiatic if this did not sound undeservedly slighting to the Japanese and Chinese), the Cadets, nevertheless, accept them as the utmost limit.

Thus, they are adjusting themselves to the Purishkeviches, cringing to them, fearing to jeopardise their position, protecting them from the people's movement, from the democracy. As *Proletarskaya Pravda* wrote: 'In effect, this means adapting oneself to the interests of the feudal-minded landlords and to the worst nationalist prejudices of the dominant nation, instead of systematically combating those prejudices.'

Being men who are familiar with history and claim to be democrats, the Cadets do not even attempt to assert that the democratic movement, which is today characteristic of both Eastern Europe and Asia and is striving to change both on the model of the civilised capitalist countries, is bound to leave intact the boundaries fixed by the feudal epoch, the epoch of the omnipotence of the Purishkeviches and the disfranchisement of wide strata of the bourgeoisie and petty bourgeoisie.

The fact that the question raised in the controversy between *Proletarskaya Pravda* and *Rech* was not merely a literary question, but one that involved a real political issue of the day, was proved, among other things, by the last conference of the Constitutional-Democratic Party held on March 23–25, 1914; in the official report of this conference in *Rech* (No. 83, of March 26, 1914) we read:

A particularly lively discussion also took place on national problems. The Kiev deputies, who were supported by N. V. Nekrasov and A. M. Kolyubakin, pointed out that the national question was becoming a key issue, which would have to be faced up to more resolutely than hitherto. F. F. Kokoshkin pointed out, however [this 'however' is like Shchedrin's 'but' – 'the ears never grow higher than the forehead, never!'] that both the programme and past political experience demanded that 'elastic formulas' of 'political self-determination of nationalities' should be handled very carefully.

This most remarkable line of reasoning at the Cadet conference deserves serious attention from all Marxists and all democrats. (We will note in parentheses that *Kievskaya Mysl*, which is evidently very well informed and no doubt presents Mr. Kokoshkin's ideas correctly, added that, of course, as a warning to his opponents, he laid special stress on the danger of the 'disintegration' of the state.)

The official report in *Rech* is composed with consummate diplomatic skill designed to lift the veil as little as possible and to conceal as much as possible. Yet, in the main, what took place at the Cadet conference is quite clear. The liberal-bourgeois delegates, who were familiar with the state of affairs in the Ukraine, and the 'Left' Cadets raised the question *precisely of the political* self-determination of nations. Otherwise, there would have been no need for Mr. Kokoshkin to urge that this 'formula' should be 'handled carefully'.

The Cadet programme, which was of course known to the delegates at the Cadet conference, speaks of 'cultural', *not* of political self-determination. Hence, Mr. Kokoshkin was *defending* the programme *against* the Ukrainian delegates, and *against* the Left Cadets; he was defending 'cultural' self-determination *as opposed* to 'political' self-determination. It is perfectly clear that in opposing 'political' self-determination, in playing up the danger of the 'disintegration of the state', and in calling the formula 'political self-determination' an '*elastic*' one (quite in keeping with Rosa Luxemburg!), Mr. Kokoshkin was defending Great-Russian national-liberalism against the more 'Left' or more democratic elements of the Constitutional-Democratic Party and also against the Ukrainian bourgeoisie.

Mr. Kokoshkin won the day at the Cadet conference, as is evident from the treacherous little word 'however' in the *Rech* report; Great-Russian national-liberalism has triumphed among the Cadets. Will not this victory help to clear the minds of those misguided individuals among the Marxists in Russia who, like the Cadets, have also begun to fear the 'elastic formulas of political self-determination of nationalities'?

Let us, 'however', examine the substance of Mr. Kokoshkin's line of thought. By referring to 'past political experience' (i.e., evidently, the experience of 1905, when the Great-Russian bourgeoisie took alarm for its national privileges and scared the Cadet Party with its fears), and also by playing up the danger of the 'disintegration of the state', Mr. Kokoshkin showed that he understood perfectly well that political self-determination can mean nothing else but the right to secede and form an independent national state. The question is – how should Mr. Kokoshkin's fears be appraised in the light of democracy in general, and the proletarian class struggle in particular?

Mr. Kokoshkin would have us believe that recognition of the right to secession increases the danger of the 'disintegration of the state'. This is the viewpoint of Constable Mymretsov, whose motto was 'grab 'em and hold 'em'. From the viewpoint of democracy in general, the very opposite is the case: recognition of the right to secession *reduces* the danger of the 'disintegration of the state'.

Mr. Kokoshkin argues exactly like the nationalists do. At their last congress they attacked the Ukrainian 'Mazeppists'. The Ukrainian movement, Mr. Savenko and Co. exclaimed, threatens to weaken the ties between the Ukraine and Russia, since Austrian Ukrainophilism is strengthening the Ukrainians' ties with Austria! It remains unexplained why Russia cannot try to 'strengthen' her ties with the Ukrainians *through the same method* that the Savenkos blame Austria for using, i.e., by granting the Ukrainians freedom to use their own language, self-government and an autonomous Diet.

The arguments of the Savenkos and Kokoshkins are exactly alike, and from the purely logical point of view they are equally ridiculous and absurd. Is it not clear that the more liberty the Ukrainian nationality enjoys in any particular country, the stronger its ties with that country will be? One would think that this truism could not be disputed without totally abandoning all the premises of democracy. Can there be greater freedom of nationality, as such, than the freedom to secede, the freedom to form an independent national state?

To clear up this question, which has been so confused by the liberals (and by those who are so misguided, as to echo them), we shall cite a very simple example. Let us take the question of divorce. In her article Rosa Luxemburg writes that the centralised democratic state, while conceding autonomy to its constituent parts, should retain the most important branches of legislation, including legislation on divorce, under the jurisdiction of the central parliament. The concern that the central authority of the democratic state should retain the power to allow divorce can be readily understood. The reactionaries are opposed to freedom of divorce; they say that it must be 'handled carefully', and loudly declare that it means the 'disintegration of the family'. The democrats, however, believe that the reactionaries are hypocrites, and that they are actually defending the omnipotence of the police and the bureaucracy, the privileges of one of the sexes, and the worst kind of oppression of women. They believe that in actual fact freedom of divorce will not cause the 'disintegration' of family ties, but, on the contrary, will strengthen them on a democratic basis, which is the only possible and durable basis in civilised society.

To accuse those who support freedom of self-determination, i.e., freedom to secede, of encouraging separatism, is as foolish and hypocritical as accusing those who advocate freedom of divorce of encouraging the destruction of family ties. Just as in bourgeois society the defenders of privilege and corruption, on which bourgeois marriage rests, oppose freedom of divorce, so, in the capitalist state, repudiation of the right to self-determination, i.e., the right of nations to secede, means nothing more than defence of the privileges of the dominant nation and police methods of administration, to the detriment of democratic methods.

No doubt, the political chicanery arising from all the relationships existing in capitalist society sometimes leads members of parliament and journalists to indulge in frivolous and even nonsensical twaddle about one or another nation seceding. But only reactionaries can allow themselves to be frightened (or pretend to be frightened) by such talk.

Those who stand by democratic principles, i.e., who insist that questions of state be decided by the mass of the population, know very well that there is a 'tremendous distance'[7] between what the politicians prate about and what the people decide. From their daily experience the masses know perfectly well the value of geographical and economic ties and the advantages of a big market and a big state. They will, therefore, resort to secession only when national oppression and national friction make joint life absolutely intolerable and hinder any and all economic intercourse. In that case, the interests of capitalist development and of the freedom of the class struggle will be best served by secession.

Thus, from whatever angle we approach Mr. Kokoshkin's arguments, they prove to be the height of absurdity and a mockery of the principles of democracy. And yet there is a modicum of logic in these arguments, the logic of the class interests of the Great-Russian bourgeoisie. Like most members of the Constitutional-Democratic Party, Mr. Kokoshkin is a lackey of the money-bags of that bourgeoisie. He defends its privileges in general, and its *state* privileges in particular. He defends them hand in hand and shoulder to shoulder with Purishkevich, the only difference being that Purishkevich puts more faith in the feudalist cudgel, while Kokoshkin and Co. realise that this cudgel was badly damaged in 1905, and rely more on bourgeois methods of fooling the masses, such as frightening the petty bourgeoisie and the peasants with the spectre of the 'disintegration of the state', and deluding them with phrases about blending 'people's freedom' with historical tradition, etc.

The liberals' hostility to the principle of political self-determination of nations can have one, and only one, real class meaning: national-liberalism, defence of the state privileges of the Great-Russian bourgeoisie. And the opportunists among the Marxists in Russia, who today, under the Third of June regime, are against the right of nations to self-determination – the liquidator Semkovsky, the Bundist Liebman, the Ukrainian petty-bourgeois Yurkevich – are *actually* following in the wake of the national-liberals, and corrupting the working class with national-liberal ideas.

The interests of the working class and of its struggle against capitalism demand complete solidarity and the closest unity of the workers of all nations; they demand resistance to the nationalist policy of the bourgeoisie of every nationality. Hence, Social-Democrats would be deviating from proletarian policy and subordinating the workers to the policy of the bourgeoisie if they were to repudiate the right of nations to self-determination, i.e., the right of an oppressed nation to secede, or if they were to support all the national demands of the bourgeoisie of oppressed nations. It makes no difference to the hired worker whether he is exploited chiefly by the Great-Russian bourgeoisie rather than the non-Russian bourgeoisie, or by the Polish bourgeoisie rather than the Jewish bourgeoisie, etc. The hired worker who has come to understand his class interests is equally indifferent to the state privileges of the Great-Russian capitalists and to the promises of the Polish or Ukrainian capitalists to set up an earthly paradise when they obtain state privileges. Capitalism is developing and will continue to develop, anyway, both in integral states with a mixed population and in separate national states.

In any case the hired worker will be an object of exploitation. Successful struggle against exploitation requires that the proletariat be free of nationalism, and be absolutely neutral, so to speak, in the fight for supremacy that is going on among the bourgeoisie of the various nations. If the proletariat of any one nation gives the slightest support to the privileges of its 'own' national bourgeoisie, that will inevitably rouse distrust among the proletariat of another nation; it will weaken the international class solidarity of the workers and divide them, to the delight of the bourgeoisie. Repudiation of the right to self-determination or to secession inevitably means, in practice, support for the privileges of the dominant nation.

We will get even more striking confirmation of this if we take the concrete case of Norway's secession from Sweden.

6. Norway's Secession from Sweden

Rosa Luxemburg cites precisely this example, and discusses it as follows:

> The latest event in the history of federative relations, the secession of Norway from Sweden – which at the time was hastily seized upon by the social-patriotic Polish press (see the Kraków *Naprzod*[8]) as a gratifying

sign of the strength and progressive nature of the tendency towards state secession – at once provided striking proof that federalism and its concomitant, separation, are in no way an expression of progress or democracy. After the so-called Norwegian 'revolution', which meant that the Swedish king was deposed and compelled to leave Norway, the Norwegians coolly proceeded to choose another king, formally rejecting, by a national referendum, the proposal to establish a republic. That which superficial admirers of all national movements and of all semblance of independence proclaimed to be a 'revolution' was simply a manifestation of peasant and petty-bourgeois particularism, the desire to have a king 'of their own' for their money instead of one imposed upon them by the Swedish aristocracy, and was, consequently, a movement that had absolutely nothing in common with revolution. At the same time, the dissolution of the union between Sweden and Norway showed once more to what extent, in this case also, the federation which had existed until then was only an expression of purely dynastic interests and, therefore, merely a form of monarchism and reaction. (*Przegiad.*)

That is literally all that Rosa Luxemburg has to say on this score! Admittedly, it would have been difficult for her to have revealed the hopelessness of her position more saliently than she has done in this particular instance.

The question was, and is: do the Social-Democrats in a mixed national state need a programme that recognises the right to self-determination or secession?

What does the example of Norway, cited by Rosa Luxemburg, tell us on this point?

Our author twists and turns, exercises her wit and rails at *Naprzod*, but she does not answer the question! Rosa Luxemburg speaks about everything under the sun so as to *avoid saying a single word* about the actual point at issue!

Undoubtedly, in wishing to have a king of their own for their money, and in rejecting, in a national referendum, the proposal to establish a republic, the Norwegian petty bourgeoisie displayed exceedingly bad philistine qualities. Undoubtedly, *Naprzod* displayed equally bad and equally philistine qualities in failing to notice this.

But what has all this to do with the case?

The question under discussion was the right of nations to self-determination and the attitude to be adopted by the socialist proletariat towards this right! Why, then, does not Rosa Luxemburg answer this question instead of beating about the bush?

To a mouse there is no stronger beast than the cat, it is said. To Rosa Luxemburg there is evidently no stronger beast than the 'Fracy'. 'Fracy' is the popular term for the 'Polish Socialist Party', its so-called revolutionary section, and the Kraków newspaper *Naprzod* shares the views of that 'section'. Rosa Luxemburg is so blinded by her fight against the nationalism of that 'section' that she loses sight of everything except *Naprzod*.

If *Naprzod* says 'yes', Rosa Luxemburg considers it her sacred duty to say an immediate 'no', without stopping to think that by so doing she does not reveal independence from *Naprzod*, but, on the contrary, her ludicrous dependence on the 'Fracy' and her inability to see things from a viewpoint any deeper and broader than that of the Kraków ant hill. *Naprzod*, of course, is a wretched and by no means Marxist organ; but that should not prevent us from properly analysing the example of Norway, once we have chosen it.

To analyse this example in Marxist fashion, we must deal, not with the vices of the awfully terrible 'Fracy', but, first, with the concrete historical features of the secession of Norway from Sweden, and secondly, with the tasks which confronted the *proletariat* of both countries in connection with this secession.

The geographic, economic and language ties between Norway and Sweden are as intimate as those between the Great Russians and many other Slav nations. But the union between Norway and Sweden was not a voluntary one, and in dragging in the question of 'federation' Rosa Luxemburg was talking at random, simply because she did not know what to say. Norway was *ceded* to Sweden by the monarchs during the Napoleonic wars, against the will of the Norwegians; and the Swedes had to bring troops into Norway to subdue her.

Despite the very extensive autonomy which Norway enjoyed (she had her own parliament, etc.), there was constant friction between Norway and Sweden for many decades after the union, and the Norwegians strove hard to throw off the yoke of the Swedish aristocracy. At last, in August 1905, they succeeded: the Norwegian parliament resolved that the Swedish king was no longer king of Norway, and in the referendum held later among the Norwegian people, the overwhelming majority (about two hundred thousand as against a few hundred) voted for complete separation from Sweden. After a short period of indecision, the Swedes resigned themselves to the fact of secession.

This example shows us on what grounds cases of the secession of nations are practicable, and actually occur, under modern economic and political relationships, and the *form* secession sometimes assumes under conditions of political freedom and democracy.

No Social-Democrat will deny – unless he would profess indifference to questions of political freedom and democracy (in which case he is naturally no longer a Social-Democrat) – that this example *virtually* proves that it is the *bounden duty* of class-conscious workers to conduct systematic propaganda and prepare the ground for the settlement of conflicts that may arise over the secession of nations, not in the 'Russian way', but *only in the way* they were settled in 1905 between Norway and Sweden. This is exactly what is meant by the demand in the programme for the recognition of the right of nations to self-determination. But Rosa Luxemburg tried to get around a fact that was repugnant to her theory by violently attacking the philistinism of the Norwegian philistines and the Kraków *Naprzod*; for she understood perfectly well that this historical fact *completely refutes* her phrases about the right of nations to self-determination being a 'utopia', or like the right 'to eat off gold plates', etc. Such phrases only express a smug and opportunist belief in the immutability of the present alignment of forces among the nationalities of Eastern Europe.

To proceed. In the question of the self-determination of nations, as in every other question, we are interested, first and foremost, in the self-determination of the proletariat within a given nation. Rosa Luxemburg modestly evaded this question too, for she realised that an analysis of it on the basis of the example of Norway, which she herself had chosen, would be disastrous to her 'theory'.

What position did the Norwegian and Swedish proletariat take, and indeed had to take, in the conflict over secession? *After* Norway seceded, the class-conscious workers of Norway would naturally have voted for a republic, and if some socialists voted otherwise it only goes to show how much dense, philistine opportunism there sometimes is in the European socialist movement.[9] There can be no two opinions about that, and we mention the point only because Rosa Luxemburg is trying to obscure the issue by speaking *off the mark*. We do not know whether the Norwegian socialist programme made it obligatory for Norwegian Social-Democrats to hold particular views on the question of secession. We will assume that it did not, and that the Norwegian socialists left it an open question as to what extent the autonomy of Norway gave sufficient scope to wage the class struggle freely, or to what extent the eternal friction and conflicts with the Swedish aristocracy hindered freedom of economic life. But it cannot be disputed that the Norwegian proletariat had to oppose this aristocracy and support Norwegian peasant democracy (with all its philistine limitations).

And the Swedish proletariat? It is common knowledge that the Swedish landed proprietors, abetted by the Swedish clergy, advocated war against Norway. Inasmuch as Norway was much weaker than Sweden, had already experienced a Swedish invasion, and the Swedish aristocracy carries enormous weight in its own country, this advocacy of war presented a grave danger. We may be sure that the Swedish Kokoshkins spent much time and energy in trying to corrupt the minds of the Swedish people by appeals to 'handle' the 'elastic formulas of political self-determination of nations carefully', by painting horrific pictures of the danger of the 'disintegration of the state' and by assuring them that 'people's freedom' was compatible with the traditions of the Swedish aristocracy. There cannot be the slightest doubt that the Swedish Social-Democrats would have betrayed the cause of socialism and democracy if they had not fought with all their might to combat both the landlord and the 'Kokoshkin' ideology and policy, and if they had failed to demand, *not only* equality of nations in general (to which the Kokoshkins also subscribe), but also the right of nations to self-determination, Norway's freedom to secede.

The close alliance between the Norwegian and Swedish workers, their complete fraternal class solidarity, *gained* from the Swedish workers' recognition of the right of the Norwegians to secede. This convinced the Norwegian workers that the Swedish workers were not infected with Swedish nationalism, and that they placed fraternity with the Norwegian proletarians above the privileges of the Swedish bourgeoisie and aristocracy. The dissolution of the ties imposed upon Norway by the monarchs of Europe and the Swedish aristocracy strengthened the ties between the Norwegian and Swedish workers. The Swedish workers have proved that in spite of *all* the vicissitudes of bourgeois policy – bourgeois relations may quite possibly bring about a repetition of the forcible subjection of the Norwegians to the Swedes! – they will be able to preserve and defend the complete equality and class solidarity of the workers of both nations in the struggle against both the Swedish and the Norwegian bourgeoisie.

Incidentally, this reveals how groundless and even frivolous are the attempts sometimes made by the 'Fracy' to 'use' our disagreements with Rosa Luxemburg against Polish Social-Democracy. The 'Fracy' are not a proletarian or a socialist party, but a petty-bourgeois nationalist party, something like Polish Social-Revolutionaries. There never has been, nor could there be, any question of unity between the Russian Social-Democrats and this party. On the other hand, no Russian Social-Democrat has ever 'repented' of the close relations and unity that have been established with the Polish Social-Democrats. The Polish Social-Democrats have rendered a great historical service by creating the first really Marxist, proletarian party in Poland, a country imbued with nationalist aspirations and passions. Yet the service the Polish Social-Democrats have rendered is a great one, not because Rosa Luxemburg has talked a lot of nonsense about § 9 of the Russian Marxists' Programme, but despite that sad circumstance.

The question of the 'right to self-determination' is of course not so important to the Polish Social-Democrats as it is to the Russian. It is quite understandable that in their zeal (sometimes a little excessive, perhaps) to combat the nationalistically blinded petty bourgeoisie of Poland the Polish Social-Democrats should overdo things. No Russian Marxist has ever thought of blaming the Polish Social-Democrats for being opposed to the secession of Poland. These Social-Democrats err only when, like Rosa Luxemburg, they try to deny the necessity of including the recognition of the right to self-determination in the Programme of the *Russian* Marxists.

Virtually, this is like attempting to apply relationships, understandable by Kraków standards, to all the peoples and nations inhabiting Russia, including the Great Russians. It means being 'Polish nationalists the wrong way round', not Russian, not international Social-Democrats.

For international Social-Democracy stands for the recognition of the right of nations to self-determination. This is what we shall now proceed to discuss.

7. The Resolution of the London International Congress, 1896

This resolution reads:

> This Congress declares that it stands for the full right of all nations to self-determination [*Selbstbestimmungsrecht*] and expresses its sympathy for the workers of every country now suffering under the yoke of military, national or other absolutism. This Congress calls upon the workers of all these countries to join the ranks of the class-conscious [*Klassenbewusste* – those who understand their class interests] workers of the whole world in order jointly to fight for the defeat of international capitalism and for the achievement of the aims of international Social-Democracy.[10]

As we have already pointed out, our opportunists – Semkovsky, Liebman and Yurkevich – are simply unaware of this resolution. But Rosa Luxemburg knows it and quotes the full text, which contains the same expression as that contained in our programme, viz., 'self-determination'.

How does Rosa Luxemburg remove this obstacle from the path of her 'original' theory?

Oh, quite simply … the whole emphasis lies in the second part of the resolution … its declarative character … one can refer to it only by mistake!

The feebleness and utter confusion of our author are simply amazing. Usually it is only the opportunists who talk about the consistent

democratic and socialist points in the programme being mere declarations, and cravenly avoid an open debate on them. It is apparently
not without reason that Rosa Luxemburg has this time found herself in
the deplorable company of the Semkovskys, Liebmans and Yurkeviches.
Rosa Luxemburg does not venture to state openly whether she regards
the above resolution as correct or erroneous. She shifts and shuffles
as if counting on the inattentive or ill-informed reader, who forgets
the first part of the resolution by the time he has started reading the
second, or who has never heard of the discussion that took place in
the socialist press *prior* to the London Congress.

Rosa Luxemburg is greatly mistaken, however, if she imagines that,
in the sight of the class-conscious workers of Russia, she can get away
with trampling upon the resolution of the International on such an
important fundamental issue, without even deigning to analyse it
critically.

Rosa Luxemburg's point of view was voiced during the discussions
which took place prior to the London Congress, mainly in the columns
of *Die Neue Zeit*, organ of the German Marxists; *in essence this point of
view was defeated in the International*! That is the crux of the matter,
which the Russian reader must particularly bear in mind.

The debate turned on the question of Poland's independence. Three
points of view were put forward:

1) That of the 'Fracy', in whose name Haecker spoke. They wanted
the International to include in *its own* programme a demand for the
independence of Poland. The motion was not carried and this point
of view was defeated in the International.

2) Rosa Luxemburg's point of view, viz., the Polish socialists should
not demand independence for Poland. This point of view entirely pre-
cluded the proclamation of the right of nations to self-determination.
It was likewise defeated in the International.

3) The point of view which was elaborated at the time by K. Kautsky,
who opposed Rosa Luxemburg and proved that her materialism was
extremely 'one-sided'; according to Kautsky, the International could
not at the time make the independence of Poland a point in its programme; but the Polish socialists were fully entitled to put forward
such a demand. From the socialists' point of view it was undoubtedly

a mistake to ignore the tasks of national liberation in a situation where national oppression existed.

The International's resolution reproduces the most essential and fundamental propositions in this point of view: on the one hand, the absolutely direct, unequivocal recognition of the full right of all nations to self-determination; on the other hand, the equally unambiguous appeal to the workers for *international* unity in their class struggle.

We think that this resolution is absolutely correct, and that, to the countries of Eastern Europe and Asia at the beginning of the twentieth century, it is this resolution, with both its parts being taken as an integral whole, that gives the only correct lead to the proletarian class policy in the national question.

Let us deal with the three above-mentioned viewpoints in somewhat greater detail.

As is known, Karl Marx and Friedrich Engels considered it the bounden duty of the whole of West-European democracy, and still more of Social-Democracy, to give active support to the demand for Polish independence. For the period of the 1840s and 1860s, the period of the bourgeois revolutions in Austria and Germany, and the period of the 'Peasant Reform' in Russia,[11] this point of view was quite correct and the only one that was consistently democratic and proletarian. So long as the masses of the people in Russia and in most of the Slav countries were still sunk in torpor, so long as *there were no* independent, mass, democratic movements in those countries, the liberation movement of the *gentry* in Poland[12] assumed an immense and paramount importance from the point of view, not only of Russian, not only of Slav, but of European democracy as a whole.[13]

But while Marx's standpoint was quite correct for the 1840s, 1850s and 1860s, or for the third quarter of the nineteenth century, it has ceased to be correct by the twentieth century. Independent democratic movements, and even an independent proletarian movement, have arisen in most Slav countries, even in Russia, one of the most backward Slav countries. Aristocratic Poland has disappeared, yielding place to capitalist Poland. Under such circumstances Poland could not but lose her *exceptional* revolutionary importance.

The attempt of the PSP (the Polish Socialist Party, the present-day

'Fracy') in 1896 to 'establish' for all time the point of view Marx had held in a *different epoch* was an attempt to use the *letter* of Marxism against the *spirit* of Marxism. The Polish Social-Democrats were therefore quite right in attacking the extreme nationalism of the Polish petty bourgeoisie and pointing out that the national question was of secondary importance to Polish workers, in creating for the first time a purely proletarian party in Poland and proclaiming the extremely important principle that the Polish and the Russian workers must maintain the closest alliance in their class struggle.

But did this mean that at the beginning of the twentieth century the International could regard the principle of political self-determination of nations, or the right to secede, as unnecessary to Eastern Europe and Asia? This would have been the height of absurdity, and (theoretically) tantamount to admitting that the bourgeois-democratic reform of the Turkish, Russian and Chinese states had been consummated; indeed, it would have been tantamount (in practice) to opportunism, towards absolutism.

No. At a time when bourgeois-democratic revolutions in Eastern Europe and Asia have begun, in this period of the awakening and intensification of national movements and of the formation of independent proletarian parties, the task of these parties with regard to national policy must be twofold: recognition of the right of all nations to self-determination, since bourgeois-democratic reform is not yet completed and since working-class democracy consistently, seriously and sincerely (and not in a liberal, Kokoshkin fashion) fights for equal rights for nations; then, a close, unbreakable alliance in the class struggle of the proletarians of all nations in a given state, throughout all the changes in its history, irrespective of any reshaping of the frontiers of the individual states by the bourgeoisie.

It is this twofold task of the proletariat that the 1896 resolution of the International formulates. That is the substance, the underlying principle, of the resolution adopted by the Conference of Russian Marxists held in the summer of 1913. Some people profess to see a 'contradiction' in the fact that while point 4 of this resolution, which recognises the right to self-determination and secession, seems to 'concede' the maximum to nationalism (in reality, the recognition of the *right of all* nations to self-determination implies the maximum of *democracy* and the minimum of nationalism), point 5 warns the workers against the nationalist slogans of the bourgeoisie of any nation and demands the unity and amalgamation of the workers of all nations in internationally united proletarian organisations. But this is a 'contradiction' only for extremely shallow minds, which, for instance, cannot grasp why the unity and class solidarity of the Swedish and the Norwegian proletariat *gained* when the Swedish workers upheld Norway's freedom to secede and form an independent state.

8. The Utopian Karl Marx and the Practical Rosa Luxemburg

Calling Polish independence a 'utopia' and repeating this *ad nauseam*, Rosa Luxemburg exclaims ironically: Why not raise the demand for the independence of Ireland?

The 'practical' Rosa Luxemburg evidently does not know what Karl Marx's attitude to the question of Irish independence was. It is worthwhile dwelling upon this, so as to show how a *concrete* demand for national independence was analysed from a genuinely Marxist, not opportunist, standpoint.

It was Marx's custom to 'sound out' his socialist acquaintances, as he expressed it, to test their intelligence and the strength of their convictions.[14] After making the acquaintance of Lopatin, Marx wrote to Engels on 5 July 1870, expressing a highly flattering opinion of the young Russian socialist but adding at the same time: '*Poland* is his weak point. On this point he speaks quite like an Englishman – say, an English Chartist of the old school – about Ireland.'[15]

Marx questions a socialist belonging to an oppressor nation about his attitude to the oppressed nation and at once reveals a defect *common* to the socialists of the dominant nations (the English and the Russian): failure to understand their socialist duties towards the downtrodden nations, their echoing of the prejudices acquired from the bourgeoisie of the 'dominant nation'.

Before passing on to Marx's positive declarations on Ireland, we must point out that in general the attitude of Marx and Engels to the national question was strictly critical, and that they recognised its historically conditioned importance. Thus, Engels wrote to Marx on 23 May 1851, that the study of history was leading him to pessimistic conclusions in regard to Poland, that the importance of Poland was temporary – only until the agrarian revolution in Russia. The role of the Poles in history was one of 'bold (hotheaded) foolishness'. 'And one cannot point to a single instance in which Poland has successfully represented progress, even in relation to Russia, or done anything at all of historical importance.' Russia contains more of civilisation, education, industry and the bourgeoisie than 'the Poland of the indolent gentry'. 'What are Warsaw and Kraków compared to St. Petersburg, Moscow, Odessa!' Engels had no faith in the success of the Polish gentry's insurrections.

But all these thoughts, showing the deep insight of genius, by no means prevented Engels and Marx from treating the Polish movement with the most profound and ardent sympathy twelve years later, when Russia was still dormant and Poland was seething.

When drafting the Address of the International in 1864, Marx wrote to Engels (on 4 November 1864) that he had to combat Mazzini's nationalism, and went on to say: 'Inasmuch as international politics occurred in the Address, I spoke of countries, not of nationalities, and denounced Russia, not the *minores gentium*.' Marx had no doubt as to the subordinate position of the national question as compared with the 'labour question'. But his theory is as far from ignoring national movements as heaven is from earth.

Then came 1866. Marx wrote to Engels about the 'Proudhonist clique' in Paris which

> declares nationalities to be an absurdity, attacks Bismarck and Garibaldi. As polemics against chauvinism their doings are useful and explicable. But as believers in Proudhon (Lafargue and Longuet, two very good friends of mine here, also belong to them), who think all Europe must and will sit quietly on their hind quarters until the gentlemen in France abolish poverty and ignorance – they are grotesque. (Letter of 7 June 1866.)

'Yesterday', Marx wrote on 20 June 1866,

there was a discussion in the International Council on the present war ... The discussion wound up, as was to be foreseen, with 'the question of nationality' in general and the attitude we take towards it ... The representatives of 'Young France' (*non-workers*) came out with the announcement that all nationalities and even nations were 'antiquated prejudices'. Proudhonised Stirnerism ... The whole world waits until the French are ripe for a social revolution ... The English laughed very much when I began my speech by saying that our friend Lafargue and others, who had done away with nationalities, had spoken 'French' to us, i.e., a language which nine-tenths of the audience did not understand. I also suggested that by the negation of nationalities he appeared, quite unconsciously, to understand their absorption by the model French nation.

The conclusion that follows from all these critical remarks of Marx's is clear: the working class should be the last to make a fetish of the national question, since the development of capitalism does not necessarily awaken *all* nations to independent life. But to brush aside the mass national movements once they have started, and to refuse to support what is progressive in them means, in effect, pandering to *nationalistic* prejudices, that is, recognising 'one's own nation' as a model nation (or, we would add, one possessing the exclusive privilege of forming a state).[16]

But let us return to the question of Ireland.

Marx's position on this question is most clearly expressed in the following extracts from his letters:

I have done my best to bring about this demonstration of the English workers in favour of Fenianism ... I used to think the separation of Ireland from England impossible. I now think it inevitable, although after the separation there may come federation.

This is what Marx wrote to Engels on 2 November 1867.

In his letter of 30 November of the same year he added:

... what shall we advise the *English* workers? In my opinion they must make the *Repeal of the Union* [Ireland with England, i.e., the separation of Ireland from England] (in short, the affair of 1783, only democratised and adapted to the conditions of the time) an article of their *pronunziamento*. This is the only legal and therefore only possible form of Irish emancipation which can be admitted in the programme of an *English* party. Experience must show later whether a mere personal union can continue to subsist between the two countries ...

... What the Irish need is:

1) Self-government and independence from England;

2) An agrarian revolution ...

Marx attached great importance to the Irish question and delivered hour-and-a-half lectures on this subject at the German Workers' Union (letter of 17 December 1867).

In a letter dated 20 November 1868, Engels spoke of 'the hatred towards the Irish found among the English workers', and almost a year later (24 October 1869), returning to this subject, he wrote:

Il n'y a qu'un pas [it is only one step] from Ireland to Russia ... Irish history shows what a misfortune it is for one nation to have subjugated another. All the abominations of the English have their origin in the Irish Pale. I have still to plough my way through the Cromwellian period, but this much seems certain to me, that things would have taken another turn in England, too, but for the necessity of military rule in Ireland and the creation of a new aristocracy there.

Let us note, in passing, Marx's letter to Engels of 18 August 1869:

The Polish workers in Posen have brought a strike to a victorious end with the help of their colleagues in Berlin. This struggle against Monsieur le Capital – even in the lower form of the strike – is a more serious way of getting rid of national prejudices than peace declamations from the lips of bourgeois gentlemen.

The policy on the Irish question pursued by Marx in the International may be seen from the following.

On 18 November 1869, Marx wrote to Engels that he had spoken for an hour and a quarter at the Council of the International on the question of the attitude of the British Ministry to the Irish Amnesty, and had proposed the following resolution:

Resolved,

that in his reply to the Irish demands for the release of the imprisoned Irish patriots Mr. Gladstone deliberately insults the Irish nation;

that he clogs political amnesty with conditions alike degrading to the victims of misgovernment and the people they belong to;

that having, in the teeth of his responsible position, publicly and enthusiastically cheered on the American slave-holders' rebellion, he now steps in to preach to the Irish people the doctrine of passive obedience;

that his whole proceedings with reference to the Irish Amnesty question are the true and genuine offspring of that *'policy of conquest'*, by the fiery denunciation of which Mr. Gladstone ousted his Tory rivals from office;

that the General Council of the International Workingmen's Association express their admiration of the spirited, firm and high-souled manner in which the Irish people carry on their Amnesty movement;

that this resolution be communicated to all branches of, and workingmen's bodies connected with, the International Workingmen's Association in Europe and America.

On 10 December 1869, Marx wrote that his paper on the Irish question to be read at the Council of the International would be couched as follows:

Quite apart from all phrases about 'international' and 'humane' justice for Ireland – which are taken for granted in the International Council – *it is in the direct and absolute interest of the English working class to get rid of their present connection with Ireland.* And this is my fullest conviction; and for reasons which in part I can *not* tell the English workers themselves. For a long time I believed that it would be possible to overthrow the Irish regime by English working-class ascendancy. I always expressed this point of view in the *New York Tribune*[17] [an American paper to which Marx contributed for a long time]. Deeper study has now convinced me of the opposite. The English working class will *never accomplish anything* until it has got rid of Ireland ... The English reaction in England had its roots in the subjugation of Ireland. [Marx's italics]

Marx's policy on the Irish question should now be quite clear to our readers.

Marx, the 'utopian', was so 'unpractical' that he stood for the separation of Ireland, which half a century later has not yet been achieved.

What gave rise to Marx's policy, and was it not mistaken?

At first Marx thought that Ireland would not be liberated by the national movement of the oppressed nation, but by the working-class movement of the oppressor nation. Marx did not make an Absolute of the national movement, knowing, as he did that only the victory of the working class can bring about the complete liberation of all nationalities. It is impossible to estimate beforehand all the possible relations between the bourgeois liberation movements of the oppressed nations and the proletarian emancipation movement of the oppressor nation (the very problem which today makes the national question in Russia so difficult).

However, it so happened that the English working class fell under the influence of the liberals for a fairly long time, became an appendage to the liberals, and by adopting a liberal-labour policy left itself leaderless. The bourgeois liberation movement in Ireland grew stronger and assumed revolutionary forms. Marx reconsidered his view and corrected it. 'What a misfortune it is for a nation to have subjugated another.' The English working class will never be free until Ireland is freed from the English yoke. Reaction in England is strengthened and fostered by the enslavement of Ireland (just as reaction in Russia is fostered by her enslavement of a number of nations').

And, in proposing in the International a resolution of sympathy with 'the Irish nation', 'the Irish people' (the clever L. Vl would probably have berated poor Marx for forgetting about the class struggle!), Marx advocated the *separation* of Ireland from England, 'although after the separation there may come federation'.

What were the theoretical grounds for Marx's conclusion? In England the bourgeois revolution had been consummated long ago. But it had not yet been consummated in Ireland; it is being consummated only now, after the lapse of half a century, by the reforms of the English Liberals. If capitalism had been overthrown in England as quickly as Marx had at first expected, there would have been no room for a bourgeois-democratic and general national movement in Ireland. But since it had arisen, Marx advised the English workers to support it, give it a revolutionary impetus and see it through in the interests of *their own* liberty.

The economic ties between Ireland and England in the 1860s were of course, even closer than Russia's present ties with Poland, the Ukraine, etc. The 'unpracticality' and 'impracticability' of the separation of Ireland (if only owing to geographical conditions and England's immense colonial power) were quite obvious. Though, in principle, an enemy of federalism, Marx in this instance granted the possibility of federation, as well, *if only* the emancipation of Ireland was achieved in a revolutionary, not reformist way, through a movement of the mass of the people of Ireland supported by the working class of England.[18] There can be no doubt that only such a solution of the historical problem would have been in the best interests of the proletariat and most conducive to rapid social progress.

Things turned out differently. Both the Irish people and the English proletariat proved weak. Only now, through the sordid deals between the English Liberals and the Irish bourgeoisie, is the Irish problem *being solved* (the example of Ulster shows with what difficulty) through the land reform (with compensation) and Home Rule (not yet introduced). Well then? Does it follow that Marx and Engels were 'utopians', that they put forward 'impracticable' national demands, or that they allowed themselves to be influenced by the Irish petty-bourgeois nationalists (for there is no doubt about the petty-bourgeois nature of the Fenian movement), etc.?

No. In the Irish question, too, Marx and Engels pursued a consistently proletarian policy, which really educated the masses in a spirit of democracy and socialism. Only such a policy could have saved both Ireland and England half a century of delay in introducing the necessary reforms, and prevented these reforms from being mutilated by the Liberals to please the reactionaries.

The policy of Marx and Engels on the Irish question serves as a splendid example of the attitude the proletariat of the oppressor nations should adopt towards national movements, an example which has lost none of its immense *practical* importance. It serves as a warning against that 'servile haste' with which the philistines of all countries, colours and languages hurry to label as 'utopian' the idea of altering the frontiers of states that were established by the violence and privileges of the landlords and bourgeoisie of one nation.

If the Irish and English proletariat had not accepted Marx's policy and had not made the secession of Ireland their slogan, this would have been the worst sort of opportunism, a neglect of their duties as democrats and socialists, and a concession to *English* reaction and the *English* bourgeoisie.

9. The 1903 Programme and its Liquidators

The Minutes of the 1903 Congress, at which the Programme of the Russian Marxists was adopted, have become a great rarity, and the vast majority of the active members of the working-class movement today are unacquainted with the motives underlying the various points (the more so since not all the literature relating to it enjoys the blessings of legality …). It is therefore necessary to analyse the debate that took place at the 1903 Congress on the question under discussion.

Let us state first of all that however meagre the Russian Social-Democratic literature on the 'right of nations to self-determination' may be, it nevertheless shows clearly that this right has always been understood to mean the right to secession. The Semkovskys, Liebmans and Yurkeviches who doubt this and declare that § 9 is 'vague', etc., do so only because of their sheer ignorance or carelessness. As far back as 1902, Plekhanov, in *Zarya*, defended 'the right to self-determination' in the draft programme, and wrote that this demand, while not obligatory upon bourgeois democrats, was 'obligatory upon Social-Democrats'. 'If we were to forget it or hesitate to advance it', Plekhanov wrote, 'for fear of offending the national prejudices of our fellow-countrymen of Great-Russian nationality, the call … "workers of all countries, unite!" would be a shameful lie on our lips …'[19]

This is a very apt description of the fundamental argument in favour of the point under consideration; so apt that it is not surprising that the 'anythingarian' critics of our programme have been timidly avoiding it. The abandonment of this point, no matter for what motives, is *actually* a 'shameful' concession to *Great-Russian* nationalism. But why Great-Russian, when it is a question of the right of *all* nations to self-determination? Because it refers to secession *from* the Great Russians. The interests of the *unity of the proletarians*, the interests of their class solidarity call for recognition of the right of *nations to secede* – that is what Plekhanov admitted twelve years ago in the words quoted above. Had our opportunists given thought to this they would probably not have talked so much nonsense about self-determination.

At the 1903 Congress, which adopted the draft programme that Plekhanov advocated, the main work was done by the *Programme Commission*. Unfortunately, no Minutes of its proceedings were kept; they would have been particularly interesting on this point, for it was *only* in the Commission that the representatives of the Polish Social-Democrats, Warszawski and Hanecki, tried to defend their views and to dispute 'recognition of the right to self-determination'. Any reader who goes to the trouble of comparing their arguments (set forth in the speech by Warszawski and the statement by him and Hanecki, pp. 134–6 and 388–90 of the Congress Minutes) with those which Rosa Luxemburg advanced in her Polish article, which we have analysed, will find them identical.

How were these arguments treated by the Programme Commission of the Second Congress, where Plekhanov, more than anyone else, spoke against the Polish Marxists? They were mercilessly ridiculed! The absurdity of proposing to the Marxists of *Russia* that they should reject the recognition of the right of nations to self-determination was demonstrated so plainly and clearly that the Polish Marxists *did not even venture to repeat their arguments at the plenary meeting of the Congress*! They left the Congress, convinced of the hopelessness of their case at the supreme assembly of Marxists – Great-Russian, Jewish, Georgian, and Armenian.

Needless to say, this historic episode is of very great importance to everyone seriously interested in *his own* programme. The fact that the Polish Marxists' arguments were completely defeated at the Programme Commission of the Congress, and that the Polish Marxists gave up the attempt to defend their views at the plenary meeting of the Congress is very significant. No wonder Rosa Luxemburg maintained a 'modest' silence about it in her article in 1908 – the recollection of the Congress must have been too unpleasant! She also kept quiet about the ridiculously inept proposal made by Warszawski and Hanecki in 1903, on behalf of all Polish Marxists, to 'amend' § 9 of the Programme, a proposal which neither Rosa Luxemburg nor the other Polish Social-Democrats have ventured (or will ever venture) to repeat.

But although Rosa Luxemburg, concealing her defeat in 1903, has maintained silence over these facts, those who take an interest in the history of their Party will make it their business to ascertain them and give thought to their significance.

On leaving the 1903 Congress, Rosa Luxemburg's friends submitted the following statement:

'We propose that Clause 7 [now Clause 9] of the draft programme read as follows: § 7. *Institutions guaranteeing full freedom of cultural development* to all nations incorporated in the state.' (p. 390 of the Minutes.)

Thus, the Polish Marxists at that time put forward views on the national question that were so vague that *instead of* self-determination they practically proposed the notorious 'cultural-national autonomy', only under another name!

This sounds almost incredible, but unfortunately it is a fact. At the Congress itself, attended though it was by five Bundists with five votes and three Caucasians with six votes, without counting Kostrov's consultative voice, *not a single* vote was cast for the *rejection* of the clause about self-determination. Three votes were cast for the proposal to add 'cultural-national autonomy' to this clause (in favour of Goldblatt's formula: 'the establishment of institutions guaranteeing the nations full freedom of cultural development') and four votes for Lieber's formula ('the right of nations to freedom in their cultural development').

Now that a Russian liberal party – the Constitutional-Democratic Party – has appeared on the scene, we know that in *its* programme the political self-determination of nations has been replaced by 'cultural self-determination'. Rosa Luxemburg's Polish friends, therefore, were '*combating*' the nationalism of the PSP, and did it so successfully that they proposed the substitution of a *liberal* programme for the Marxist programme! And in the same breath they accused our programme of being opportunist; no wonder this accusation was received with laughter by the Programme Commission of the Second Congress!

How was 'self-determination' understood by the delegates to the Second Congress, of whom, as we have seen, *not one* was opposed to 'self-determination of nations'?

The following three extracts from the Minutes provide the answer:

'*Martynov* is of the opinion that the term 'self-determination' should not be given a broad interpretation; it merely means the right of a nation to establish itself as a separate polity, not regional self-government' (p. 171). Martynov was a member of the Programme Commission, in which the arguments of Rosa Luxemburg's friends were repudiated and ridiculed. Martynov was then an Economist in his views, and a violent opponent of *Iskra;* had he expressed an opinion that was not shared by the majority of the Programme Commission he would certainly have been repudiated.

Bundist Goldblatt was the first to speak when the Congress, after the Commission had finished its work, discussed § 8 (the present Clause 9) of the Programme.

He said:

> No objections can be raised to the 'right to self-determination'. When a nation is fighting for independence, that should not he opposed. If Poland refuses to enter into lawful marriage with Russia, she should not be interfered with, as Plekhanov put it. I agree with this opinion within these limits [pp. 175–6].

Plekhanov had not spoken on this subject at all at the plenary meeting of the Congress. Goldblatt was referring to what Plekhanov had said at the Programme Commission, where the 'right to self-determination' had been explained in a simple yet detailed manner to mean the right to secession. Lieber, who spoke after Goldblatt, remarked:

'Of course, if any nationality finds that it cannot live within the frontiers of Russia, the *Party* will not place any obstacles in its way' (p. 176).

The reader will see that at the Second Congress of the Party, which adopted the programme, it was unanimously understood that self-determination meant 'only' the right to secession. Even the Bundists grasped this truth at the time, and it is only in our own deplorable times of continued counter-revolution and all sorts of 'apostasy' that we can find people who, bold in their ignorance, declare that the programme is 'vague'. But before devoting time to these sorry would-be Social-Democrats, let us first finish with the attitude of the Poles to the programme.

They came to the Second Congress (1903) declaring that unity was necessary and imperative. But they left the Congress after their 'reverses' in the Programme Commission, and their *last word* was a written statement, printed in the Minutes of the Congress, containing the above-mentioned proposal to *substitute* cultural-national autonomy for self-determination.

In 1906 the Polish Marxists joined the Party; *neither* upon joining *nor* afterwards (at the Congress of 1907, the conferences of 1907 and 1908, or the plenum of 1910) *did they introduce* a single proposal to amend § 9 of the Russian Programme!

That is a fact.

And, despite all utterances and assurances, this fact definitely proves that Rosa Luxemburg's friends regarded the question as having been settled by the debate at the Programme Commission of the Second Congress, as well as by the decision of that Congress, and that they tacitly acknowledged their mistake and corrected it by joining the Party in 1906, after they had left the Congress in 1903, without a single attempt to raise the question of amending § 9 of the Programme through *Party* channels.

Rosa Luxemburg's article appeared over her signature in 1908 – of course, it never entered anyone's head to deny Party publicists the right to criticise the programme – and, *since* the Writing of this article, *not a single* official body of the Polish Marxists has raised the question of revising § 9.

Trotsky was therefore rendering a great disservice to certain admirers of Rosa Luxemburg when he wrote, on behalf of the editors of *Borba*, in issue No. 2 of that publication (March 1914):

'The Polish Marxists consider that "the right to national self-determination" is entirely devoid of political content and should be deleted from the programme' (p. 25).

The obliging Trotsky is more dangerous than an enemy! Trotsky could produce *no* proof, except 'private conversations' (i.e., simply gossip, on which Trotsky always subsists), for classifying 'Polish Marxists' in general as supporters of every article by Rosa Luxemburg. Trotsky presented the 'Polish Marxists' as people devoid of honour and conscience, incapable of respecting even their own convictions and the programme of their Party. How obliging Trotsky is!

When, in 1903, the representatives of the Polish Marxists walked out of the Second Congress *over* the right to self-determination, Trotsky could have said *at the time* that they regarded this right as devoid of content and subject to deletion from the programme.

But after that the Polish Marxists *joined* the Party whose programme this was, and they have never introduced a motion to amend it.[20]

Why did Trotsky withhold these facts from the readers of his journal? Only because it pays him to speculate on fomenting differences between the Polish and the Russian opponents of liquidationism and to deceive the Russian workers on the question of the programme.

Trotsky has never yet held a firm opinion on any important question of Marxism. He always contrives to worm his way into the cracks of any given difference of opinion, and desert one side for the other. At the present moment he is in the company of the Bundists and the liquidators. And these gentlemen do not stand on ceremony where the Party is concerned.

Listen to the Bundist Liebman.

'When, fifteen years ago,' this gentleman writes,

the Russian Social-Democrats included the point about the right of every nationality to 'self-determination' in their programme, everyone [!] asked himself: What does this fashionable [!] term really mean? No answer was forthcoming [!]. This word was left [!] wrapped in mist. And indeed, at the time, it was difficult to dispel that mist. The moment had not come when this point could be made concrete – it was said – so let it remain wrapped in mist [!] for the time being and practice will show what content should be put into it.

Isn't it magnificent, the way this 'ragamuffin'[21] mocks at the Party programme?

And why does he mock at it?

Because he is an absolute ignoramus, who has never learnt anything or even read any Party history, but merely happened to land in liquidationist circles where going about in the nude is considered the 'right' thing to do as far as knowledge of the Party and everything it stands for is concerned.

Pomyalovsky's seminary student boasts of having 'spat into a barrel of sauerkraut'.[22] The Bundist gentlemen have gone one better. They let the Liebmans loose to spit publicly into their own barrel. What do the Liebmans care about the fact that the International Congress has passed a decision, that at the Congress of their own Party the representatives of their own Bund proved that they were quite able (and what 'severe' critics and determined enemies of *Iskra* they were!) to understand the meaning of 'self-determination' and were even in agreement with it? And will it not be easier to liquidate the Party if the 'Party publicists' (no jokes, please!) treat its history and programme after the fashion of the seminary student?

Here is a second 'ragamuffin', Mr. Yurkevich of *Dzvin*. Mr. Yurkevich must have had the Minutes of the Second Congress before him, because he quotes Plekhanov, as repeated by Goldblatt, and shows that he is aware of the fact that self-determination can only mean the right to secession. This, however, does not prevent him from spreading slander about the Russian Marxists among the Ukrainian petty bourgeoisie, alleging that they stand for the 'state integrity' of Russia. (No. 7–8, 1913, p. 83, etc.) Of course, the Yurkeviches could not have invented a better method than such slander to alienate the Ukrainian democrats from the Great-Russian democrats. And such alienation is in line with the entire policy of the group of *Dzvin* publicists who advocate the *separation* of the Ukrainian workers *in a special* national organisation![23]

It is quite appropriate, of course, that a group of nationalist philistines, who are engaged in splitting the ranks of the proletariat – and objectively this is the role of *Dzvin* – should disseminate such hopeless confusion on the national question. Needless to say, the Yurkeviches and Liebmans, who are 'terribly' offended when they are called 'near Party men', do not say a word, not a single word, as to how *they* would like the problem of the right to secede to be settled in the programme.

But here is the third and principal 'ragamuffin', Mr. Semkovsky, who, addressing a Great-Russian audience through the columns of a liquidationist newspaper, lashes at § 9 of the Programme and at the same time declares that 'for certain reasons he does not approve of the proposal' to delete this clause!

This is incredible, but it is a fact.

In August 1912, the liquidators' conference raised the national question officially. For eighteen months not a single article has appeared on the question of § 9, except the one written by Mr. Semkovsky. And in this article the author *repudiates* the programme, 'without approving', however, 'for *certain* reasons' (is this a secrecy disease?) the proposal to amend it! We may be sure that it would be difficult to find anywhere in the world similar examples of opportunism, or even worse – renunciation of the Party, and a desire to liquidate it.

A single example will suffice to show what Semkovsky's arguments are like:

'What are we to do,' he writes,

> if the Polish proletariat wants to fight side by side with the proletariat of all Russia within the framework of a single state, while the reactionary classes of Polish society, on the contrary, want to separate Poland from Russia and obtain a majority of votes in favour of secession by referendum? Should we, Russian Social-Democrats in the central parliament, vote together with our Polish comrades *against* secession, or – in order not to violate the 'right to self-determination' – vote *for* secession? [*Novaya Rabochaya Gazeta* No. 71.]

From this it is evident that Mr. Semkovsky does not even understand the *point at issue*! It did not occur to him that the right to secession presupposes the settlement of the question by a parliament (Diet, referendum, etc.) of the *seceding* region, *not* by a central parliament.

The childish perplexity over the question, 'What are we to do?', if under democracy the majority are for reaction, serves to screen the real and live issue when *both* the Purishkeviches and the Kokoshkins consider the very idea of secession criminal! Perhaps the proletarians of *all* Russia ought not to fight the Purishkeviches and the Kokoshkins today, but should bypass them and fight the reactionary classes of Poland!

Such is the sheer rubbish published in the liquidators' organ of which Mr. L. Martov is one of the ideological leaders, the self-same L. Martov who drafted the programme and spoke in favour of its adoption in 1903, and even subsequently wrote in favour of the right to secede. Apparently, L. Martov is now arguing according to the rule:

No clever man is needed there;

Better send Read,

And I shall wait and see.[24]

He sends Read-Semkovsky along and allows our programme to be distorted, and endlessly muddled up in a daily paper whose new readers are unacquainted with it!

Yes. Liquidationism has gone a long way – there are even very many prominent ex-Social-Democrats who have not a trace of Party spirit left in them.

Rosa Luxemburg cannot, of course, be classed with the Liebmans, Yurkeviches and Semkovskys, but the fact that it was this kind of people who seized upon her error shows with particular clarity the opportunism she has lapsed into.

10. Conclusion

To sum up.

As far as the theory of Marxism in general is concerned, the question of the right to self-determination presents no difficulty. No one can seriously question the London resolution of 1896, or the fact that self-determination implies only the right to secede, or that the formation of independent national states is the tendency in all bourgeois-democratic revolutions.

A difficulty is to some extent created by the fact that in Russia the proletariat of both the oppressed and oppressor nations are fighting, and must fight, side by side. The task is to preserve the unity of the proletariat's class struggle for socialism, and to resist all bourgeois and Black-Hundred nationalist influences. Where the oppressed nations are concerned, the separate organisation of the proletariat as an independent party sometimes leads to such a bitter struggle against local nationalism that the perspective becomes distorted and the nationalism of the oppressor nation is lost sight of.

But this distortion of perspective cannot last long. The experience of the joint struggle waged by the proletarians of various nations has demonstrated all too clearly that we must formulate political issues from the all-Russia, not the 'Kraków' point of view. And in all-Russia politics it is the Purishkeviches and the Kokoshkins who are in the saddle. Their ideas predominate, and their persecution of non-Russians for 'separatism', for *thinking* about secession, is being preached, and practised in the Duma, in the schools, in the churches, in the barracks, and in hundreds and thousands of newspapers. It is this Great-Russian nationalist poison that is polluting the entire all-Russia political atmosphere. This is the misfortune of one nation, which, by subjugating other nations, is strengthening reaction throughout Russia. The memories of 1849 and 1863 form a living political tradition, which, unless great storms arise, threatens to hamper every democratic and *especially* every Social-Democratic movement for decades to come.

There can be no doubt that however natural the point of view of certain Marxists belonging to the oppressed nations (whose 'misfortune' is sometimes that the masses of the population are blinded by the idea of their 'own' national liberation) may appear at times, *in reality* the objective alignment of class forces in Russia makes refusal to advocate the right to self-determination tantamount to the worst opportunism, to the infection of the proletariat with the ideas of the Kokoshkins. And these ideas are, essentially, the ideas and the policy of the Purishkeviches.

Therefore, although Rosa Luxemburg's point of view could at first have been excused as being specifically Polish, 'Kraków' narrow-mindedness, it is inexcusable today, when nationalism and, above all, governmental Great-Russian nationalism, has everywhere gained ground, and when policy is being shaped by this *Great-Russian nationalism*.[25] In actual fact; it is being seized upon by the opportunists of *all* nations, who fight shy of the idea of 'storms' and 'leaps', believe that the bourgeois-democratic revolution is over, and follow in the wake of the liberalism of the Kokoshkins.

Like any other nationalism, Great-Russian nationalism passes through various phases, according to the classes that are dominant in the bourgeois country at any given time. Up to 1905, we almost exclusively knew national-reactionaries. After the revolution, *national-liberals* arose in our country.

In our country this is virtually the stand adopted both by the Octobrists and by the Cadets (Kokoshkin), i.e., by the whole of the present-day bourgeoisie.

Great-Russian national-democrats will *inevitably* appear later on. Mr. Peshekhonov, one of the founders of the 'Popular Socialist' Party, already expressed this point of view (in the issue of *Russkoye Bogatstvo* for August 1906) when he called for caution in regard to the peasants' nationalist prejudices. However much others may slander us Bolsheviks and accuse us of 'idealising' the peasant, we always have made and always will make a clear distinction between peasant intelligence and peasant prejudice, between peasant strivings for democracy and opposition to Purishkevich, and the peasant desire to make peace with the priest and the landlord.

Even now, and probably for a fairly long time to come, proletarian democracy must reckon with the nationalism of the Great-Russian peasants (not with the object of making concessions to it, but in order to combat it).[26] The awakening of nationalism among the oppressed nations, which became so pronounced after 1905 (let us recall, say, the group of 'Federalist-Autonomists' in the First Duma, the growth of the Ukrainian movement, of the Moslem movement, etc.) will inevitably lead to greater nationalism among the Great-Russian petty bourgeoisie in town and countryside. The slower the democratisation of Russia, the more persistent, brutal and bitter will be the national persecution and bickering among the bourgeoisie of the various nations. The particularly reactionary nature of the Russian Purishkeviches will simultaneously give rise to (and strengthen) 'separatist' tendencies among the various oppressed nationalities, which sometimes enjoy far greater freedom in neighbouring states.

In this situation, the proletariat, of Russia is faced with a twofold or, rather, a two-sided task: to combat nationalism of every kind, above all, Great-Russian nationalism; to recognise, not only fully equal rights, for all nations in general, but also equality of rights as regards polity, i.e., the right of nations to self-determination, to secession. And at the same time, it is their task, in the interests of a successful struggle against all and every kind of nationalism among all nations, to preserve the unity of the proletarian struggle and the proletarian organisations, amalgamating these organisations into a close-knit international association, despite bourgeois strivings for national exclusiveness.

Complete equality of rights for all nations; the right of nations to self-determination; the unity of the workers of all nations – such is the national programme that Marxism, the experience of the whole world, and the experience of Russia, teach the workers.

This article had been set up when I received No. 3 of *Nasha Rabochaya Gazeta*, in which Mr. Vl. Kosovsky writes the following about the recognition of the right of all nations to self-determination:

> Taken mechanically from the resolution of the First Congress of the Party (1898), which in turn had borrowed it from the decisions of international socialist congresses, it was given, as is evident from the debate, the same meaning at the 1903 Congress as was ascribed to it by the Socialist International, i.e., political self-determination, the self-determination of nations in the field of political independence. Thus the formula: national self-determination, which implies the right to territorial separation, does not in any way affect the question of how national relations *within* a given state organism should be regulated for nationalities that cannot or have no desire to leave the existing state.

It is evident from this that Mr. Vl. Kosovsky has seen the Minutes of the Second Congress of 1903 and understands perfectly well the real (and only) meaning of the term self-determination. Compare this with the fact that the editors of the Bund newspaper *Zeit* let Mr. Liebman loose to scoff at the programme and to declare that it is vague! Queer 'party' ethics among these Bundists ... The Lord alone knows why Kosovsky should declare that the Congress took over the principle of self-determination *mechanically*. Some people want to 'object', but how, why, and for what reason – they do not know.

The Revolutionary Proletariat and the Right of Nations to Self-Determination[1]

Like most programmes or tactical resolutions of the Social-Democratic parties, the Zimmerwald Manifesto proclaims the 'right of nations to self-determination'. In Nos. 252 and 253 of *Berner Tagwacht*, Parabellum[2] has called 'illusory' 'the struggle for the non-existent right to self-determination', and *has contraposed* to it 'the proletariat's revolutionary mass struggle against capitalism', while at the same time assuring us that 'we are against annexations' (an assurance is repeated five times in Parabellum's article), and against all violence against nations.

The arguments advanced by Parabellum in support of his position boil down to an assertion that today all national problems, like those of Alsace-Lorraine, Armenia, etc., are problems of imperialism; that capital has outgrown the framework of national states; that it is impossible to turn the clock of history back to the obsolete ideal of national states, etc.

Let us see whether Parabellum's reasoning is correct.

First of all, it is Parabellum who is looking backward, not forward, when, in opposing working-class acceptance 'of the ideal of the national state', he looks towards Britain, France, Italy, Germany, i.e., countries where the movement for national liberation is a thing of the past, and not towards the East, towards Asia, Africa, and the colonies, where this movement is a thing of the present and the future. Mention of India, China, Persia, and Egypt will be sufficient.

Furthermore, imperialism means that capital has outgrown the framework of national states; it means that national oppression has been extended and heightened on a new historical foundation. Hence, it follows that, despite Parabellum, we must *link* the revolutionary struggle for socialism with a revolutionary programme on the national question.

From what Parabellum says, it appears that, *in the name of* the socialist revolution, he scornfully rejects a consistently revolutionary programme in the sphere of democracy. He is wrong to do so. The proletariat cannot be victorious except through democracy, i.e., by giving full effect to democracy and by linking with each step of its struggle democratic demands formulated in the most resolute terms. It is absurd to *contrapose* the socialist revolution and the revolutionary struggle against capitalism to a *single* problem of democracy, in this case, the national question. We must *combine* the revolutionary struggle against capitalism with a revolutionary programme and tactics on all democratic demands: a republic, a militia, the popular election of officials, equal rights for women, the self-determination of nations, etc. While capitalism exists, these demands – all of them – can only be accomplished as an exception, and even then in an incomplete and distorted form. Basing ourselves on the democracy already achieved, and exposing its incompleteness under capitalism, we demand the overthrow of capitalism, the expropriation of the bourgeoisie, as a necessary basis both for the abolition of the poverty of the masses and for the *complete* and *all-round* institution of *all* democratic reforms. Some of these reforms will be started before the overthrow of the bourgeoisie, others *in the course* of that overthrow, and still others after it. The social revolution is not a single battle, but a period covering a series of battles over all sorts of problems of economic and democratic reform, which are consummated only by the expropriation of the bourgeoisie. It is for the sake of this final aim that we must formulate *every one* of our democratic demands in a consistently revolutionary way. It is quite conceivable that the workers of some particular country will overthrow the bourgeoisie *before* even a single fundamental democratic reform has been fully achieved. It is, however, quite inconceivable that the proletariat, as a historical class, will be able to defeat the bourgeoisie, unless it is prepared for that by being educated in the spirit of the most consistent and resolutely revolutionary democracy.

Imperialism means the progressively mounting oppression of the nations of the world by a handful of Great Powers; it means a period of wars between the latter to extend and consolidate the oppression of nations; it means a period in which the masses of the people are deceived by hypocritical social-patriots, i.e., individuals who, under the pretext of the 'freedom of nations', 'the right of nations to self-determination', and 'defence of the fatherland', justify and defend the oppression of the majority of the world's nations by the Great Powers.

That is why the focal point in the Social-Democratic programme must be that division of nations into oppressor and oppressed which forms the *essence* of imperialism, and is *deceitfully* evaded by the social-chauvinists and Kautsky. This division is not significant from the angle of bourgeois pacifism or the philistine Utopia of peaceful competition among independent nations under capitalism, but it is most significant from the angle of the revolutionary struggle against imperialism. It is from this division that *our* definition of the 'right of nations to self-determination' must follow, a definition that is consistently democratic, revolutionary, and in *accord* with the general task of the immediate struggle for socialism. It is for that right, and in a struggle to achieve sincere recognition for it, that the Social-Democrats of the oppressor nations must demand that the oppressed nations should have the right of secession, for otherwise recognition of equal rights for nations and of international working-class solidarity would in fact be merely empty phrase-mongering, sheer hypocrisy. On the other hand, the Social-Democrats of the oppressed nations must attach prime significance to the unity and the merging of the workers of the oppressed nations with those of the oppressor nations; otherwise these Social-Democrats will involuntarily become the allies of their own national *bourgeoisie*, which always betrays the interests of the people and of democracy, and is *always* ready, in its turn, to annex territory and oppress other nations.

The way in which the national question was posed at the end of the sixties of the past century may serve as an instructive example. The petty-bourgeois democrats, to whom any thought of the class struggle and of the socialist revolution was wholly alien, pictured to themselves a Utopia of peaceful competition among free and equal nations, under capitalism. In examining the immediate tasks of the social revolution, the Proudhonists totally 'negated' the national question and the right of nations to self-determination. Marx ridiculed French Proudhonism and showed the affinity between it and French chauvinism. ('All Europe must and will sit quietly on their hindquarters until the gentlemen in France abolish "poverty" … By the negation of nationalities they appeared, quite unconsciously, to understand their absorption by the model French nation.') Marx demanded *the separation of Ireland* from Britain 'although after the separation there may come federation', demanding it, not from the standpoint of the petty-bourgeois Utopia of a peaceful capitalism, or from considerations of 'justice for Ireland',[3] but from the standpoint of the interests of the revolutionary struggle of the proletariat of the *oppressor, i.e., British, nation* against capitalism. The freedom of that nation has been cramped and mutilated by the fact that it has oppressed another nation. The British proletariat's internationalism would remain a hypocritical phrase if *they* did not demand the separation of Ireland. Never in favour of petty states, or the splitting up of states in general, or the principle of federation, Marx considered the separation of an oppressed nation to be a step towards federation, and consequently, not towards a split, but towards concentration, both political and economic, but concentration on the basis of democracy. As Parabellum sees it, Marx was probably waging an 'illusory struggle' in demanding separation for Ireland. Actually, however, this demand alone presented a consistently revolutionary programme; it alone was in accord with internationalism; it alone advocated concentration along *non*-imperialist lines.

The imperialism of our days has led to a situation in which the Great-Power oppression of nations has become general. The view that a struggle must be conducted against the social-chauvinism of the dominant nations, who are now engaged in an imperialist war to enhance the oppression of nations, and are oppressing most of the world's nations and most of the earth's population – this view must be decisive, cardinal and basic in the national programme of Social-Democracy.

Take a glance at the present trends in Social-Democratic thinking on this subject. The petty-bourgeois Utopians, who dreamt of equality and peace among nations under capitalism, have been succeeded by the social-imperialists. In combating the former, Parabellum is tilting at windmills, thereby unwittingly playing in the hands of the social-imperialists. What is the social-chauvinists' programme on the national question?

They either entirely deny the right to self-determination, using arguments like those advanced by Parabellum (Cunow, Parvus, the Russian opportunists Semkovsky, Liebman, and others), or they recognise that right in a patently hypocritical fashion, namely, without applying it to those very nations that are oppressed by their own nation or by her military allies (Plekhanov, Hyndman, all the pro-French patriots, then Scheidemann, etc., etc.). The most plausible formulation of the social-chauvinist lie, one that is therefore most dangerous to the proletariat, is provided by Kautsky. In word, he is in favour of the self-determination of nations; in word, he is for the Social-Democratic Party '*die Selbstandigkeit der Nationen allseitig* [!] *und rückhaltlos* [?] *achtet und fordert*'[4] (*Die Neue Zeit* No. 33, II, S. 241, 21 May 1915). In deed, however, he has adapted the national programme to the prevailing social-chauvinism, distorted and docked it; he gives no precise definition of the duties of the socialists in the oppressor nations, and patently falsifies the democratic principle itself when he says that to demand 'state independence' (*staatliche Selb standigkeit*) for every nation would mean demanding 'too much' ('*zu viel*', *Die Neue Zeit* No. 33, II, S. 77, 16 April 1915). 'National autonomy', if you please, is enough! The principal question, the one the imperialist bourgeoisie will not permit discussion of, namely, the question of the *boundaries of a state* that is built upon the oppression of nations, is evaded by Kautsky, who, to please that bourgeoisie, has thrown out of the programme what is most essential. The bourgeoisie are ready to promise all the 'national equality' and 'national autonomy' you please, so long as the proletariat remain within the framework of legality and 'peacefully' submit to them on the question of the state *boundaries*! Kautsky has formulated the national programme of Social-Democracy in a reformist, not a revolutionary manner.

Parabellum's national programme, or, to be more precise, his *assurances* that 'we are against annexations', has the wholehearted backing of the *Parteivorstand*,[5] Kautsky, Plekhanov and Co., for the very reason that the programme does not expose the dominant social-patriots. Bourgeois pacifists would also endorse that programme. Parabellum's splendid *general* programme ('a revolutionary mass struggle against capitalism') serves him – as it did the Proudhonists of the 1860s – not for the drawing up, in conformity with it and in its spirit, of a programme on the national question that is uncompromising and equally revolutionary, but in order to leave the way open to the social-patriots. In our imperialist times most socialists throughout the world are members of nations that oppress other nations and strive to extend that oppression. That is why our 'struggle against annexations' will be meaningless and will not scare the social-patriots in the least, unless we declare that a socialist of an oppressor nation who does not conduct both peacetime and wartime propaganda in favour of freedom of secession for oppressed nations, is no socialist and no internationalist, but a chauvinist! The socialist of an oppressor nation who fails to conduct such propaganda in defiance of government bans, i.e., in the free, i.e., in the illegal press, is a hypocritical advocate of equal rights for nations!

Parabellum has only a single sentence on Russia, which has not yet completed its bourgeois-democratic revolution:

> Even economically very backward Russia has proved, in the stand taken
> by the Polish, Lettish and Armenian bourgeoisie that it is not only the
> military guard that keeps together the peoples in that 'prison of peoples',
> but also the need for capitalist expansion, for which the vast territory is
> a splendid ground for development.

That is not a 'Social-Democratic standpoint' but a liberal-bourgeois one, not an internationalist, but a Great-Russian chauvinist standpoint. Parabellum, who is such a fine fighter against the German social-patriots, seems to have little knowledge of Russian chauvinism. For Parabellum's wording to be converted into a Social-Democratic postulate and for Social-Democratic conclusions to be drawn from it, it should be modified and supplemented as follows:

Russia is a prison of peoples, not only because of the military-feudal character of tsarism and not only because the Great-Russian bourgeoisie support tsarism, but also because the Polish, etc., bourgeoisie have sacrificed the freedom of nations and democracy in general for the interests of capitalist expansion. The Russian proletariat cannot march at the head of the people towards a victorious democratic revolution (which is its immediate task), or fight alongside its brothers, the proletarians of Europe, for a socialist revolution, without immediately demanding, fully and unreservedly, for all nations oppressed by tsarism, the freedom to secede from Russia. This we demand, not independently of our revolutionary struggle for socialism, but because this struggle will remain a hollow phrase if it is not linked up with a revolutionary approach to all questions of democracy, including the national question. We demand freedom of self-determination, i.e., independence, i.e., freedom of secession for the oppressed nations, not because we have dreamt of splitting up the country economically, or of the ideal of small states, but, on the contrary, because we want large states and the closer unity and even fusion of nations, only on a truly democratic, truly internationalist basis, which is inconceivable without the freedom to secede. Just as Marx, in 1869, demanded the separation of Ireland, not for a split between Ireland and Britain, but for a subsequent free union between them, not so as to secure 'justice for Ireland', but in the interests of the revolutionary struggle of the British proletariat, we in the same way consider the refusal of Russian socialists to demand freedom of self-determination for nations, in the sense we have indicated above, to be a direct betrayal of democracy, internationalism and socialism.

Imperialism, the Highest Stage of Capitalism: A Popular Outline

Preface

The pamphlet here presented to the reader was written in the spring of 1916, in Zurich. In the conditions in which I was obliged to work there I naturally suffered somewhat from a shortage of French and English literature and from a serious dearth of Russian literature. However, I made use of the principal English work on imperialism, the book by J. A. Hobson, with all the care that, in my opinion, that work deserves.

This pamphlet was written with an eye to the tsarist censorship. Hence, I was not only forced to confine myself strictly to an exclusively theoretical, specifically economic analysis of facts, but to formulate the few necessary observations on politics with extreme caution, by hints, in an allegorical language – in that accursed Aesopian language – to which tsarism compelled all revolutionaries to have recourse whenever they took up the pen to write a 'legal' work.

It is painful, in these days of liberty, to re-read the passages of the pamphlet which have been distorted, cramped, compressed in an iron vice on account of the censor. That the period of imperialism is the eve of the socialist revolution; that social-chauvinism (socialism in words, chauvinism in deeds) is the utter betrayal of socialism, complete desertion to the side of the bourgeoisie; that this split in the working-class movement is bound up with the objective conditions of imperialism, etc. – on these matters I had to speak in a 'slavish' tongue, and I must refer the reader who is interested in the subject to the articles I wrote abroad in 1914–17, a new edition of which is soon to appear. In order to show the reader, in a guise acceptable to the censors, how shame-lessly untruthful the capitalists and the social-chauvinists who have deserted to their side (and whom Kautsky opposes so inconsistently) are on the question of annexations; in order to show how shamelessly they *screen* the annexations of *their* capitalists, I was forced to quote as an example – Japan! The careful reader will easily substitute Russia for Japan, and Finland, Poland, Courland, the Ukraine, Khiva, Bokhara, Estonia or other regions peopled by non-Great Russians, for Korea.

I trust that this pamphlet will help the reader to understand the fundamental economic question, that of the economic essence of impe-rialism, for unless this is studied, it will be impossible to understand and appraise modern war and modern politics.

Petrograd, 26 April 1917

Preface to the French and German Editions

I

As was indicated in the preface to the Russian edition, this pamphlet was written in 1916, with an eye to the tsarist censorship. I am unable to revise the whole text at the present time, nor, perhaps, would this be advisable, since the main purpose of the book was, and remains, to present, on the basis of the summarised returns of irrefutable bourgeois statistics, and the admissions of bourgeois scholars of all countries, *a composite picture* of the world capitalist system in its international relationships at the beginning of the twentieth century – on the eve of the first world imperialist war.

To a certain extent it will even be useful for many Communists in advanced capitalist countries to convince themselves by the example of this pamphlet, legal from the standpoint of the tsarist censor, of the possibility, and necessity, of making use of even the slight remnants of legality which still remain at the disposal of the Communists, say, in contemporary America or France, after the recent almost wholesale arrests of Communists, in order to explain the utter falsity of social-pacifist views and hopes for 'world democracy'. The most essential of what should be added to this censored pamphlet I shall try to present in this preface.

II

It is proved in the pamphlet that the war of 1914–18 was imperialist (that is, an annexationist, predatory war of plunder) on the part of both sides; it was a war for the division of the world, for the partition and repartition of colonies and spheres of influence of finance capital, etc.

Proof of what was the true social, or rather, the true class character of the war is naturally to be found, not in the diplomatic history of the war, but in an analysis of the *objective* position of the ruling *classes* in *all* the belligerent countries. In order to depict this objective position, one must not take examples or isolated data (in view of the extreme complexity of the phenomena of social life it is always possible to select any number of examples or separate data to prove any proposition), but *all* the data on the *basis* of economic life in *all* the belligerent countries and the whole world.

It is precisely irrefutable summarised data of this kind that I quoted in describing the *partition of the world* in 1876 and 1914 (in Chapter VI) and the division of the world's *railways* in 1890 and 1913 (in Chapter VII). Railways are a summation of the basic capitalist industries, coal, iron and steel; a summation and the most striking index of the development of world trade and bourgeois-democratic civilisation. How the railways are linked up with large-scale industry with monopolies, syndicates, cartels, trusts, banks and the financial oligarchy is shown in the preceding chapters of the book. The uneven distribution of the railways, their uneven development – sums up, as it were, modern monopolist capitalism on a world-wide scale. And this summary proves that imperialist wars are absolutely inevitable under such an economic system, *as long as* private property in the means of production exists.

The building of railways seems to be a simple, natural, democratic, cultural and civilising enterprise; that is what it is in the opinion of the bourgeois professors who are paid to depict capitalist slavery in bright colours, and in the opinion of petty-bourgeois philistines. But as a matter of fact the capitalist threads, which in thousands of different intercrossings bind these enterprises with private property in the means of production in general, have converted this railway construction into an instrument for oppressing *a thousand million* people (in the colonies and semi-colonies), that is, more than half the population of the globe that inhabits the dependent countries, as well as the wage-slaves of capital in the 'civilised' countries.

Private property based on the labour of the small proprietor, free competition, democracy, all the catchwords with which the capitalists and their press deceive the workers and the peasants are things of the distant past. Capitalism has grown into a world system of colonial oppression and of the financial strangulation of the overwhelming majority of the population of the world by a handful of 'advanced' countries. And this 'booty' is shared between two or three powerful world plunderers armed to the teeth (America, Great Britain, Japan), who are drawing the whole world into *their* war over the division of *their* booty.

III

The Treaty of Brest-Litovsk dictated by monarchist Germany, and the subsequent much more brutal and despicable Treaty of Versailles dictated by the 'democratic' republics of America and France and also by 'free' Britain, have rendered a most useful service to humanity by exposing both imperialism's hired coolies of the pen and petty-bourgeois reactionaries who, although they call themselves pacifists and socialists, sang praises to 'Wilsonism', and insisted that peace and reforms were possible under imperialism.

The tens of millions of dead and left maimed by the war – a war to decide whether the British or German group of financial plunderers is to receive the most booty – and those two 'peace treaties', are with unprecedented rapidity opening the eyes of the millions and tens of millions of people who are downtrodden, oppressed, deceived and duped by the bourgeoisie. Thus, out of the universal ruin caused by the war a world-wide revolutionary crisis is arising which, however prolonged and arduous its stages may be, cannot end otherwise than in a proletarian revolution and in its victory.

The Basle Manifesto of the Second International, which in 1912 gave an appraisal of the very war that broke out in 1914 and not of war in general (there are different kinds of wars, including revolutionary wars) – this Manifesto is now a monument exposing to the full the shameful bankruptcy and treachery of the heroes of the Second International.

That is why I reproduce this Manifesto as a supplement to the present edition, and again and again I urge the reader to note that the heroes of the Second International are as assiduously avoiding the passages of this Manifesto which speak precisely, clearly and definitely of the connection between that impending war and the proletarian revolution, as a thief avoids the scene of his crime.[1]

IV

Special attention has been devoted in this pamphlet to a criticism of Kautskyism, the international ideological trend represented in all countries of the world by the 'most prominent theoreticians', the leaders of the Second International (Otto Bauer and Co. in Austria, Ramsay MacDonald and others in Britain, Albert Thomas in France, etc., etc.) and a multitude of socialists, reformists, pacifists, bourgeois democrats and parsons.

This ideological trend is, on the one hand, a product of the disintegration and decay of the Second International, and, on the other hand, the inevitable fruit of the ideology of the petty bourgeoisie, whose entire way of life holds them captive to bourgeois and democratic prejudices.

The views held by Kautsky and his like are a complete renunciation of those same revolutionary principles of Marxism that writer has championed for decades, especially, by the way, in his struggle against socialist opportunism (of Bernstein, Millerand, Hyndman, Gompers, etc.). It is not a mere accident, therefore, that Kautsky's followers all over the world have now united in practical politics with the extreme opportunists (through the Second, or Yellow, International) and with the bourgeois governments (through bourgeois coalition governments in which socialists take part).

The growing world proletarian revolutionary movement in general, and the communist movement in particular, cannot dispense with an analysis and exposure of the theoretical errors of Kautskyism. The more so since pacifism and 'democracy' in general, which lay no claim to Marxism whatever, but which, like Kautsky and Co., are obscuring the profundity of the contradictions of imperialism and the inevitable revolutionary crisis to which it gives rise, are still very widespread all over the world. To combat these tendencies is the bounden duty of the party of the proletariat, which must win away from the bourgeoisie the small proprietors who are duped by them, and the millions of working people who enjoy more or less petty-bourgeois conditions of life.

V

A few words must be said about Chapter VIII, 'Parasitism and Decay of Capitalism'. As already pointed out in the text, Hilferding, ex-'Marxist', and now a comrade-in-arms of Kautsky and one of the chief exponents of bourgeois, reformist policy in the Independent Social-Democratic Party of Germany, has taken a step backward on this question compared with the *frankly* pacifist and reformist Englishman, Hobson. The international split of the entire working-class movement is now quite evident (the Second and the Third Internationals). The fact that armed struggle and civil war is now raging between the two trends is also evident – the support given to Kolchak and Denikin in Russia by the Mensheviks and Socialist-Revolutionaries against the Bolsheviks; the fight the Scheidemanns and Noskes have conducted in conjunction with the bourgeoisie against the Spartacists in Germany; the same thing in Finland, Poland, Hungary, etc. What is the economic basis of this world-historical phenomenon?

It is precisely the parasitism and decay of capitalism, characteristic of its highest historical stage of development, i.e., imperialism. As this pamphlet shows, capitalism has now singled out a *handful* (less than one-tenth of the inhabitants of the globe; less than one-fifth at a most 'generous' and liberal calculation) of exceptionally rich and powerful states which plunder the whole world simply by 'clipping coupons'. Capital exports yield an income of eight to ten thousand million francs per annum, at pre-war prices and according to pre-war bourgeois statistics. Now, of course, they yield much more.

Obviously, out of such enormous *superprofits* (since they are obtained over and above the profits which capitalists squeeze out of the workers of their 'own' country) it is *possible to bribe* the labour leaders and the upper stratum of the labour aristocracy. And that is just what the capitalists of the 'advanced' countries are doing: they are bribing them in a thousand different ways, direct and indirect, overt and covert.

This stratum of workers-turned-bourgeois, or the labour aristocracy, who are quite philistine in their mode of life, in the size of their earnings and in their entire outlook, is the principal prop of the Second International, and in our days, the principal *social* (not military) *prop of the bourgeoisie*. For they are the real *agents of the bourgeoisie in the working-class* movement, the labour lieutenants of the capitalist class, real vehicles of reformism and chauvinism. In the civil war between the proletariat and the bourgeoisie they inevitably, and in no small numbers, take the side of the bourgeoisie, the 'Versaillais' against the 'Communards'.

Unless the economic roots of this phenomenon are understood and its political and social significance is appreciated, not a step can be taken toward the solution of the practical problem of the communist movement and of the impending social revolution.

Imperialism is the eve of the social revolution of the proletariat. This has been confirmed since 1917 on a world-wide scale.

6 July 1920

During the last fifteen to twenty years, especially since the Spanish-American War (1898) and the Anglo-Boer War (1899–1902), the economic and also the political literature of the two hemispheres has more and more often adopted the term 'imperialism' in order to describe the present era. In 1902, a book by the English economist J. A. Hobson, *Imperialism*, was published in London and New York. This author, whose point of view is that of bourgeois social-reformism and pacifism which, in essence, is identical with the present point of view of the ex-Marxist, Karl Kautsky, gives a very good and comprehensive description of the principal specific economic and political features of imperialism. In 1910, there appeared in Vienna the work of the Austrian Marxist, Rudolf Hilferding, *Finance Capital* (Russian edition, Moscow, 1912). In spite of the mistake the author makes on the theory of money, and in spite of a certain inclination on his part to reconcile Marxism with opportunism, this work gives a very valuable theoretical analysis of 'the latest phase of capitalist development', as the subtitle runs. Indeed, what has been said of imperialism during the last few years, especially in an enormous number of magazine and newspaper articles, and also in the resolutions, for example, of the Chemnitz and Basle congresses which took place in the autumn of 1912, has scarcely gone beyond the ideas expounded, or more exactly, summed up by the two writers mentioned above ...

Later on, I shall try to show briefly, and as simply as possible, the connection and relationships between the *principal* economic features of imperialism. I shall not be able to deal with the non-economic aspects of the question, however much they deserve to be dealt with. References to literature and other notes which, perhaps, would not interest all readers, are to be found at the end of this pamphlet.

I. Concentration of Production and Monopolies

The enormous growth of industry and the remarkably rapid concentration of production in ever-larger enterprises are one of the most characteristic features of capitalism. Modern production censuses give most complete and most exact data on this process.

In Germany, for example, out of every 1,000 industrial enterprises, large enterprises, i.e., those employing more than 50 workers, numbered 3 in 1882, 6 in 1895 and 9 in 1907; and out of every 100 workers employed, this group of enterprises employed 22, 30 and 37, respectively. Concentration of production, however, is much more intense than the concentration of workers, since labour in the large enterprises is much more productive. This is shown by the figures on steam-engines and electric motors. If we take what in Germany is called industry in the broad sense of the term, that is, including commerce, transport, etc., we get the following picture. Large-scale enterprises, 30,588 out of a total of 3,265,623, that is to say, 0.9 per cent. These enterprises employ 5,700,000 workers out of a total of 14,400,000, i.e., 39.4 per cent; they use 6,600,000 steam horse power out of a total of 8,800,000, i.e., 75.3 per cent, and 1,200,000 kilowatts of electricity out of a total of 1,500,000, i.e., 77.2 per cent.

Less than one-hundredth of the total number of enterprises utilise *more than three-fourths* of the total amount of steam and electric power! 2,970,000 small enterprises (employing up to 5 workers), constituting 91 per cent of the total, utilise only 7 per cent of the total amount of steam and electric power! Tens of thousands of huge enterprises are everything; millions of small ones are nothing.

In 1907, there were in Germany 586 establishments employing 1,000 and more workers, nearly *one-tenth* (1,380,000) of the total number of workers employed in industry, and they consumed *almost one-third* (32 per cent) of the total amount of steam and electric power.[2] As we shall see, money capital and the banks make this superiority of a handful of the largest enterprises still more overwhelming, in the most literal sense of the word, i.e., millions of small, medium and even some big 'proprietors' are in fact in complete subjection to some hundreds of millionaire financiers.

In another advanced country of modern capitalism, the United States of America, the growth of the concentration of production is still greater. Here statistics single out industry in the narrow sense of the word and classify enterprises according to the value of their annual output. In 1904 large-scale enterprises with an output valued at one million dollars and over, numbered 1,900 (out of 216,180, i.e., 0.9 per cent). These employed 1,400,000 workers (out of 5,500,000, i.e., 25.6 per cent) and the value of their output amounted to $5,600,000,000 (out of $14,800,000,000, i.e., 38 per cent). Five years later, in 1909, the corresponding figures were: 3,060 enterprises (out of 268,491, i.e., 1.1 per cent) employing 2,000,000 workers (out of 6,600,000, i.e., 30.5 per cent) with an output valued at $9,000,000,000 (out of $20,700,000,000, i.e., 43.8 per cent).[3]

Almost half the total production of all the enterprises of the country was carried on by *one-hundredth part* of these enterprises! These 3,000 giant enterprises embrace 258 branches of industry. From this it can be seen that at a certain stage of its development concentration itself, as it were, leads straight to monopoly, for a score or so of giant enterprises can easily arrive at an agreement, and on the other hand, the hindrance to competition, the tendency towards monopoly, arises from the huge size of the enterprises. This transformation of competition into monopoly is one of the most important – if not the most important – phenomena of modern capitalist economy, and we must deal with it in greater detail. But first we must clear up one possible misunderstanding.

American statistics speak of 3,000 giant enterprises in 250 branches of industry, as if there were only a dozen enterprises of the largest scale for each branch of industry.

But this is not the case. Not in every branch of industry are there large-scale enterprises; and moreover, a very important feature of capitalism in its highest stage of development is so-called *combination* of production, that is to say, the grouping in a single enterprise of different branches of industry, which either represent the consecutive stages in the processing of raw materials (for example, the smelting of iron ore into pig-iron, the conversion of pig-iron into steel, and then, perhaps, the manufacture of steel goods) – or are auxiliary to one another (for example, the utilisation of scrap, or of by-products, the manufacture of packing materials, etc.).

'Combination', writes Hilferding,

> levels out the fluctuations of trade and therefore assures to the combined enterprises a more stable rate of profit. Secondly, combination

has the effect of eliminating trade. Thirdly, it has the effect of rendering possible technical improvements, and, consequently, the acquisition of superprofits over and above those obtained by the 'pure' (i.e., non-combined) enterprises. Fourthly, it strengthens the position of the combined enterprises relative to the 'pure' enterprises, strengthens them in the competitive struggle in periods of serious depression, when the fall in prices of raw materials does not keep pace with the fall in prices of manufactured goods.[4]

The German bourgeois economist, Heymann, who has written a book especially on 'mixed' – that is, combined – enterprises in the German iron industry, says: 'Pure enterprises perish, they are crushed between the high price of raw material and the low price of the finished product.' Thus, we get the following picture:

> There remain, on the one hand, the big coal companies, producing millions of tons yearly, strongly organised in their coal syndicate, and on the other, the big steel plants, closely allied to the coal mines, having their own steel syndicate. These giant enterprises, producing 400,000 tons of steel per annum, with a tremendous output of ore and coal and producing finished steel goods, employing 10,000 workers quartered in company houses, and sometimes owning their own railways and ports, are the typical representatives of the German iron and steel industry. And concentration goes on further and further. Individual enterprises are becoming larger and larger. An ever-increasing number of enterprises in one, or in several different industries, join together in giant enterprises, backed up and directed by half a dozen big Berlin banks. In relation to the German mining industry, the truth of the teachings of Karl Marx on concentration is definitely proved; true, this applies to a country where industry is protected by tariffs and freight rates. The German mining industry is ripe for expropriation.[5]

Such is the conclusion which a bourgeois economist who, by way of exception, is conscientious, had to arrive at. It must be noted that he seems to place Germany in a special category because her industries are protected by higher tariffs. But this is a circumstance which only accelerates concentration and the formation of monopolist manufacturers' associations, cartels, syndicates, etc. It is extremely important to note that in free-trade Britain, concentration also leads to monopoly, although somewhat later and perhaps in another form. Professor Hermann Levy, in his special work of research entitled *Monopolies, Cartels and Trusts,* based on data on British economic development, writes as follows:

> In Great Britain it is the size of the enterprise and its high technical level which harbour a monopolist tendency. This, for one thing, is due to the great investment of capital per enterprise, which gives rise to increasing demands for new capital for the new enterprises and thereby renders their launching more difficult. Moreover (and this seems to us to be the more important point), every new enterprise that wants to keep pace with the gigantic enterprises that have been formed by concentration would here produce such an enormous quantity of surplus goods that it could dispose of them only by being able to sell them profitably as a result of an enormous increase in demand; otherwise, this surplus would force prices down to a level that would be unprofitable both for the new enterprise and for the monopoly combines.

Britain differs from other countries where protective tariffs facilitate the formation of cartels in that monopolist manufacturers' associations, cartels and trusts arise in the majority of cases only when the number of the chief competing enterprises has been reduced to 'a couple of dozen or so'. 'Here the influence of concentration on the formation of large industrial monopolies in a whole sphere of industry stands out with crystal clarity.'[6]

Half a century ago, when Marx was writing *Capital,* free competition appeared to the overwhelming majority of economists to be a 'natural law'. Official science tried, by a conspiracy of silence, to kill the works of Marx, who by a theoretical and historical analysis of capitalism had proved that free competition gives rise to the concentration of production, which, in turn, at a certain stage of development, leads to monopoly. Today, monopoly has become a fact. Economists are writing mountains of books in which they describe the diverse manifestations of monopoly and continue to declare in chorus that 'Marxism is refuted'. But facts are stubborn things, as the English proverb says, and they have to be reckoned with, whether we like it or not. The facts show that differences between capitalist countries, e.g., in the matter of protection or free trade, only give rise to insignificant variations in the form of monopolies or in the moment of their appearance; and that the rise of monopolies, as the result of the concentration of production, is a general and fundamental law of the present stage of development of capitalism.

For Europe, the time when the new capitalism *definitely* superseded the old can be established with fair precision; it was the beginning of the twentieth century. In one of the latest compilations on the history of the 'formation of monopolies', we read:

Isolated examples of capitalist monopoly could be cited from the period preceding 1860; in these could be discerned the embryo of the forms that are so common today; but all this undoubtedly represents the prehistory of the cartels. The real beginning of modern monopoly goes back, at the earliest, to the sixties. The first important period of development of monopoly commenced with the international industrial depression of the seventies and lasted until the beginning of the nineties ... If we examine the question on a European scale, we will find that the development of free competition reached its apex in the sixties and seventies. It was then that Britain completed the construction of her old-style capitalist organisation. In Germany, this organisation had entered into a fierce struggle with handicraft and domestic industry, and had begun to create for itself its own forms of existence.

The great revolution commenced with the crash of 1873, or rather, the depression which followed it and which, with hardly discernible interruptions in the early eighties, and the unusually violent, but short-lived boom round about 1889, marks twenty-two years of European economic history ... During the short boom of 1889–90, the system of cartels was widely resorted to in order to take advantage of favourable business conditions. An ill-considered policy drove prices up still more rapidly and still higher than would have been the case if there had been no cartels, and nearly all these cartels perished ingloriously in the smash. Another five-year period of bad trade and low prices followed, but a new spirit reigned in industry; the depression was no longer regarded as something to be taken for granted: it was regarded as nothing more than a pause before another boom.

The cartel movement entered its second epoch: instead of being a transitory phenomenon, the cartels have become one of the foundations of economic life. They are winning one field of industry after another, primarily, the raw materials industry. At the beginning of the nineties the cartel system had already acquired in the organisation of the coke syndicate on the model of which the coal syndicate was later formed – a cartel technique which has hardly been improved on. For the first time the great boom at the close of the nineteenth century and the crisis of 1900–3 occurred entirely – in the mining and iron industries at least – under the aegis of the cartels. And while at that time it appeared to be something novel, now the general public takes it for granted that large spheres of economic life have been, as a general rule, removed from the realm of free competition.[7]

Thus, the principal stages in the history of monopolies are the following: (1) 1860–70, the highest stage, the apex of development of free competition; monopoly is in the barely discernible, embryonic stage. (2) After the crisis of 1873, a lengthy period of development of cartels; but they are still the exception. They are not yet durable. They are still a transitory phenomenon. (3) The boom at the end of the nineteenth century and the crisis of 1900–3. Cartels become one of the foundations of the whole of economic life. Capitalism has been transformed into imperialism.

Cartels come to an agreement on the terms of sale, dates of payment, etc. They divide the markets among themselves. They fix the quantity of goods to be produced. They fix prices. They divide the profits among the various enterprises, etc.

The number of cartels in Germany was estimated at about 250 in 1896 and at 385 in 1905, with about 12,000 firms participating.[8] But it is generally recognised that these figures are underestimations. From the statistics of German industry for 1907 we quoted above, it is evident that even these 12,000 very big enterprises probably consume more than half the steam and electric power used in the country. In the United States of America, the number of trusts in 1900 was estimated at 185 and in 1907, 250. American statistics divide all industrial enterprises into those belonging to individuals, to private firms or to corporations. The latter in 1904 comprised 23.6 per cent, and in 1909, 25.9 per cent, i.e., more than one-fourth of the total industrial enterprises in the country. These employed in 1904, 70.6 per cent, and in 1909, 75.6 per cent, i.e., more than three-fourths of the total wage-earners. Their output at these two dates was valued at $10,900,000,000 and $16,300,000,000, i.e., 73 7 per cent and 79.0 per cent of the total, respectively.

At times cartels and trusts concentrate in their hands seven- or eight-tenths of the total output of a given branch of industry. The Rhine-Westphalian Coal Syndicate, at its foundation in 1893, concentrated 86.7 per cent of the total coal output of the area, and in 1910 it already concentrated 95.4 per cent.[9] The monopoly so created assures enormous profits, and leads to the formation of technical production units of formidable magnitude. The famous Standard Oil Company in the United States was founded in 1900:

It has an authorised capital of $150,000,000. It issued $100,000,000 common and $106,000,000 preferred stock. From 1900 to 1907 the following dividends were paid on the latter: 48, 48, 45, 44, 36, 40, 40, 40 per cent in the respective years, i.e., in all, $367,000,000. From 1882 to 1907, out of total net profits amounting to $889,000,000, $606,000,000 were distributed in dividends, and the rest went to reserve capital.

… In 1907 the various works of the United States Steel Corporation employed no less than 210,180 people. The largest enterprise in the German mining industry, Gelsenkirchener Bergwerksgesellschaft, in 1908 had a staff of 46,048 workers and office employees.[10]

In 1902, the United States Steel Corporation already produced 9,000,000 tons of steel.[11] Its output constituted in 1901, 66.3 per cent, and in 1908, 56.1 per cent of the total output of steel in the United States.[12] The output of ore was 43.9 per cent and 46.3 per cent, respectively.

The report of the American Government Commission on Trusts states:

Their superiority over competitors is due to the magnitude of their enterprises and their excellent technical equipment. Since its inception, the Tobacco Trust has devoted all its efforts to the universal substitution of mechanical for manual labour. With this end in view it has bought up all patents that have anything to do with the manufacture of tobacco and has spent enormous sums for this purpose. Many of these patents at first proved to be of no use, and had to be modified by the engineers employed by the trust. At the end of 1906, two subsidiary companies were formed solely to acquire patents. With the same object in view, the trust has built its own foundries, machine shops and repair shops. One of these establishments, that in Brooklyn, employs on the average 300 workers; here experiments are carried out on inventions concerning the manufacture of cigarettes, cheroots, snuff, tinfoil for packing, boxes, etc. Here, also, inventions are perfected.

... Other trusts also employ what are called development engineers whose business it is to devise new methods of production and to test technical improvements. The United States Steel Corporation grants big bonuses to its workers and engineers for all inventions that raise technical efficiency, or reduce cost of production.[13]

In German large-scale industry, e.g., in the chemical industry, which has developed so enormously during these last few decades, the promotion of technical improvement is organised in the same way. By 1908 the process of concentration of production had already given rise to two main 'groups' which, in their way, were also in the nature of monopolies. At first these groups constituted 'dual alliances' of two pairs of big factories, each having a capital of from twenty to twenty-one million marks on the one hand, the former Meister Factory in Hochst and the Casella Factory in Frankfurt am Main; and on the other hand, the aniline and soda factory at Ludwigshafen and the former Bayer Factory at Elberfeld. Then, in 1905, one of these groups, and in 1908 the other group, each concluded an agreement with yet another big factory. The result was the formation of two 'triple alliances', each with a capital of from forty to fifty million marks. And these 'alliances' have already begun to 'approach' each other, to reach 'an understanding' about prices, etc.[14]

Competition becomes transformed into monopoly. The result is immense progress in the socialisation of production. In particular, the process of technical invention and improvement becomes socialised.

This is something quite different from the old free competition between manufacturers, scattered and out of touch with one another, and producing for an unknown market. Concentration has reached the point at which it is possible to make an approximate estimate of all sources of raw materials (for example, the iron ore deposits) of a country and even, as we shall see, of several countries, or of the whole world. Not only are such estimates made, but these sources are captured by gigantic monopolist associations. An approximate estimate of the capacity of markets is also made, and the associations 'divide' them up amongst themselves by agreement. Skilled labour is monopolised, the best engineers are engaged; the means of transport are captured – railways in America, shipping companies in Europe and America. Capitalism in its imperialist stage leads directly to the most comprehensive socialisation of production; it, so to speak, drags the capitalists, against their will and consciousness, into some sort of a new social order, a transitional one from complete free competition to complete socialisation.

Production becomes social, but appropriation remains private. The social means of production remain the private property of a few. The general framework of formally recognised free competition remains, and the yoke of a few monopolists on the rest of the population becomes a hundred times heavier, more burdensome and intolerable.

The German economist, Kestner, has written a book especially devoted to 'the struggle between the cartels and outsiders', i.e., the capitalists outside the cartels. He entitled his work *Compulsory Organisation*, although, in order to present capitalism in its true light, he should, of course, have written about compulsory submission to monopolist associations. It is instructive to glance at least at the list of the methods the monopolist associations resort to in the present-day, the latest, the civilised struggle for 'organisation': (1) stopping supplies of raw materials ... ('one of the most important methods of compelling adherence to the cartel'); (2) stopping the supply of labour by means of 'alliances' (i.e., of agreements between the capitalists and the trade unions by which the latter permit their members to work only in cartelised enterprises); (3) stopping deliveries; (4) closing trade outlets; (5) agreements with the buyers, by which the latter undertake to trade only with the cartels; (6) systematic price cutting (to ruin 'outside' firms, i.e., those which refuse to submit to the monopolists. Millions are spent in order to sell goods for a certain time below their cost price; there were instances when the price of petrol was thus reduced from 40 to 22 marks, i.e., almost by half!); (7) stopping credits; (8) boycott.

Here we no longer have competition between small and large, between technically developed and backward enterprises. We see here the monopolists throttling those who do not submit to them, to their yoke, to their dictation. This is how this process is reflected in the mind of a bourgeois economist:

'Even in the purely economic sphere,' writes Kestner,

a certain change is taking place from commercial activity in the old sense of the word towards organisational-speculative activity. The greatest success no longer goes to the merchant whose technical and commercial experience enables him best of all to estimate the needs of the buyer, and who is able to discover and, so to speak, 'awaken' a latent demand; it goes to the speculative genius [?!] who knows how to estimate, or even only to sense in advance, the organisational development and the possibilities of certain connections between individual enterprises and the banks ...

Translated into ordinary human language this means that the development of capitalism has arrived at a stage when, although commodity production still 'reigns' and continues to be regarded as the basis of economic life, it has in reality been undermined and the bulk of the profits go to the 'geniuses' of financial manipulation. At the basis of these manipulations and swindles lies socialised production; but the immense progress of mankind, which achieved this socialisation, goes to benefit ... the speculators. We shall see later how 'on these grounds' reactionary, petty-bourgeois critics of capitalist imperialism dream of going *back* to 'free,' 'peaceful' and 'honest' competition.

'The prolonged raising of prices which results from the formation of cartels', says Kestner, has hitherto been observed only in respect of the most important means of production, particularly coal, iron and potassium, but never in respect of manufactured goods. Similarly, the increase in profits resulting from this raising of prices has been limited only to the industries which produce means of production. To this observation we must add that the industries which process raw materials (and not semi-manufactures) not only secure advantages from the cartel formation in the shape of high profits, to the detriment of the finished goods industry, but have also secured a *dominating position* over the latter, which did not exist under free competition.[15]

The words which I have italicised reveal the essence of the case which the bourgeois economists admit so reluctantly and so rarely, and which the present-day defenders of opportunism, led by Kautsky, so zealously try to evade and brush aside. Domination, and the violence that is associated with it, such are the relationships that are typical of the 'latest phase of capitalist development' this is what inevitably had to result, and has resulted, from the formation of all-powerful economic monopolies.

I shall give one more example of the methods employed by the cartels. Where it is possible to capture all or the chief sources of raw materials, the rise of cartels and formation of monopolies is particularly easy. It would be wrong, however, to assume that monopolies do not arise in other industries in which it is impossible to corner the sources of raw materials. The cement industry, for instance, can find its raw materials everywhere. Yet in Germany this industry too is strongly cartelised. The cement manufacturers have formed regional syndicates: South German, Rhine-Westphalian, etc. The prices fixed are monopoly prices: 230 to 280 marks a car-load, when the cost price is 180 marks! The enterprises pay a dividend of from 12 to 16 per cent – and it must not be forgotten that the 'geniuses' of modern speculation know how to pocket big profits besides what they draw in dividends. In order to prevent competition in such a profitable industry, the monopolists even resort to various stratagems: they spread false rumours about the bad situation in their industry; anonymous warnings are published in the newspapers, like the following: 'Capitalists, don't invest your capital in the cement industry!'; lastly, they buy up 'outsiders' (those outside the syndicates) and pay them compensation of 60,000, 80,000 and even 150,000 marks.[16] Monopoly hews a path for itself everywhere without scruple as to the means, from paying a 'modest' sum to buy off competitors, to the American device of employing dynamite against them.

The statement that cartels can abolish crises is a fable spread by bourgeois economists who at all costs desire to place capitalism in a favourable light. On the contrary, the monopoly created in *certain* branches of industry increases and intensifies the anarchy inherent in capitalist production *as a whole*. The disparity between the development of agriculture and that of industry, which is characteristic of capitalism in general, is increased. The privileged position of the most highly cartelised, so-called *heavy* industry, especially coal and iron, causes 'a still greater lack of co-ordination' in other branches of industry – as Jeidels, the author of one of the best works on 'the relationship of the German big banks to industry', admits.[17]

'The more developed an economic system is,' writes Liefmann, an unblushing apologist of capitalism, 'the more it resorts to risky enterprises, or enterprises in other countries, to those which need a great deal of time to develop, or finally, to those which are only of local importance.'[18] The increased risk is connected in the long run with a prodigious increase of capital, which, as it were, overflows the brim, flows abroad, etc. At the same time the extremely rapid rate of technical progress gives rise to increasing elements of disparity between the various spheres of national economy, to anarchy and crises. Liefmann is obliged to admit that: 'In all probability mankind will see further important technical revolutions in the near future which will also affect the organisation of the economic system' (For example, electricity and aviation.) 'As a general rule, in such periods of radical economic change, speculation develops on a large scale.' ...[19]

Crises of every kind – economic crises most frequently, but not only these – in their turn increase very considerably the tendency towards concentration and towards monopoly. In this connection, the following reflections of Jeidels on the significance of the crisis of 1900, which, as we have already seen, marked the turning-point in the history of modern monopoly, are exceedingly instructive:

Side by side with the gigantic plants in the basic industries, the crisis of 1900 still found many plants organised on lines that today would be considered obsolete, the 'pure' (non-combined) plants, which were brought into being at the height of the industrial boom. The fall in prices and the falling off in demand put these 'pure' enterprises in a precarious position, which did not affect the gigantic combined enterprises at all or only affected them for a very short time. As a consequence of this the crisis of 1900 resulted in a far greater concentration of industry than the crisis of 1873: the latter crisis also produced a sort of selection of the best-equipped enterprises, but owing to the level of technical development at that time, this selection could not place the firms which successfully emerged from the crisis in a position of monopoly. Such a durable monopoly exists to a high degree in the gigantic enterprises in the modern iron and steel and electrical industries owing to their very complicated technique, far-reaching organisation and magnitude of capital, and, to a lesser degree, in the engineering industry, certain branches of the metallurgical industry, transport, etc.[20]

Monopoly! This is the last word in the 'latest phase of capitalist development'. But we shall only have a very insufficient, incomplete, and poor notion of the real power and the significance of modern monopolies if we do not take into consideration the part played by the banks.

II. Banks and Their New Role

The principal and primary function of banks is to serve as middlemen in the making of payments. In so doing they transform inactive money capital into active, that is, into capital yielding a profit; they collect all kinds of money revenues and place them at the disposal of the capitalist class.

As banking develops and becomes concentrated in a small number of establishments, the banks grow from modest middlemen into powerful monopolies having at their command almost the whole of the money capital of all the capitalists and small businessmen and also the larger part of the means of production and sources of raw materials in

Table 1. Percentage of Total Deposits

	In 9 big Berlin banks	In the other 48 banks with a capital of more than 10 million marks	In 115 banks with a capital of 1–10 million marks	In small banks (with a capital of less than a million marks)
1907–8	47	32.5	16.5	4
1912–13	49	36	12	3

any one country and in a number of countries. This transformation of numerous modest middlemen into a handful of monopolists is one of the fundamental processes in the growth of capitalism into capitalist imperialism; for this reason, we must first of all examine the concentration of banking.

In 1907–8, the combined deposits of the German joint-stock banks, each having a capital of more than a million marks, amounted to 7,000 million marks; in 1912–13, these deposits already amounted to 9,800 million marks, an increase of 40 per cent in five years; and of the 2,800 million increase, 2,750 million was divided among 57 banks, each having a capital of more than 10 million marks. The distribution of the deposits between big and small banks was as follows:[21]

The small banks are being squeezed out by the big banks, of which only nine concentrate in their hands almost half the total deposits. But we have left out of account many important details – for instance, the transformation of numerous small banks into actual branches of the big banks, etc. I shall speak of this later.

At the end of 1913, Schulze-Gaevernitz estimated the deposits in the nine big Berlin banks at 5,100 million marks, out of a total of about 10,000 million marks. Taking into account not only the deposits, but the total bank capital, this author wrote:

> At the end of 1909, the nine big Berlin banks, together with their affiliated banks, controlled 11,300 million marks, that is, about 83 per cent of the total German bank capital. The Deutsche Bank, which together with its affiliated banks controls nearly 3,000 million marks, represents, parallel to the Prussian State Railway Administration, the biggest and also the most decentralised accumulation of capital in the Old World.[22]

I have emphasised the reference to the 'affiliated' banks because it is one of the most important distinguishing features of modern capitalist concentration. The big enterprises, and the banks in particular, not only completely absorb the small ones, but also 'annex' them, subordinate them, bring them into their 'own' group or 'concern' (to use the technical term) by acquiring 'holdings' in their capital, by purchasing or exchanging shares, by a system of credits, etc., etc. Professor Liefmann has written a voluminous 'work' of about 500 pages describing modern 'holding and finance companies',[23] unfortunately adding very dubious 'theoretical' reflections to what is frequently undigested raw material. To what results this 'holding' system leads in respect of concentration is best illustrated in the book written on the big German banks by Riesser, himself a banker. But before examining his data, let us quote a concrete example of the 'holding' system.

The Deutsche Bank 'group' is one of the biggest, if not the biggest, of the big banking groups. In order to trace the main threads which connect all the banks in this group, a distinction must be made between holdings of the first and second and third degree, or what amounts to the same thing, between dependence (of the lesser banks on the Deutsche Bank) in the first, second and third degree. We then obtain the following picture:[24]

Table 2

The Deutsche Bank has holdings:	Direct or 1st degree dependence	2nd degree dependence	3rd degree dependence
Permanently	in 17 other banks	9 of the 17 have holdings in 34 other banks	4 of the 9 have holdings in 7 other banks
For an indefinite period	in 5 other banks	—	—
Occasionally	in 8 other banks	5 of the 8 have holdings in 14 other banks	2 of the 5 have holdings in 2 other banks
Totals	in 30 other banks	14 of the 30 have holdings in 48 other banks	6 of the 14 have holdings in 9 other banks

Included in the eight banks 'occasionally' dependent on the Deutsche Bank in the 'first degree', are three foreign banks: one Austrian (the Wiener Bankverein) and two Russian (the Siberian Commercial Bank and the Russian Bank for Foreign Trade). Altogether, the Deutsche Bank group comprises, directly and indirectly, partially and totally, eighty-seven banks; and the total capital – its own and that of others which it controls – is estimated at between two and three thousand million marks.

It is obvious that a bank which stands at the head of such a group, and which enters into agreement with half a dozen other banks only slightly smaller than itself for the purpose of conducting exceptionally big and profitable financial operations like floating state loans, has already outgrown the part of 'middleman' and has become an association of a handful of monopolists.

The rapidity with which the concentration of banking proceeded in Germany at the turn of the twentieth century is shown by the following data which we quote in an abbreviated form from Riesser:

Table 3. Six Big Berlin Banks

Year	Branches in Germany	Deposit banks and exchange offices	Constant holdings in German joint-stock banks	Total establishments
1895	16	14	1	42
1900	21	40	8	80
1911	104	276	63	450

We see the rapid expansion of a close network of channels which cover the whole country, centralising all capital and all revenues, transforming thousands and thousands of scattered economic enterprises into a single national capitalist, and then into a world capitalist economy. The 'decentralisation' that Schulze-Gaevernitz, as an exponent of present-day bourgeois political economy, speaks of in the passage previously quoted, really means the subordination to a single centre of an increasing number of formerly relatively 'independent', or rather, strictly local economic units. In reality it is centralisation, the enhancement of the role, importance and power of monopolist giants.

In the older capitalist countries this 'banking network' is still more close. In Great Britain and Ireland, in 1910, there were in all 7,151 branches of banks. Four big banks had more than 400 branches each (from 447 to 689); four had more than 200 branches each, and eleven more than 100 each.

In France, three very big banks, Crédit Lyonnais, the Comptoir National and the Société Générale extended their operations and their network of branches in the following manner.[25]

Table 4

Year	Number of branches and offices			Capital (000,000 francs)	
	In the provinces	In Paris	Total	Own Capital	Deposits used as capital
1895	47	17	64	200	427
1900	192	66	258	265	1,245
1911	1,033	196	1,229	887	4,363

In order to show the 'connections' of a big modern bank, Riesser gives the following figures of the number of letters dispatched and received by the Disconto-Gesellschaft, one of the biggest banks in Germany and in the world (its capital in 1914 amounted to 300 million marks):

Table 5

Year	Letters received	Letters dispatched
1852	6,135	6,292
1870	85,800	87,513
1900	533,102	626,043

The number of accounts of the big Paris bank, the Crédit Lyonnais, increased from 28,535 in 1875 to 633,539 in 1912.[26]

These simple figures show perhaps better than lengthy disquisitions how the concentration of capital and the growth of bank turnover are radically changing the significance of the banks. Scattered capitalists are transformed into a single collective capitalist. When carrying the current accounts of a few capitalists, a bank, as it were, transacts a purely technical and exclusively auxiliary operation. When, however, this operation grows to enormous dimensions we find that a handful of monopolists subordinate to their will all the operations, both commercial and industrial, of the whole of capitalist society; for they are enabled by means of their banking connections, their current accounts and other financial operations – first, to ascertain exactly the financial position of the various capitalists, then to control them, to influence them by restricting or enlarging, facilitating or hindering credits, and finally to entirely determine their fate, determine their income, deprive them of capital, or permit them to increase their capital rapidly and to enormous dimensions, etc.

We have just mentioned the 300 million marks capital of the Disconto-Gesellschaft of Berlin. This increase of the capital of the bank was one of the incidents in the struggle for hegemony between two of the biggest Berlin banks – the Deutsche Bank and the Disconto. In 1870, the first was still a novice and had a capital of only 15 million marks, while the second had a capital of 30 million marks. In 1908, the first had a capital of 200 million, while the second had 170 million. In 1914, the first increased its capital to 250 million and the second, by merging with another first-class big bank, the Schaaffhausenscher Bankverein, increased its capital to 300 million. And, of course, this struggle for hegemony went hand in hand with the more and more frequent conclusion of 'agreements' of an increasingly durable character between the two banks. The following are the conclusions that this development forces upon banking specialists who regard economic questions from a standpoint which does not in the least exceed the bounds of the most moderate and cautious bourgeois reformism.

Commenting on the increase of the capital of the Disconto Gesellschaft to 300 million marks, the German review, *Die Bank*, wrote:

Other banks will follow this same path and in time the three hundred men, who today govern Germany economically, will gradually be reduced to fifty, twenty-five or still fewer. It cannot be expected that this latest move towards concentration will be confined to banking. The close relations that exist between individual banks naturally lead to the bringing together of the industrial syndicates which these banks favour … One fine morning we shall wake up in surprise to see nothing but trusts before our eyes, and to find ourselves faced with the necessity of substituting state monopolies for private monopolies. However, we have nothing to reproach ourselves with, except that we have allowed things to follow their own course, slightly accelerated by the manipulation of stocks.[27]

This is an example of the impotence of bourgeois journalism which differs from bourgeois science only in that the latter is less sincere and strives to obscure the essence of the matter, to hide the forest behind the trees. To be 'surprised' at the results of concentration, to 'reproach' the government of capitalist Germany, or capitalist 'society' ('ourselves'), to fear that the introduction of stocks and shares might 'accelerate' concentration in the same way as the German 'cartel' specialist Tschierschky fears the American trusts and 'prefers' the German cartels on the grounds that they 'may not, like the trusts, excessively accelerate technical and economic progress' - is not all this a sign of impotence?[28]

But facts remain facts. There are no trusts in Germany; there are 'only' cartels - but Germany is governed by not more than three hundred magnates of capital, and the number of these is constantly diminishing. At all events, banks greatly intensify and accelerate the process of concentration of capital and the formation of monopolies in all capitalist countries, notwithstanding all the differences in their banking laws.

The banking system 'possesses, indeed, the form of universal bookkeeping and distribution of means of production on a social scale, but solely the form,' wrote Marx in *Capital* half a century ago (Russ. trans., Vol. III, part II, p. 144.[29]) The figures we have quoted on the growth of bank capital, on the increase in the number of the branches and offices of the biggest banks, the increase in the number of their accounts, etc., present a concrete picture of this 'universal book-keeping' of the whole capitalist class; and not only of the capitalists, for the banks collect, even though temporarily, all kinds of money revenues - of small businessmen, office clerks, and of a tiny upper stratum of the working class. 'Universal distribution of means of production' - that, from the formal aspect, is what grows out of the modern banks, which, numbering some three to six of the biggest in France, and six to eight in Germany, control millions and millions. In substance, however, the distribution of means of production is not at all 'universal', but private, i.e., it conforms to the interests of big capital, and primarily, of huge, monopoly capital, which operates under conditions in which the masses live in want, in which the whole development of agriculture hopelessly lags behind the development of industry, while within industry itself the 'heavy industries' exact tribute from all other branches of industry.

In the matter of socialising capitalist economy, the savings-banks and post-offices are beginning to compete with the banks; they are more 'decentralised', i.e., their influence extends to a greater number of local-ities, to more remote places, to wider sections of the population. Here is the data collected by an American commission on the comparative growth of deposits in banks and savings-banks:[30]

Table 6. Deposits (000,000,000 marks)

	Britain		France		Germany		
Year	Banks	Savings-banks	Banks	Savings-banks	Banks	Credit Societies	Savings-banks
1880	8.4	1.6	?	0.9	0.5	0.4	2.6
1888	12.4	2.0	1.5	2.1	1.1	0.4	4.5
1908	23.2	4.2	3.7	4.2	7.1	2.2	13.9

As they pay interest at the rate of 4 per cent and 4.25 per cent on deposits, the savings-banks must seek 'profitable' investments for their capital, they must deal in bills, mortgages, etc. The boundaries between the banks and the savings-banks 'become more and more obliterated'. The Chambers of Commerce of Bochum and Erfurt, for example, demand that savings-banks be 'prohibited' from engaging in 'purely' banking business, such as discounting bills; they demand the limitation of the 'banking' operations of the post-office.[31] The banking magnates seem to be afraid that state monopoly will steal upon them from an unexpected quarter. It goes without saying, however, that this fear is no more than an expression of the rivalry, so to speak, between two department managers in the same office; for, on the one hand, the millions entrusted to the savings-banks are in the final analysis actually controlled by these very same bank capital magnates, while, on the other hand, state monopoly in capitalist society is merely a means of increasing and guaranteeing the income of m llionaires in some branch of industry who are on the verge of bankruptcy.

The change from the old type of capitalism, in which free competition predominated, to the new capitalism, in which monopoly reigns, is expressed, among other things, by a decline in the importance of the Stock Exchange. The review, *Die Bank*, writes: "The Stock Exchange has long ceased to be the indispensable medium of circulation that it formerly was when the banks were not yet able to place the bulk of new issues with their clients."[32]

"'Every bank is a Stock Exchange", and the bigger the bank, and the more successful the concentration of banking, the truer does this modern aphorism ring.'[33]

> While formerly, in the 1870s, the Stock Exchange, flushed with the exuberance of youth [a 'subtle' allusion to the Stock Exchange crash of 1873, the company promotion scandals,[34] etc.] opened the era of the industrialisation of Germany, nowadays the banks and industry are able to 'manage it alone'. The domination of our big banks over the Stock Exchange ... is nothing else than the expression of the completely organised German industrial state. If the domain of the automatically functioning economic laws is thus restricted, and if the domain of conscious regulation by the banks is considerably enlarged, the national economic responsibility of a few guiding heads is immensely increased.

So writes the German Professor Schulze-Gaevernitz,[35] an apologist of German imperialism, who is regarded as an authority by the imperialists of all countries, and who tries to gloss over the 'mere detail' that the 'conscious regulation' of economic life by the banks consists in the fleecing of the public by a handful of 'completely organised' monopolists. The task of a bourgeois professor is not to lay bare the entire mechanism, or to expose all the machinations of the bank monopolists, but rather to present them in a favourable light.

In the same way, Riesser, a still more authoritative economist and himself a banker, makes shift with meaningless phrases in order to explain away undeniable facts: '... the Stock Exchange is steadily losing the feature which is absolutely essential for national economy as a whole and for the circulation of securities in particular – that of being not only a most exact measuring-rod, but also an almost automatic regulator of the economic movements which converge on it.'[36]

In other words, the old capitalism, the capitalism of free competition with its indispensable regulator, the Stock Exchange, is passing away. A new capitalism has come to take its place, bearing obvious features of something transient, a mixture of free competition and monopoly. The question naturally arises: into what is this new capitalism 'developing'? But the bourgeois scholars are afraid to raise this question.

'Thirty years ago, businessmen, freely competing against one another, performed nine-tenths of the work connected with their business other than manual labour. At the present time, nine-tenths of this "brain work" is performed by employees. Banking is in the forefront of this evolution.'[37] This admission by Schulze-Gaevernitz brings us once again to the question: into what is this new capitalism, capitalism in its imperialist stage, developing?

Among the few banks which remain at the head of all capitalist economy as a result of the process of concentration, there is naturally to be observed an increasingly marked tendency towards monopolist agreements, towards a bank trust. In America, not nine, but two very big banks, those of the multimillionaires Rockefeller and Morgan, control a capital of eleven thousand million marks.[38] In Germany the absorption of the Schaaffhausenscher Bankverein by the Disconto-Gesellschaft to which I referred above, was commented on in the following terms by the Frankfurter Zeitung,[39] an organ of Stock Exchange interests:

> The concentration movement of the banks is narrowing the circle of establishments from which it is possible to obtain credits, and is consequently increasing the dependence of big industry upon a small number of banking groups. In view of the close connection between industry and the financial world, the freedom of movement of industrial companies which need banking capital is restricted. For this reason, big industry is watching the growing trustification of the banks with mixed feelings.

Indeed, we have repeatedly seen the beginnings of certain agreements between the individual big banking concerns, which aim at restricting competition.[40]

Again and again, the final word in the development of banking is monopoly.

As regards the close connection between the banks and industry, it is precisely in this sphere that the new role of the banks is, perhaps, most strikingly felt. When a bank discounts a bill for a firm, opens a current account for it, etc., these operations, taken separately, do not in the least diminish its independence, and the bank plays no other part than that of a modest middleman. But when such operations are multiplied and become an established practice, when the bank 'collects' in its own hands enormous amounts of capital, when the running of a current account for a given firm enables the bank – and this is what happens – to obtain fuller and more detailed information about the economic position of its client, the result is that the industrial capitalist becomes more completely dependent on the bank.

At the same time a personal link-up, so to speak, is established between the banks and the biggest industrial and commercial enterprises, the merging of one with another through the acquisition of shares, through the appointment of bank directors to the Supervisory Boards (or Boards of Directors) of industrial and commercial enterprises, and vice versa. The German economist Jeidels has compiled most detailed data on this form of concentration of capital and of enterprises. Six of the biggest Berlin banks were represented by their directors in 344 industrial companies; and by their board members in 407 others, making a total of 751 companies. In 289 of these companies, they either had two of their representatives on each of the respective Supervisory Boards, or held the posts of chairmen. We find these industrial and commercial companies in the most diverse branches of industry: insurance, transport, restaurants, theatres, art industry, etc. On the other hand, on the Supervisory Boards of these six banks (in 1910) were fifty-one of the biggest industrialists, including the director of Krupp, of the powerful 'Hapag' (Hamburg-Amerika Line), etc., etc. From 1895 to 1910, each of these six banks participated in the share and bond issues of many hundreds of industrial companies (the number ranging from 281 to 419).[41]

The 'personal link-up' between the banks and industry is supplemented by the 'personal link-up' between both of them and the government. 'Seats on Supervisory Boards', writes Jeidels, 'are freely offered to persons of title, also to ex-civil servants, who are able to do a great deal to facilitate (!!) relations with the authorities ... Usually, on the Supervisory Board of a big bank, there is a member of parliament or a Berlin city councillor.'

The building and development, so to speak, of the big capitalist monopolies is therefore going on full steam ahead in all 'natural' and 'supernatural' ways. A sort of division of labour is being systematically developed amongst the several hundred kings of finance who reign over modern capitalist society:

Simultaneously with this widening of the sphere of activity of certain big industrialists (joining the boards of banks, etc.) and with the assignment of provincial bank managers to definite industrial regions, there is a growth of specialisation among the directors of the big banks. Generally speaking, this specialisation is only conceivable when banking is conducted on a large scale, and particularly when it has widespread connections with industry. This division of labour proceeds along two lines: on the one hand, relations with industry as a whole are entrusted to one director, as his special function; on the other, each director assumes the supervision of several separate enterprises, or of a group of enterprises in the same branch of industry or having similar interests ... (Capitalism has already reached the stage of organised supervision of individual enterprises.) One specialises in German industry, sometimes even in West German industry alone (the West is the most industrialised part of Germany), others specialise in relations with foreign states and foreign industry, in information on the characters of industrialists and others, in Stock Exchange questions, etc. Besides, each bank director is often assigned a special locality or a special branch of industry; one works chiefly on Supervisory Boards of electric companies, another, on chemical, brewing, or beet sugar plants, a third, in a few isolated industrial enterprises, but at the same time works on the Supervisory

Boards of insurance companies ... In short, there can be no doubt that
the growth in the dimensions and diversity of the big banks' operations is accompanied by an increase in the division of labour among
their directors with the object (and result) of, so to speak, lifting them
somewhat out of pure banking and making them better experts, better
judges of the general problems of industry and the special problems
of each branch of industry, thus making them more capable of acting
within the respective bank's industrial sphere of influence. This system
is supplemented by the banks' endeavours to elect to their Supervisory
Boards men who are experts in industrial affairs, such as industrialists,
former officials, especially those formerly in the railway service or in
mining [etc.].[42]

We find the same system only in a slightly different form in French
banking. For instance, one of the three biggest French banks, the
Crédit Lyonnais, has organised a financial research service (*service des
études financières*), which permanently employs over fifty engineers,
statisticians, economists, lawyers, etc. This costs from six to seven
hundred thousand francs annually. The service is in turn divided
into eight departments: one specialises in collecting information on
industrial establishments, another studies general statistics, a third,
railway and steamship companies, a fourth, securities, a fifth, financial
reports, etc.[43]

The result is, on the one hand, the ever-growing merger, or, as N. I.
Bukharin aptly calls it, coalescence, of bank and industrial capital and,
on the other hand, the growth of the banks into institutions of a truly
'universal character'. On this question I find it necessary to quote the
exact terms used by Jeidels, who has best studied the subject:

An examination of the sum total of industrial relationships reveals the
universal character of the financial establishments working on behalf
of industry. Unlike other kinds of banks, and contrary to the demand
sometimes expressed in the literature that banks should specialise in one
kind of business or in one branch of industry in order to prevent the
ground from slipping from under their feet – the big banks are striving to
make their connections with industrial enterprises as varied as possible

in respect of the locality or branches of industry and are striving to eliminate the unevenness in the distribution of capital among localities and branches of industry resulting from the historical development of individual enterprises ... One tendency is to make the connections with industry general; another tendency is to make them durable and close. In the six big banks both these tendencies are realised, not in full, but to a considerable extent and to an equal degree.

Quite often industrial and commercial circles complain of the 'terrorism' of the banks. And it is not surprising that such complaints are heard, for the big banks 'command', as will be seen from the following example. On 19 November 1901, one of the big, so-called Berlin 'D' banks (the names of the four biggest banks begin with the letter D) wrote to the Board of Directors of the German Central Northwest Cement Syndicate in the following terms:

As we learn from the notice you published in a certain newspaper of the 18th inst., we must reckon with the possibility that the next general meeting of your syndicate, to be held on the 30th of this month, may decide on measures which are likely to effect changes in your enterprise which are unacceptable to us. We deeply regret that, for these reasons, we are obliged henceforth to withdraw the credit which had hitherto been allowed you ... But if the said next general meeting does not decide upon measures which are unacceptable to us, and if we receive suitable guarantees on this matter for the future, we shall be quite willing to open negotiations with you on the grant of a new credit.[44]

As a matter of fact, this is small capital's old complaint about being oppressed by big capital, but, in this case, it was a whole syndicate that fell into the category of 'small' capital! The old struggle between small and big capital is being resumed at a new and immeasurably higher stage of development. It stands to reason that the big banks' enterprises, worth many millions, can accelerate technical progress with means that cannot possibly be compared with those of the past. The banks, for example, set up special technical research societies, and, of course, only 'friendly' industrial enterprises benefit from their work. To this category belong the Electric Railway Research Association, the Central Bureau of Scientific and Technical Research, etc.

The directors of the big banks themselves cannot fail to see that new conditions of national economy are being created; but they are powerless in the face of these phenomena.

'Anyone who has watched, in recent years writes Jeidels,

> the changes of incumbents of directorships and seats on the Supervisory Boards of the big banks, cannot fail to have noticed that power is gradually passing into the hands of men who consider the active intervention of the big banks in the general development of industry to be necessary and of increasing importance. Between these new men and the old bank directors, disagreements on this subject of a business and often of a personal nature are growing. The issue is whether or not the banks, as credit institutions, will suffer from this intervention in industry, whether they are sacrificing tried principles and an assured profit to engage in a field of activity which has nothing in common with their role as middlemen in providing credit, and which is leading the banks into a field where they are more than ever before exposed to the blind forces of trade fluctuations. This is the opinion of many of the older bank directors, while most of the young men consider active intervention in industry to be a necessity as great as that which gave rise, simultaneously with big modern industry, to the big banks and modern industrial banking. The two parties are agreed only on one point: that there are neither firm principles nor a concrete aim in the new activities of the big banks.[45]

The old capitalism has had its day. The new capitalism represents a transition towards something. It is hopeless, of course, to seek for 'firm principles and a concrete aim' for the purpose of 'reconciling' monopoly with free competition. The admission of the practical men has quite a different ring from the official praises of the charms of 'organised' capitalism sung by its apologists, Schulze-Gaevernitz, Liefmann and similar 'theoreticians'.

At precisely what period were the 'new activities' of the big banks finally established? Jeidels gives us a fairly exact answer to this important question:

The connections between the banks and industrial enterprises, with their new content, their new forms and their new organs, namely, the big banks which are organised on both a centralised and a decentralised basis, were scarcely a characteristic economic phenomenon before the nineties; in one sense, indeed, this initial date may be advanced to the year 1897, when the important mergers took place and when, for the first time, the new form of decentralised organisation was introduced to suit the industrial policy of the banks. This starting-point could perhaps be placed at an even later date, for it was the crisis of 1900 that enormously accelerated and intensified the process of concentration of industry and of banking, consolidated that process, for the first time transformed the connection with industry into the actual monopoly of the big banks, and made this connection much closer and more active.[46]

Thus, the twentieth century marks the turning-point from the old capitalism to the new, from the domination of capital in general to the domination of finance capital.

III. Finance Capital and the Financial Oligarchy

'A steadily increasing proportion of capital in industry', writes Hilferding,

> ceases to belong to the industrialists who employ it. They obtain the use of it only through the medium of the banks which, in relation to them, represent the owners of the capital. On the other hand, the bank is forced to sink an increasing share of its funds in industry. Thus, to an ever-greater degree the banker is being transformed into an industrial capitalist. This bank capital, i.e., capital in money form, which is thus actually transformed into industrial capital, I call 'finance capital' ... Finance capital is capital controlled by banks and employed by industrialists.[47]

This definition is incomplete insofar as it is silent on one extremely important fact – on the increase of concentration of production and of capital to such an extent that concentration is leading, and has led, to monopoly. But throughout the whole of his work, and particularly in the two chapters preceding the one from which this definition is taken, Hilferding stresses the part played by capitalist monopolies.

The concentration of production; the monopolies arising therefrom; the merging or coalescence of the banks with industry – such is the history of the rise of finance capital and such is the content of that concept.

We now have to describe how, under the general conditions of commodity production and private property, the 'business operations' of capitalist monopolies inevitably lead to the domination of a financial oligarchy. It should be noted that German – and not only German – bourgeois scholars, like Riesser, Schulze-Gaevernitz, Liefmann and others, are all apologists of imperialism and of finance capital. Instead of revealing the 'mechanics' of the formation of an oligarchy, its methods, the size of its revenues 'impeccable and peccable', its connections with parliaments etc., etc., they obscure or gloss over them. They evade these 'vexed questions' by pompous and vague phrases, appeals to the 'sense of responsibility' of bank directors, by praising 'the sense of duty' of Prussian officials, giving serious study to the petty details of absolutely ridiculous parliamentary bills for the 'supervision' and 'regulation' of monopolies, playing spillikins with theories, like, for example, the following 'scholarly' definition, arrived at by Professor Liefmann: '*Commerce is an occupation having for its object the collection, storage and supply of goods.*'[48] (The Professor's bold-face italics.) … From this it would follow that commerce existed in the time of primitive man, who knew nothing about exchange, and that it will exist under socialism!

But the monstrous facts concerning the monstrous rule of the financial oligarchy are so glaring that in all capitalist countries, in America, France and Germany, a whole literature has sprung up, written from the bourgeois point of view, but which, nevertheless, gives a fairly truthful picture and criticism – petty-bourgeois, naturally – of this oligarchy.

Paramount importance attaches to the 'holding system', already briefly referred to above. The German economist Heymann, probably the first to call attention to this matter, describes the essence of it in this way:

The head of the concern controls the principal company (literally: the 'mother company'); the latter reigns over the subsidiary companies ('daughter companies'), which in their turn control still other subsidiaries ('grandchild companies'), etc. In this way, it is possible with a comparatively small capital to dominate immense spheres of production. Indeed, if holding 50 per cent of the capital is always sufficient to control a company, the head of the concern needs only one million to control eight million in the second subsidiaries. And if this 'interlocking' is extended, it is possible with one million to control sixteen million, thirty-two million, etc.[49]

As a matter of fact, experience shows that it is sufficient to own 40 per cent of the shares of a company in order to direct its affairs,[50] since in practice a certain number of small, scattered shareholders find it impossible to attend general meetings, etc. The 'democratisation' of the ownership of shares, from which the bourgeois sophists and opportunist so-called 'Social-Democrats' expect (or say that they expect) the 'democratisation of capital', the strengthening of the role and significance of small-scale production, etc., is, in fact, one of the ways of increasing the power of the financial oligarchy. Incidentally, this is why, in the more advanced, or in the older and more 'experienced' capitalist countries, the law allows the issue of shares of smaller denomination. In Germany, the law does not permit the issue of shares of less than one thousand marks denomination, and the magnates of German finance look with an envious eye at Britain, where the issue of one-pound shares (= 20 marks, about 10 roubles) is permitted. Siemens, one of the biggest industrialists and 'financial kings' in Germany, told the Reichstag on 7 June 1900 that 'the one-pound share is the basis of British imperialism.'[51] This merchant has a much deeper and more 'Marxist' understanding of imperialism than a certain disreputable writer who is held to be one of the founders of Russian Marxism[52] and believes that imperialism is a bad habit of a certain nation ...

But the 'holding system' not only serves enormously to increase the power of the monopolists; it also enables them to resort with impunity to all sorts of shady and dirty tricks to cheat the public, because formally the directors of the 'mother company' are not legally responsible for the 'daughter company', which is supposed to be 'independent', and through the medium of which they can 'pull off' anything. Here is an example taken from the German review, *Die Bank*, for May 1914:

The Spring Steel Company of Kassel was regarded some years ago as being one of the most profitable enterprises in Germany. Through bad management its dividends fell from 15 per cent to nil. It appears that the Board, without consulting the shareholders, had loaned six million marks to one of its 'daughter companies', the Hassia Company, which had a nominal capital of only some hundreds of thousands of marks. This commitment, amounting to nearly treble the capital of the 'mother company', was never mentioned in its balance-sheets. This omission was quite legal and could be hushed up for two whole years because it did not violate any point of company law. The chairman of the Supervisory Board, who as the responsible head had signed the false balance-sheets, was, and still is, the president of the Kassel Chamber of Commerce. The shareholders only heard of the loan to the Hassia Company long afterwards, when it had been proved to be a mistake [the writer should put this word in inverted commas] ... and when Spring Steel shares dropped nearly 100 per cent, because those in the know were getting rid of them ...

This typical example of balance-sheet jugglery, quite common in joint-stock companies, explains why their Boards of Directors are willing to undertake risky transactions with a far lighter heart than individual businessmen. Modern methods of drawing up balance-sheets not only make it possible to conceal doubtful undertakings from the ordinary shareholder, but also allow the people most concerned to escape the consequence of unsuccessful speculation by selling their shares in time when the individual businessman risks his own skin in everything he does ...

The balance-sheets of many joint-stock companies put us in mind of the palimpsests of the Middle Ages from which the visible inscription had first to be erased in order to discover beneath it another inscription giving the real meaning of the document. [Palimpsests are parchment documents from which the original inscription has been erased and another inscription imposed.]

The simplest and, therefore, most common procedure for making balance-sheets indecipherable is to divide a single business into several parts by setting up 'daughter companies' – or by annexing them. The advantages of this system for various purposes – legal and illegal – are so evident that big companies which do not employ it are quite the exception.[53]

As an example of a huge monopolist company that extensively employs this system, the author quotes the famous General Electric Company (the A.E.G., to which I shall refer again later on). In 1912, it was calculated that this company held shares in 175 to 200 other companies, dominating them, of course, and thus controlling a total capital of about 1,500 million marks.[54]

None of the rules of control, the publication of balance-sheets, the drawing up of balance-sheets according to a definite form, the public auditing of accounts, etc., the things about which well-intentioned professors and officials – that is, those imbued with the good intention of defending and prettifying capitalism – discourse to the public, are of any avail; for private property is sacred, and no one can be prohibited from buying, selling, exchanging or hypothecating shares, etc.

The extent to which this 'holding system' has developed in the big Russian banks may be judged by the figures given by E. Agalid, who for fifteen years was an official of the Russo-Chinese Bank and who, in May 1914, published a book, not altogether correctly entitled *Big Banks and the World Market*.[55] The author divides the big Russian banks into two main groups: (a) banks that come under the 'holding system', and (b) 'independent' banks – 'independence', however, being arbitrarily taken to mean independence of foreign banks. The author divides the first group into three subgroups: (1) German holdings, (2) British holdings, and (3) French holdings, having in view the 'holdings' and domination of the big foreign banks of the particular country mentioned. The author divides the capital of the banks into 'productively' invested capital (industrial and commercial undertakings), and 'speculatively' invested capital (in Stock Exchange and financial operations), assuming, from his petty-bourgeois reformist point of view, that it is possible, under capitalism, to separate the first form of investment from the second and to abolish the second form.

Here are the figures he supplies:

Table 7. Bank Assets (According to Reports for October–November 1912
000,000 roubles

Groups of Russian banks	Capital Invested		
	Productively	Speculatively	Total
a 1) Four banks: Siberian Commercial, Russian, International, and Discount Bank	413.7	859.1	1,272.8
a 2) Two banks: Commercial and Industrial, and Russo-British	239.3	169.1	408.4
a 3) Five banks: Russian-Asiatic, St. Petersburg Private, Azov-Don, Union Moscow, Russo-French Commercial	711.8	661.2	1,373.0
(11 banks) (*Total*) =	1,364.8	1,689.4	3,054.2
b) Eight banks: Moscow Merchants, Volga-Kama, Junker and Co., St. Petersburg Commercial (formerly Wawelberg), Bank of Moscow (formerly Ryabushinsky), Moscow Discount, Moscow Commercial, Moscow Private	504.2	391.1	895.3
(10 banks) *Total*	1,869.0	2,080.5	3,949.5

According to these figures, of the approximately 4,000 million roubles making up the 'working' capital of the big banks, more than three-fourths, more than 3,000 million, belonged to banks which in reality were only 'daughter companies' of foreign banks, and chiefly of Paris banks (the famous trio: Union Parisienne, Paris et Pays-Bas and Société Générale), and of Berlin banks (particularly the Deutsche Bank and Disconto-Gesellschaft). Two of the biggest Russian banks, the Russian (Russian Bank for Foreign Trade) and the International (St. Petersburg International Commercial Bank), between 1906 and 1912 increased their capital from 44 to 98 million roubles, and their reserves from 15 million to 39 million, 'employing three-fourths German capital'. The first bank belongs to the Berlin Deutsche Bank 'concern' and the second to the Berlin Disconto-Gesellschaft. The worthy Agahd is deeply indignant at the majority of the shares being held by the Berlin banks, so that the Russian shareholders are, therefore, powerless. Naturally, the country which exports capital skims the cream; for example, the Berlin Deutsche Bank, before placing the shares of the Siberian Commercial

Bank on the Berlin market, kept them in its portfolio for a whole year, and then sold them at the rate of 193 for 100, that is, at nearly twice their nominal value, 'earning' a profit of nearly six million roubles, which Hilferding calls 'promoter's profits'.

Our author puts the total 'capacity' of the principal St. Petersburg banks at 8,235 million roubles, well over 8,000 million, and the 'holdings', or rather, the extent to which foreign banks dominated them, he estimates as follows: French banks, 55 per cent; British, 10 per cent; German, 35 per cent. The author calculates that of the total of 8,235 million roubles of functioning capital, 3,687 million roubles, or over 40 per cent, fall to the share of the Produgol and Prodamet syndicates[56] and the syndicates in the oil, metallurgical and cement industries. Thus, owing to the formation of capitalist monopolies, the merging of bank and industrial capital has also made enormous strides in Russia.

Finance capital, concentrated in a few hands and exercising a virtual monopoly, exacts enormous and ever-increasing profits from the floating of companies, issue of stock, state loans, etc., strengthens the domination of the financial oligarchy and levies tribute upon the whole of society for the benefit of monopolists. Here is an example, taken from a multitude of others, of the 'business' methods of the American trusts, quoted by Hilferding. In 1887, Havemeyer founded the Sugar Trust by amalgamating fifteen small firms, whose total capital amounted to 6,500,000 dollars. Suitably 'watered', as the Americans say, the capital of the trust was declared to be 50 million dollars. This 'overcapitalisation' anticipated the monopoly profits, in the same way as the United States Steel Corporation anticipates its monopoly profits in buying up as many iron ore fields as possible. In fact, the Sugar Trust set up monopoly prices, which secured it such profits that it could pay 10 per cent dividend on capital 'watered' sevenfold, or about 70 per cent on the capital actually invested at the time the trust was formed! In 1909, the capital of the Sugar Trust amounted to 90 million dollars. In twenty-two years, it had increased its capital more than tenfold.

In France the domination of the 'financial oligarchy' (*Against the Financial Oligarchy in France*, the title of the well-known book by Lysis, the fifth edition of which was published in 1908) assumed a form that was only slightly different. Four of the most powerful banks enjoy, not a relative, but an 'absolute monopoly' in the issue of bonds. In reality, this is a 'trust of big banks'. And monopoly ensures monopoly profits from bond issues. Usually a borrowing country does not get more than 90 per cent of the sum of the loan, the remaining 10 per cent goes to the banks and other middlemen. The profit made by the banks out of the Russo-Chinese loan of 400 million francs amounted to 8 per cent; out of the Russian (1904) loan of 800 million francs the profit amounted to 10 per cent; and out of the Moroccan (1904) loan of 62,500,000 francs it amounted to 18.75 per cent. Capitalism, which began its development with petty usury capital, is ending its development with gigantic usury capital. 'The French', says Lysis, 'are the usurers of Europe.' All the conditions of economic life are being profoundly modified by this transformation of capitalism. With a stationary population, and stagnant industry, commerce and shipping, the 'country' can grow rich by usury. 'Fifty persons representing a capital of eight million francs, can control 2,000 million francs deposited in four banks.' The 'holding system', with which we are already familiar, leads to the same result. One of the biggest banks, the Société Générale for instance, issues 64,000 bonds for its 'daughter company', the Egyptian Sugar Refineries. The bonds are issued at 150 per cent, i.e., the bank gains 50 centimes on the franc. The dividends of the new company were found to be fictitious, the 'public' lost from 90 to 100 million francs. 'One of the directors of the Société Générale was a member of the board of directors of the Sugar Refineries.' It is not surprising that the author is driven to the conclusion that 'the French Republic is a financial monarchy'; 'it is the complete domination of the financial oligarchy; the latter dominates over the press and the government.'[57]

The extraordinarily high rate of profit obtained from the issue of bonds, which is one of the principal functions of finance capital, plays a very important part in the development and consolidation of the financial oligarchy. 'There is not a single business of this type within the country that brings in profits even approximately equal to those obtained from the floatation of foreign loans,' says *Die Bank*.[58]

'No banking operation brings in profits comparable with those obtained from the issue of securities!' According to the German Economist, the average annual profits made on the issue of industrial stock were as follows:

Table 8

Year	Per Cent
1895	38.6
1896	36.1
1897	66.7
1898	67.7
1899	66.9
1900	55.2

'In the ten years from 1891 to 1900, more than a thousand million marks were "earned" by issuing German industrial stock.'[59]

During periods of industrial boom, the profits of finance capital are immense, but during periods of depression, small and unsound businesses go out of existence, and the big banks acquire 'holdings' in them by buying them up for a mere song, or participate in profitable schemes for their 'reconstruction' and 'reorganisation'. In the 'reconstruction' of undertakings which have been running at a loss, 'the share capital is written down, that is, profits are distributed on a smaller capital and continue to be calculated on this smaller basis. Or, if the income has fallen to zero, new capital is called in, which, combined with the old and less remunerative capital, will bring in an adequate return.' 'Incidentally,' adds Hilferding, 'all these reorganisations and reconstructions have a twofold significance for the banks: first, as profitable transactions; and secondly, as opportunities for securing control of the companies in difficulties.'[60]

Here is an instance. The Union Mining Company of Dortmund was founded in 1872. Share capital was issued to the amount of nearly 40 million marks and the market price of the shares rose to 170 after it had paid a 12 per cent dividend for its first year. Finance capital skimmed the cream and earned a trifle of something like 28 million marks. The principal sponsor of this company was that very big German Disconto-Gesellschaft which so successfully attained a capital of 300 million marks. Later, the dividends of the Union declined to nil; the shareholders had to consent to a 'writing down' of capital, that is, to losing some of it in order not to lose it all. By a series of 'reconstructions', more than 73 million marks were written off the books of the Union in the course of thirty years. 'At the present time, the original shareholders of the company possess only 5 per cent of the nominal value of their shares'[61] but the banks 'earned something' out of every 'reconstruction'.

Speculation in land situated in the suburbs of rapidly growing big towns is a particularly profitable operation for finance capital. The monopoly of the banks merges here with the monopoly of ground-rent and with monopoly of the means of communication, since the rise in the price of land and the possibility of selling it profitably in lots, etc., is mainly dependent on good means of communication with the centre of the town; and these means of communication are in the hands of large companies which are connected with these same banks through the holding system and the distribution of seats on the boards. As a result we get what the German writer L. Eschwege, a contributor to *Die Bank* who has made a special study of real estate business and mortgages, etc., calls a 'bog'. Frantic speculation in suburban building lots; collapse of building enterprises like the Berlin firm of Boswau and Knauer, which acquired as much as 100 million marks with the help of the 'sound and solid' Deutsche Bank – the latter, of course, acting through the holding system, i.e., secretly, behind the scenes – and got out of it with a loss of 'only' 12 million marks, then the ruin of small proprietors and of workers who get nothing from the fictitious building firms, fraudulent deals with the 'honest' Berlin police and administration for the purpose of gaining control of the issue of cadastral certificates, building licences, etc., etc.[62]

'American ethics', which the European professors and well-meaning bourgeois so hypocritically deplore, have, in the age of finance capital, become the ethics of literally every large city in any country.

At the beginning of 1914, there was talk in Berlin of the formation of a 'transport trust', i.e., of establishing 'community of interests' between the three Berlin transport undertakings: the city electric railway, the tramway company and the omnibus company. 'We have been aware', wrote *Die Bank*,

that this plan was contemplated ever since it became known that the majority of the shares in the bus company had been acquired by the other two transport companies ... We may fully believe those who are pursuing this aim when they say that by uniting the transport services, they will secure economies, part of which will in time benefit the public. But the question is complicated by the fact that behind the transport trust that is being formed are the banks, which, if they desire, can subordinate the means of transportation, which they have monopolised, to the interests of their real estate business. To be convinced of the reasonableness of such a conjecture, we need only recall that the interests of the big banks that encouraged the formation of the Electric Railway Company were already involved in it at the time the company was formed. That is to say: the interests of this transport undertaking were interlocked with the real estate interests. The point is that the eastern line of this railway was to run across land which this bank sold at an enormous profit for itself and for several partners in the transactions when it became certain the line was to be laid down.[63]

A monopoly, once it is formed and controls thousands of millions, inevitably penetrates into every sphere of public life, regardless of the form of government and all other 'details'. In German economic literature one usually comes across obsequious praise of the integrity of the Prussian bureaucracy, and allusions to the French Panama scandal[64] and to political corruption in America. But the fact is that even bourgeois literature devoted to German banking matters constantly has to go far beyond the field of purely banking operations; it speaks, for instance, about 'the attraction of the banks' in reference to the increasing frequency with which public officials take employment with the banks, as follows: 'How about the integrity of a state official who in his innermost heart is aspiring to a soft job in the Behrenstrasse?'[65] (The Berlin street where the head office of the Deutsche Bank is situated.) In 1909, the publisher of *Die Bank*, Alfred Lansburgh, wrote an article entitled 'The Economic Significance of Byzantinism', in which he incidentally referred to Wilhelm II's tour of Palestine, and to 'the immediate result of this journey, the construction of the Baghdad railway, that fatal "great product of German enterprise", which is more responsible for the "encirclement" than all our political blunders put together'.[66] (By encirclement is meant the policy of Edward VII to isolate Germany and surround her with an imperialist anti-German alliance.) In 1911, Eschwege, the contributor to this same magazine to whom I have already referred, wrote an article entitled 'Plutocracy and Bureaucracy', in which he exposed, for example, the case of a German official named Völker, who was a zealous member of the Cartel Committee and who, it turned out some time later, obtained a lucrative post in the biggest cartel, the Steel Syndicate. Similar cases, by no means casual, forced this bourgeois author to admit that 'the economic liberty guaranteed by the German Constitution has become in many departments of economic life, a meaningless phrase' and that under the existing rule of the plutocracy, 'even the widest political liberty cannot save us from being converted into a nation of unfree people'.[67]

As for Russia, I shall confine myself to one example. Some years ago, all the newspapers announced that Davydov, the director of the Credit Department of the Treasury, had resigned his post to take employment with a certain big bank at a salary which, according to the contract, would total over one million roubles in the course of several years. 'The function of the Credit Department is to "co-ordinate the activities of all the credit instutions of the country"; it also grants subsidies to bans in St Peterburg and Moscow amounting to between 800 and 1000 million rubles.'[68]

It is characteristic of capitalism in general that the ownership of capital is separated from the application of capital to production, that money capital is separated from industrial or productive capital, and that the rentier who lives entirely on income obtained from money capital, is separated from the entrepreneur and from all who are directly concerned in the management of capital. Imperialism, or the domination of finance capital, is that highest stage of capitalism in which this separation reaches vast proportions. The supremacy of finance capital over all other forms of capital means the predominance of the rentier and of the financial oligarchy; it means that a small number of financially 'powerful' states stand out among all the rest. The extent to which this process is going on may be judged from the statistics on emissions, i.e., the issue of all kinds of securities.

In the Bulletin of the International Statistical Institute, A. Neymarck[69] has published very comprehensive, complete and comparative figures covering the issue of securities all over the world, which have been repeatedly quoted in part in economic literature. The following are the totals he gives for four decades:

Table 9. Total Issues
in Francs per Decade
(000,000,000)

Year	
1871–80	76.1
1881–90	64.5
1891–1900	100.4
1901–10	197.8

In the 1870s the total amount of issues for the whole world was high, owing particularly to the loans floated in connection with the Franco-Prussian War, and the company-promotion boom which set in in Germany after the war. On the whole, the increase was relatively not very rapid during the three last decades of the nineteenth century, and only in the first ten years of the twentieth century is an enormous increase of almost 100 per cent to be observed. Thus, the beginning of the twentieth century marks the turning-point, not only in the growth of monopolies (cartels, syndicates, trusts), of which we have already spoken, but also in the growth of finance capital.

Neymarck estimates the total amount of issued securities current in the world in 1910 at about 815,000 million francs. Deducting from this sum amounts which might have been duplicated, he reduces the total to 575,000–600,000 million, which is distributed among the various countries as follows (I take 600,000 million):

Table 10. Financial Securities Current in 1910
(000,000,000 Francs)

Great Britain	142	Holland	12.5
United States	132	Belgium	7.5
France	110	Spain	7.5
Germany	95	Switzerland	6.25
Russia	31	Denmark	3.75
Austria-Hungary	24	Sweden,	2.5
Italy	14	Norway,	
Japan	12	Romania, etc.	

From these figures we at once see standing out in sharp relief four of the richest capitalist countries, each of which holds securities to amounts ranging approximately from 100,000 to 150,000 million francs. Of these four countries, two, Britain and France, are the oldest capitalist countries, and, as we shall see, possess the most colonies; the other two, the United States and Germany, are capitalist countries leading in the rapidity of development and the degree of extension of capitalist monopolies in industry. Together, these four countries own 479,000 million francs, that is, nearly 80 per cent of the world's finance capital. In one way or another, nearly the whole of the rest of the world is more or less the debtor to and tributary of these international banker countries, these four 'pillars' of world finance capital.

It is particularly important to examine the part which the export of capital plays in creating the international network of dependence on and connections of finance capital.

IV. Export of Capital

Typical of the old capitalism, when free competition held undivided sway, was the export of goods. Typical of the latest stage of capitalism, when monopolies rule, is the export of capital.

Capitalism is commodity production at its highest stage of development, when labour-power itself becomes a commodity. The growth of internal exchange, and, particularly, of international exchange, is a characteristic feature of capitalism. The uneven and spasmodic development of individual enterprises, individual branches of industry and individual countries is inevitable under the capitalist system. England became a capitalist country before any other, and by the middle of the nineteenth century, having adopted free trade, claimed to be the 'workshop of the world', the supplier of manufactured goods to all countries, which in exchange were to keep her provided with raw materials. But in the last quarter of the nineteenth century, this monopoly was already undermined; for other countries, sheltering themselves with 'protective' tariffs, developed into independent capitalist states. On the threshold of the twentieth century, we see the formation of a new type of monopoly: firstly, monopolist associations of capitalists in all capitalistically developed countries; secondly, the monopolist position of a few very rich countries, in which the accumulation of capital has reached gigantic proportions. An enormous 'surplus of capital' has arisen in the advanced countries.

It goes without saying that if capitalism could develop agriculture, which today is everywhere lagging terribly behind industry, if it could raise the living standards of the masses, who in spite of the amazing technical progress are everywhere still half-starved and poverty-stricken, there could be no question of a surplus of capital. This 'argument' is very often advanced by the petty-bourgeois critics of capitalism. But if capitalism did these things, it would not be capitalism; for both uneven development and a semi-starvation level of existence of the masses are fundamental and inevitable conditions and constitute premises of this mode of production. As long as capitalism remains what it is, surplus capital will be utilised not for the purpose of raising the standard of living of the masses in a given country, for this would mean a decline in profits for the capitalists, but for the purpose of increasing profits by exporting capital abroad to the backward countries. In these backward countries profits are usually high, for capital is scarce, the price of land is relatively low, wages are low, raw materials are cheap. The export of capital is made possible by a number of backward countries having already been drawn into world capitalist intercourse; main railways have either been or are being built in those countries, elementary conditions for industrial development have been created, etc. The need to export capital arises from the fact that in a few countries, capitalism has become 'overripe' and (owing to the backward state of agriculture and the poverty of the masses) capital cannot find a field for 'profitable' investment.

Here are approximate figures showing the amount of capital invested abroad by the three principal countries:[70]

Table 11. Capital Invested Abroad
(000,000,000 francs)

Year	Great Britain	France	Germany
1862	3.6	—	—
1872	15.0	10 (1869)	—
1882	22.0	15 (1880)	?
1893	42.0	20(1890)	?
1902	62.0	27–37	12.5
1914	75–100.0	00	44.0

This table shows that the export of capital reached enormous dimensions only at the beginning of the twentieth century. Before the war the capital invested abroad by the three principal countries amounted to between 175,000 million and 200,000 million francs. At the modest rate of 5 per cent, the income from this sum should reach from 8,000 to 10,000 million francs a year – a sound basis for the imperialist oppression and exploitation of most of the countries and nations of the world, for the capitalist parasitism of a handful of wealthy states!

How is this capital invested abroad distributed among the various countries? *Where* is it invested? Only an approximate answer can be given to these questions, but it is one sufficient to throw light on certain general relations and connections of modern imperialism.

Table 12. Distribution (Approximate) of Foreign Capital in Different Parts of the Globe (circa 1910) (000,000,000 marks)

	Great Britain	France	Germany	Total
Europe	4	23	18	45
America	37	4	10	51
Asia, Africa, and Australia	29	8	7	44
Total	70	35	35	140

The principal spheres of investment of British capital are the British colonies, which are very large also in America (for example, Canada), not to mention Asia, etc. In this case, enormous exports of capital are bound up most closely with vast colonies, of the importance of which for imperialism I shall speak later. In the case of France, the situation is different. French capital exports are invested mainly in Europe, primarily in Russia (at least ten thousand million francs). This is mainly loan capital, government loans, and not capital invested in industrial undertakings. Unlike British colonial imperialism, French imperialism might be termed usury imperialism. In the case of Germany, we have a third type; colonies are inconsiderable, and German capital invested abroad is divided most evenly between Europe and America.

The export of capital influences and greatly accelerates the development of capitalism in those countries to which it is exported. While, therefore, the export of capital may tend to a certain extent to arrest development in the capital-exporting countries, it can only do so by expanding and deepening the further development of capitalism throughout the world.

The capital-exporting countries are nearly always able to obtain certain 'advantages', the character of which throws light on the peculiarity of the epoch of finance capital and monopoly. The following passage, for instance, appeared in the Berlin review, *Die Bank*, for October 1913:

> A comedy worthy of the pen of Aristophanes is lately being played on the international capital market. Numerous foreign countries, from Spain to the Balkan states, from Russia to Argentina, Brazil and China, are openly or secretly coming into the big money market with demands, sometimes very persistent, for loans. The money markets are not very bright at the moment and the political outlook is not promising. But not a single money market dares to refuse a loan for fear that its neighbour may forestall it, consent to grant a loan and so secure some reciprocal service. In these international transactions the creditor nearly always manages to secure some extra benefit: a favourable clause in a commercial treaty, a coating station, a contract to construct a harbour, a fat concession, or an order for guns.[71]

Finance capital has created the epoch of monopolies, and monopolies introduce everywhere monopolist principles: the utilisation of 'connections' for profitable transactions takes the place of competition on the open market. The most usual thing is to stipulate that part of the loan granted shall be spent on purchases in the creditor country, particularly on orders for war materials, or for ships, etc. In the course of the last two decades (1890–1910), France has very often resorted to this method. The export of capital thus becomes a means of encouraging the export of commodities. In this connection, transactions between particularly big firms assume a form which, as Schilder[72] 'mildly' puts it, 'borders on corruption'. Krupp in Germany, Schneider in France, Armstrong in Britain are instances of firms which have close connections with powerful banks and governments and which cannot easily be 'ignored' when a loan is being arranged.

France, when granting loans to Russia, 'squeezed' her in the commercial treaty of 16 September 1905, stipulating for certain concessions to run till 1917. She did the same in the commercial treaty with Japan of 19 August 1911. The tariff war between Austria and Serbia, which lasted, with a seven months' interval, from 1906 to 1911, was partly caused by Austria and France competing to supply Serbia with war materials. In January 1912, Paul Deschanel stated in the Chamber of Deputies that from 1908 to 1911 French firms had supplied war materials to Serbia to the value of 45 million francs.

A report from the Austro-Hungarian Consul at São-Paulo (Brazil) states: 'The Brazilian railways are being built chiefly by French, Belgian, British and German capital. In the financial operations connected with the construction of these railways the countries involved stipulate for orders for the necessary railway materials.'

Thus, finance capital, literally, one might say, spreads its net over all countries of the world. An important role in this is played by banks founded in the colonies and by their branches. German imperialists look with envy at the 'old' colonial countries which have been particularly 'successful' in providing for themselves in this respect. In 1904, Great Britain had 50 colonial banks with 2,279 branches (in 1910 there were 72 banks with 5,449 branches), France had 20 with 136 branches; Holland, 16 with 68 branches; and Germany had 'only' 13 with 70 branches.[73] The American capitalists, in their turn, are jealous of the English and German: 'In South America', they complained in 1915,

> five German banks have forty branches and five British banks have seventy branches ... Britain and Germany have invested in Argentina, Brazil, and Uruguay in the last twenty-five years approximately four thousand million dollars, and as a result together enjoy 46 per cent of the total trade of these three countries.[74]

The capital-exporting countries have divided the world among themselves in the figurative sense of the term. But finance capital has led to the *actual* division of the world.

V. Division of the World Among Capitalist Associations

Monopolist capitalist associations, cartels, syndicates and trusts first divided the home market among themselves and obtained more or less complete possession of the industry of their own country. But under capitalism the home market is inevitably bound up with the foreign market. Capitalism long ago created a world market. As the export of capital increased, and as the foreign and colonial connections and 'spheres of influence' of the big monopolist associations expanded in all ways, things 'naturally' gravitated towards an international agreement among these associations, and towards the formation of international cartels.

This is a new stage of world concentration of capital and production, incomparably higher than the preceding stages. Let us see how this supermonopoly develops.

The electrical industry is highly typical of the latest technical achievements and is most typical of capitalism at the end of the nineteenth and the beginning of the twentieth centuries. This industry has developed most in the two leaders of the new capitalist countries, the United States and Germany. In Germany, the crisis of 1900 gave a particularly strong impetus to its concentration. During the crisis, the banks, which by that time had become fairly well merged with industry, enormously accelerated and intensified the ruin of relatively small firms and their absorption by the large ones. 'The banks', writes Jeidels, 'refused a helping hand to the very firms in greatest need of capital, and brought on first a frenzied boom and then the hopeless failure of the companies which had not been connected with them closely enough.'[75]

As a result, after 1900, concentration in Germany progressed with giant strides. Up to 1900 there had been seven or eight 'groups' in the electrical industry. Each consisted of several companies (altogether there were twenty-eight) and each was backed by two to eleven banks. Between 1908 and 1912 all these groups were merged into two, or one. The following diagram shows the process:

Groups in the Electrical Industry

Prior to 1900	Felten & Guillaume	Lahmeyer	Union A.E.G.	Siemens & Halske	Schuckert & Co.	Bergmann	Kummer

	Felten & Lahmeyer	A.E.G. (G.E.C.)	Siemens & Halske-Schuckert	Bergmann	Failed in 1900

By 1912: A.E.G. (G.E.C.) Siemens & Halske-Schuckert

(In close "co-operation" since 1908)

The famous A.E.G. (General Electric Company), which grew up in this way, controls 175 to 200 companies (through the 'holding' system), and a total capital of approximately *1,500 million* marks. Of direct agencies abroad alone, it has thirty-four, of which twelve are joint-stock companies, in more than ten countries. As early as 1904 the amount of capital invested abroad by the German electrical industry was estimated at 233 million marks. Of this sum, 62 million were invested in Russia. Needless to say, the A.E.G. is a huge 'combine' – its manufacturing companies alone number no less than sixteen – producing the most diverse articles, from cables and insulators to motor-cars and flying machines.

General Electric Company

United States:	Thomson-Houston Co. establishes a firm in Europe	Edison Co. establishes in Europe the French Edison Co. which transfers its patents to the German firm
Germany:	Union Electric Co.	General Electric Co. (A.E.G.)

General Electric Co. (A.E.G.)

But concentration in Europe was also a component part of the process of concentration in America, which developed in the following way:

Thus, *two* electrical 'great powers' were formed: 'There are no other electrical companies in the world *completely* independent of them,' wrote Heinig in his article 'The Path of the Electric Trust.' An idea, although far from complete, of the turnover and the size of the enterprises of the two 'trusts' can be obtained from the following figures:

Table 13

	Turnover (000,000 marks)	Number of employees	Net profits (000,000 marks)
America: General Electric Co: (G.E.C)			
1907	252	28,000	35.4
1910	298	32,000	45.6
Germany: General Electric Co: (A.E.G.)			
1907	216	30,700	14.5
1911	362	60,800	21.7

And then, in 1907, the German and American trusts concluded an agreement by which they divided the world between them. Competition between them ceased. The American General Electric Company (G.E.C.) 'got' the United States and Canada. The German General Electric Company (A.E.G.) 'got' Germany, Austria, Russia, Holland, Denmark, Switzerland, Turkey and the Balkans. Special agreements, naturally secret, were concluded regarding the penetration of 'daughter companies' into new branches of industry, into 'new' countries formally not yet allotted. The two trusts were to exchange inventions and experiments.[76]

The difficulty of competing against this trust, actually a single worldwide trust controlling a capital of several thousand million, with 'branches', agencies, representatives, connections, etc., in every corner of the world, is self-evident. But the division of the world between two powerful trusts does not preclude redivision if the relation of forces changes as a result of uneven development, war, bankruptcy, etc.

An instructive example of an attempt at such a redivision, of the struggle for redivision, is provided by the oil industry.

'The world oil market', wrote Jeidels in 1905, 'is even today still divided between two great financial groups – Rockefeller's American Standard Oil Co., and Rothschild and Nobel, the controlling interests of the Russian oilfields in Baku. The two groups are closely connected. But for several years five enemies have been threatening their monopoly':[77] (1) the exhaustion of the American oilfields; (2) the competition of the firm of Mantashev of Baku; (3) the Austrian oilfields; (4) the Romanian oilfields; (5) the overseas oilfields, particularly in the Dutch colonies (the extremely rich firms, Samuel and Shell, also connected with British capital). The three last groups are connected with the big German banks, headed by the huge Deutsche Bank. These banks independently and systematically developed the oil industry in Romania, for example, in order to have a foothold of their 'own'. In 1907, the foreign capital invested in the Romanian oil industry was estimated at 185 million francs, of which 74 million was German capital.[78]

A struggle began for the 'division of the world', as, in fact, it is called in economic literature. On the one hand, the Rockefeller 'oil trust' wanted to lay its hands on *everything*; it formed a 'daughter company' *right in* Holland, and bought up oilfields in the Dutch Indies, in order to strike at its principal enemy, the Anglo-Dutch Shell trust. On the other hand, the Deutsche Bank and the other German banks aimed at 'retaining' Romania 'for themselves' and at uniting her with Russia against Rockefeller. The latter possessed far more capital and an excellent system of oil transportation and distribution. The struggle had to end, and did end in 1907, with the utter defeat of the Deutsche Bank, which was confronted with the alternative: either to liquidate its 'oil interests' and lose millions, or submit. It chose to submit, and concluded a very disadvantageous agreement with the 'oil trust'. The Deutsche Bank agreed 'not to attempt anything which might injure American interests'. Provision was made, however, for the annulment of the agreement in the event of Germany establishing a state oil monopoly.

Then the 'comedy of oil' began. One of the German finance kings, von Gwinner, a director of the Deutsche Bank, through his private secretary, Stauss, launched a campaign *for* a state oil monopoly. The gigantic machine of the huge German bank and all its wide 'connections' were set in motion. The press bubbled over with 'patriotic' indignation against the 'yoke' of the American trust, and, on 15 March 1911, the Reichstag, by an almost unanimous vote, adopted a motion asking the government to introduce a bill for the establishment of an oil monopoly. The government seized upon this 'popular' idea, and the game of the Deutsche Bank, which hoped to cheat its American counterpart and improve its business by a state monopoly, appeared to have been won. The German oil magnates already saw visions of enormous profits, which would not be less than those of the Russian sugar refiners ... But, firstly, the big German banks quarrelled among themselves over the division of the spoils. The Disconto-Gesellschaft exposed the covetous aims of the Deutsche Bank; secondly, the government took fright at the prospect of a struggle with Rockefeller, for it was very doubtful whether Germany could be sure of obtaining oil from other sources (the Romanian output was small); thirdly, just at that time the 1913 credits of a thousand million marks were voted for Germany's war preparations. The oil monopoly project was postponed. The Rockefeller 'oil trust' came out of the struggle, for the time being, victorious.

The Berlin review, *Die Bank*, wrote in this connection that Germany could fight the oil trust only by establishing an electricity monopoly and by converting water-power into cheap electricity. 'But', the author added,

the electricity monopoly will come when the producers need it, that is to say, when the next great crash in the electrical industry is imminent, and when the gigantic, expensive power stations now being put up at great cost everywhere by private electrical concerns, which are already obtaining certain franchises from towns, from states, etc., can no longer work at a profit. Water-power will then have to be used. But it will be impossible to convert it into cheap electricity at state expense; it will also have to be handed over to a 'private monopoly controlled by the state', because private industry has already concluded a number of contracts and has stipulated for heavy compensation ... So it was with the nitrate monopoly, so it is with the oil monopoly, so it will be with the electric power monopoly. It is time our state socialists, who allow themselves to be blinded by a beautiful principle, understood, at last, that in Germany the monopolies have never pursued the aim, nor have they had the result, of benefiting the consumer, or even of handing over to the state part of the promoter's profits; they have served only to facilitate, at the expense of the state, the recovery of private industries which were on the verge of bankruptcy.[79]

Such are the valuable admissions which the German bourgeois economists are forced to make. We see plainly here how private and state monopolies are interwoven in the epoch of finance capital; how both are but separate links in the imperialist struggle between the big monopolists for the division of the world.

In merchant shipping, the tremendous development of concentration has ended also in the division of the world. In Germany two powerful companies have come to the fore: the Hamburg-Amerika and the Norddeutscher Lloyd, each having a capital of 200 million marks (in stocks and bonds) and possessing shipping tonnage to the value of 185 to 189 million marks. On the other hand, in America, on 1 January 1903, the International Mercantile Marine Co., known as the Morgan trust, was formed; it united nine American and British steamship companies, and possessed a capital of 120 million dollars (480 million marks). As early as 1903, the German giants and this American-British trust concluded an agreement to divide the world with a consequent division of profits. The German companies undertook not to compete in the Anglo-American traffic. Which ports were to be 'allotted' to each was precisely stipulated; a joint committee of control was set up, etc. This agreement was concluded for twenty years, with the prudent provision for its annulment in the event of war.[80]

Extremely instructive also is the story of the formation of the International Rail Cartel. The first attempt of the British, Belgian and German rail manufacturers to form such a cartel was made as early as 1884, during a severe industrial depression. The manufacturers agreed not to compete with one another in the home markets of the countries involved, and they divided the foreign markets in the following quotas: Great Britain, 66 per cent; Germany, 27 per cent; Belgium, 7 per cent. India was reserved entirely for Great Britain. Joint war was declared against a British firm which remained outside the cartel, the cost of which was met by a percentage levy on all sales. But in 1886 the cartel collapsed when two British firms retired from it. It is characteristic that agreement could not be achieved during subsequent boom periods.

At the beginning of 1904, the German steel syndicate was formed. In November 1904, the International Rail Cartel was revived, with the following quotas: Britain, 53.5 per cent; Germany, 28.83 per cent; Belgium, 17.67 per cent. France came in later and received 4.8 per cent, 5.8 per cent and 6.4 per cent in the first, second and third year respectively, over and above the 100 per cent limit, i.e., out of a total of 104.8

per cent, etc. In 1905, the United States Steel Corporation entered the cartel; then Austria and Spain. 'At the present time', wrote Vogelstein in 1910, 'the division of the world is complete, and the big consumers, primarily the state railways – since the world has been parcelled out without consideration for their interests – can now dwell like the poet in the heavens of Jupiter.'[81]

Let me also mention the International Zinc Syndicate which was established in 1909 and which precisely apportioned output among five groups of factories: German, Belgian, French, Spanish and British; and also the International Dynamite Trust, which, Liefmann says, is 'quite a modern, close alliance of all the German explosives manufacturers who, with the French and American dynamite manufacturers, organised in a similar manner, have divided the whole world among themselves, so to speak.'[82]

Liefmann calculated that in 1897 there were altogether about forty international cartels in which Germany had a share, while in 1910 there were about a hundred.

Certain bourgeois writers (now joined by Karl Kautsky, who has completely abandoned the Marxist position he had held, for example, in 1909) have expressed the opinion that international cartels, being one of the most striking expressions of the internationalisation of capital, give the hope of peace among nations under capitalism. Theoretically, this opinion is absolutely absurd, while in practice it is sophistry and a dishonest defence of the worst opportunism. International cartels show to what point capitalist monopolies have developed, and *the object* of the struggle between the various capitalist associations. This last circumstance is the most important; it alone shows us the historico-economic meaning of what is taking place; for the *forms* of the struggle may and do constantly change in accordance with varying, relatively specific and temporary causes, but the *substance* of the struggle, its class *content*, positively *cannot* change while classes exist. Naturally, it is in the interests of, for example, the German bourgeoisie, to whose side Kautsky has in effect gone over in his theoretical arguments (I shall deal with this later), to obscure the *substance* of the present economic struggle (the division of the world) and to emphasise now this and now another *form* of the struggle. Kautsky makes the same mistake. Of course, we have in mind not only the German bourgeoisie, but the bourgeoisie all over the world. The capitalists divide the world, not out of any particular malice, but because the degree of concentration which has been reached forces them to adopt this method in order to obtain profits. And they divide it 'in proportion to capital', 'in proportion to strength', because there cannot be any other method of division under commodity production and capitalism. But strength varies with the degree of economic and political development. In order to understand what is taking place, it is necessary to know what questions are settled by the changes in strength. The question as to whether these changes are 'purely' economic or non-economic (e.g., military) is a secondary one, which cannot in the least affect fundamental views on the latest epoch of capitalism. To substitute the question of the form of the struggle and agreements (today peaceful, tomorrow warlike, the next day warlike again) for the question of the substance of the struggle and agreements between capitalist associations is to sink to the role of a sophist.

The epoch of the latest stage of capitalism shows us that certain relations between capitalist associations grow up, *based* on the economic division of the world; while parallel to and in connection with it, certain relations grow up between political alliances, between states, on the basis of the territorial division of the world, of the struggle for colonies, of the 'struggle for spheres of influence'.

VI. Division of the World Among the Great Powers

In his book, *The Territorial Development of the European Colonies*, A. Supan,[83] the geographer, gives the following brief summary of this development at the end of the nineteenth century:

Table 14. Percentage of Territory Belonging to the European Colonial Powers (Including the United States)

	1876	1900	Increase or decrease
Africa	10.8	90.4	+79.6
Polynesia	56.8	98.9	+42.1
Asia	51.5	56.6	+5.1
Australia	100.0	100.0	—
America	27.5	27.2	-0.3

'The characteristic feature of this period', he concludes, 'is, therefore, the division of Africa and Polynesia.' As there are no unoccupied territories – that is, territories that do not belong to any state in Asia and America, it is necessary to amplify Supan's conclusion and say that the characteristic feature of the period under review is the final partitioning of the globe – final, not in the sense that *repartition* is impossible; on the contrary, repartitions are possible and inevitable – but in the sense that the colonial policy of the capitalist countries has *completed* the seizure of the unoccupied territories on our planet. For the first time the world is completely divided up, so that in the future *only* redivision is possible, i.e., territories can only pass from one 'owner' to another, instead of passing as ownerless territory to an owner.

Hence, we are living in a peculiar epoch of world colonial policy, which is most closely connected with the 'latest stage in the development of capitalism', with finance capital. For this reason, it is essential first of all to deal in greater detail with the facts, in order to ascertain as exactly as possible what distinguishes this epoch from those preceding it, and what the present situation is. In the first place, two questions of fact arise here: is an intensification of colonial policy, a sharpening of the struggle for colonies, observed precisely in the epoch of finance capital? And how, in this respect, is the world divided at the present time?

The American writer, Morris, in his book on the history of colonisation,[84] made an attempt to sum up the data on the colonial possessions of Great Britain, France and Germany during different periods of the nineteenth century. The following is a brief summary of the results he has obtained:

Table 15. Colonial Possessions

Year	Great Britain		France		Germany	
	Area (000,000 sq. m.)	Pop. (000,000)	Area (000,000 sq. m.)	Pop. (000,000)	Area (000,000 sq. m.)	Pop. (000,000)
1815–30	?	126.4	0.02	0.5	—	—
1860	2.5	145.1	0.2	3.4	—	—
1880	7.7	267.9	0.7	7.5	—	—
1899	9.3	309.0	3.7	56.4	1.0	14.7

For Great Britain, the period of the enormous expansion of colonial conquests was that between 1860 and 1880, and it was also very considerable in the last twenty years of the nineteenth century. For France and Germany this period falls precisely in these twenty years. We saw above that the development of premonopoly capitalism, of capitalism in which free competition was predominant, reached its limit in the 1860s and 1870s. We now see that it is *precisely after that period* that the tremendous 'boom' in colonial conquests begins, and that the struggle for the territorial division of the world becomes extraordinarily sharp. It is beyond doubt, therefore, that capitalism's transition to the stage of monopoly capitalism, to finance capital, *is connected* with the intensification of the struggle for the partitioning of the world.

Hobson, in his work on imperialism, marks the years 1884–1900 as the epoch of intensified 'expansion' of the chief European states. According to his estimate, Great Britain during these years acquired 3,700,000 square miles of territory with 57,000,000 inhabitants; France, 3,600,000 square miles with 36,500,000; Germany, 1,000,000 square miles with 14,700,000; Belgium, 900,000 square miles with 30,000,000; Portugal, 800,000 square miles with 9,000,000 inhabitants. The scramble for colonies by all the capitalist states at the end of the nineteenth century and particularly since the 1880s is a commonly known fact in the history of diplomacy and of foreign policy.

In the most flourishing period of free competition in Great Britain, i.e., between 1840 and 1860, the leading British bourgeois politicians were *opposed* to colonial policy and were of the opinion that the liberation of the colonies, their complete separation from Britain, was inevitable and desirable. M. Beer, in an article, 'Modern British Imperialism',[85] published in 1898, shows that in 1852, Disraeli, a statesman who was generally inclined towards imperialism, declared: 'The colonies are millstones round our necks.' But at the end of the nineteenth century the British heroes of the hour were Cecil Rhodes and Joseph Chamberlain, who openly advocated imperialism and applied the imperialist policy in the most cynical manner!

It is not without interest to observe that even then these leading British bourgeois politicians saw the connection between what might be called the purely economic and the socio-political roots of modern imperialism. Chamberlain advocated imperialism as a 'true, wise and economical policy', and pointed particularly to the German, American and Belgian competition which Great Britain was encountering in the world market. Salvation lies in monopoly, said the capitalists as they formed cartels, syndicates and trusts. Salvation lies in monopoly, echoed the political leaders of the bourgeoisie, hastening to appropriate the parts of the world not yet shared out. And Cecil Rhodes, we are informed by his intimate friend, the journalist Stead, expressed his imperialist views to him in 1895 in the following terms:

> I was in the East End of London (a working-class quarter) yesterday and attended a meeting of the unemployed. I listened to the wild speeches, which were just a cry for 'bread! bread!' and on my way home I pondered over the scene and I became more than ever convinced of the importance of imperialism ... My cherished idea is a solution for the social problem, i.e., in order to save the 40,000,000 inhabitants of the United Kingdom from a bloody civil war, we colonial statesmen must acquire new lands to settle the surplus population, to provide new markets for the goods produced in the factories and mines. The Empire, as I have always said, is a bread and butter question. If you want to avoid civil war, you must become imperialists.[86]

That was said in 1895 by Cecil Rhodes, millionaire, a king of finance, the man who was mainly responsible for the Anglo-Boer War. True, his defence of imperialism is crude and cynical, but in substance it does not differ from the 'theory' advocated by Messrs. Maslov, Südekum, Potresov, David, the founder of Russian Marxism and others. Cecil Rhodes was a somewhat more honest social-chauvinist ...

To present as precise a picture as possible of the territorial division of the world and of the changes which have occurred during the last decades in this respect, I shall utilise the data furnished by Supan in the work already quoted on the colonial possessions of all the powers of the world. Supan takes the years 1876 and 1900; I shall take the year 1876 – a year very aptly selected, for it is precisely by that time that the pre-monopolist stage of development of West-European capitalism can be said to have been, in the main, completed – and the year 1914, and instead of Supan's figures I shall quote the more recent statistics of Hübner's *Geographical and Statistical Tables*. Supan gives figures only for colonies; I think it useful, in order to present a complete picture of the division of the world, to add brief data on non-colonial and semi-colonial countries, in which category I place Persia, China and Turkey: the first of these countries is already almost completely a colony, the second and third are becoming such.

We thus get the following result:

Table 16. Colonial Possessions of the Great Powers (000,000 square kilometers and 000,000 inhabitants)

	Colonies				Metropolitan countries		Total	
	1876		1914		1914		1914	
	Area	Pop.	Area	Pop.	Area	Pop.	Area	Pop.
Great Britain	22.5	251.9	33.5	393.5	0.3	46.5	33.8	444.0
Russia	17.0	15.9	17.4	33.2	5.4	136.2	22.8	169.4
France	0.9	6.0	10.6	55.5	0.5	39.6	11.1	95.1
Germany	—	—	2.9	12.3	0.5	64.9	3.4	77.2
United States	—	—	0.3	9.7	9.4	97.0	9.7	106.7
Japan	—	—	0.3	19.2	0.4	53.0	0.7	72.2
Total for 6 Great Powers	40.4	273.8	65.0	523.4	16.5	437.2	81.5	960.6
Colonies of other powers (Belgium, Holland, etc.)		9.9	45.3					
Semi-colonial countries (Persia, China, Turkey)		14.5	361.2					
Other countries		28.0	289.9					
Total for the world		133.9	1,657.0					

We clearly see from these figures how 'complete' was the partition of the world at the turn of the twentieth century. After 1876 colonial possessions increased to enormous dimensions, by more than fifty per cent, from 40,000,000 to 65,000,000 square kilometres for the six biggest powers; the increase amounts to 25,000,000 square kilometres, fifty per cent more than the area of the metropolitan countries (16,500,000 square kilometres). In 1876 three powers had no colonies, and a fourth, France, had scarcely any. By 1914 these four powers had acquired colonies with an area of 14,100,000 square kilometres, i.e., about half as much again as the area of Europe, with a population of nearly 100,000,000. The unevenness in the rate of expansion of colonial possessions is very great. If, for instance, we compare France, Germany and Japan, which do not differ very much in area and population, we see that the first has acquired almost three times as much colonial territory as the other two combined. In regard to finance capital, France, at the beginning of the period we are considering, was also, perhaps, several times richer than Germany and Japan put together. In addition to, and on the basis of, purely economic conditions, geographical and other conditions also affect the dimensions of colonial possessions. However strong the process of levelling the world, of levelling the economic and living conditions in different countries, may have been in the past decades as a result of the pressure of large-scale industry, exchange and finance capital, considerable differences still remain; and among the six countries mentioned we see, firstly, young capitalist countries (America, Germany, Japan) whose progress has been extraordinarily rapid; secondly, countries with an old capitalist development (France and Great Britain), whose progress lately has been much slower than that of the previously mentioned countries, and thirdly, a country most backward economically (Russia), where modern capitalist imperialism is enmeshed, so to speak, in a particularly close network of pre-capitalist relations.

Alongside the colonial possessions of the Great Powers, we have placed the small colonies of the small states, which are, so to speak, the next objects of a possible and probable 'redivision' of colonies. These small states mostly retain their colonies only because the big powers are torn by conflicting interests, friction, etc., which prevent them from coming to an agreement on the division of the spoils. As to the 'semi-colonial' states, they provide an example of the transitional forms which are to be found in all spheres of nature and society. Finance capital is such a great, such a decisive, you might say, force in all economic and in all international relations, that it is capable of subjecting, and actually does subject, to itself even states enjoying the fullest political independence; we shall shortly see examples of this. Of course, finance capital finds most 'convenient', and derives the greatest profit from, a *form* of subjection which involves the loss of the political independence of the subjected countries and peoples. In this respect, the semi-colonial countries provide a typical example of the 'middle stage'. It is natural that the struggle for these semi-dependent countries should have become particularly bitter in the epoch of finance capital, when the rest of the world has already been divided up.

Colonial policy and imperialism existed before the latest stage of capitalism, and even before capitalism. Rome, founded on slavery, pursued a colonial policy and practised imperialism. But 'general' disquisitions on imperialism, which ignore, or put into the background, the fundamental difference between socio-economic formations, inevitably turn into the most vapid banality or bragging, like the comparison: 'Greater Rome and Greater Britain.'[87] Even the capitalist colonial policy of *previous* stages of capitalism is essentially different from the colonial policy of finance capital.

The principal feature of the latest stage of capitalism is the domination of monopolist associations of big employers. These monopolies are most firmly established when *all* the sources of raw materials are captured by one group, and we have seen with what zeal the international capitalist associations exert every effort to deprive their rivals of all opportunity of competing, to buy up, for example, iron fields, oilfields, etc. Colonial possession alone gives the monopolies complete guarantee against all contingencies in the struggle against competitors, including the case of the adversary wanting to be protected by a law establishing a state monopoly. The more capitalism is developed, the more strongly the shortage of raw materials is felt, the more intense the competition and the hunt for sources of raw materials throughout the whole world, the more desperate the struggle for the acquisition of colonies.

'It may be asserted,' writes Schilder, 'although it may sound paradoxical to some, that in the more or less foreseeable future the growth of the urban and industrial population is more likely to be hindered by a shortage of raw materials for industry than by a shortage of food.' For example, there is a growing shortage of timber – the price of which is steadily rising – of leather, and of raw materials for the textile industry.

'Associations of manufacturers are making efforts to create an equilibrium between agriculture and industry in the whole of world economy; as an example of this we might mention the International Federation of Cotton Spinners' Associations in several of the most important industrial countries, founded in 1904, and the European Federation of Flax Spinners' Associations, founded on the same model in 1910.'[88]

Of course, the bourgeois reformists, and among them particularly the present-day adherents of Kautsky, try to belittle the importance of facts of this kind by arguing that raw materials 'could be' obtained in the open market without a 'costly and dangerous' colonial policy; and that the supply of raw materials 'could be' increased enormously by 'simply' improving conditions in agriculture in general. But such arguments become an apology for imperialism, an attempt to paint it in bright colours, because they ignore the principal feature of the latest stage of capitalism: monopolies. The free market is becoming more and more a thing of the past; monopolist syndicates and trusts are restricting it with every passing day, and 'simply' improving conditions in agriculture means improving the conditions of the masses, raising wages and reducing profits. Where, except in the imagination of sentimental reformists, are there any trusts capable of concerning themselves with the condition of the masses instead of the conquest of colonies?

Finance capital is interested not only in the already discovered sources of raw materials but also in potential sources, because present-day technical development is extremely rapid, and land which is useless today may be improved tomorrow if new methods are devised (to this end a big bank can equip a special expedition of engineers, agricultural experts, etc.), and if large amounts of capital are invested. This also applies to prospecting for minerals, to new methods of processing up and utilising raw materials, etc., etc. Hence, the inevitable striving of finance capital to enlarge its spheres of influence and even its actual territory. In the same way that the trusts capitalise their property at two or three times its value, taking into account its 'potential' (and not actual) profits and the further results of monopoly, so finance capital in general strives to seize the largest possible amount of land of all kinds in all places, and by every means, taking into account potential sources of raw materials and fearing to be left behind in the fierce struggle for the last remnants of independent territory, or for the repartition of those territories that have been already divided.

The British capitalists are exerting every effort to develop cotton growing in *their* colony, Egypt (in 1904, out of 2,300,000 hectares of land under cultivation, 600,000, or more than one-fourth, were under cotton); the Russians are doing the same in *their* colony, Turkestan, because in this way they will be in a better position to defeat their foreign competitors, to monopolise the sources of raw materials and form a more economical and profitable textile trust in which *all* the processes of cotton production and manufacturing will be 'combined' and concentrated in the hands of one set of owners.

The interests pursued in exporting capital also give an impetus to the conquest of colonies, for in the colonial market it is easier to employ monopoly methods (and sometimes they are the only methods that can be employed) to eliminate competition, to ensure supplies, to secure the necessary 'connections', etc.

The non-economic superstructure which grows up on the basis of finance capital, its politics and its ideology, stimulates the striving for colonial conquest. 'Finance capital does not want liberty, it wants domination', as Hilferding very truly says. And a French bourgeois writer, developing and supplementing, as it were, the ideas of Cecil Rhodes quoted above,[89] writes that social causes should be added to the economic causes of modern colonial policy:

> Owing to the growing complexities of life and the difficulties which weigh not only on the masses of the workers, but also on the middle classes, 'impatience, irritation and hatred are accumulating in all the countries of the old civilisation and are becoming a menace to public order; the energy which is being hurled out of the definite class channel must be given employment abroad in order to avert an explosion at home'.[90]

Since we are speaking of colonial policy in the epoch of capitalist imperialism, it must be observed that finance capital and its foreign policy, which is the struggle of the great powers for the economic and political division of the world, give rise to a number of *transitional* forms of state dependence. Not only are the two main groups of countries, those owning colonies, and the colonies themselves, but also the diverse forms of dependent countries which, politically, are formally independent, but in fact, are enmeshed in the net of financial and diplomatic dependence, typical of this epoch. We have already referred to one form of dependence – the semi-colony. An example of another is provided by Argentina.

'South America, and especially Argentina', writes Schulze-Gaevernitz in his work on British imperialism, 'is so dependent financially on London that it ought to be described as almost a British commercial colony.'[91] Basing himself on the reports of the Austro-Hungarian Consul at Buenos Aires for 1909, Schilder estimated the amount of British capital invested in Argentina at 8,750 million francs. It is not difficult to imagine what strong connections British finance capital (and its faithful 'friend', diplomacy) thereby acquires with the Argentine bourgeoisie, with the circles that control the whole of that country's economic and political life.

A somewhat different form of financial and diplomatic dependence, accompanied by political independence, is presented by Portugal. Portugal is an independent sovereign state, but actually, for more than two hundred years, since the war of the Spanish Succession (1701–14), it has been a British protectorate. Great Britain has protected Portugal and her colonies in order to fortify her own positions in the fight against her rivals, Spain and France. In return Great Britain has received commercial privileges, preferential conditions for importing goods and especially capital into Portugal and the Portuguese colonies, the right to use the ports and islands of Portugal, her telegraph cables, etc., etc.[92] Relations of this kind have always existed between big and little states, but in the epoch of capitalist imperialism they become a general system, they form part of the sum total of 'divide the world' relations and become links in the chain of operations of world finance capital.

In order to finish with the question of the division of the world, I must make the following additional observation. This question was raised quite openly and definitely not only in American literature after the Spanish-American War, and in English literature after the

Anglo-Boer War, at the very end of the nineteenth century and the beginning of the twentieth; not only has German literature, which has 'most jealously' watched 'British imperialism', systematically given its appraisal of this fact. This question has also been raised in French bourgeois literature as definitely and broadly as is thinkable from the bourgeois point of view. Let me quote Driault, the historian, who, in his book *Political and Social Problems at the End of the Nineteenth Century*, in the chapter 'The Great Powers and the Division of the World', wrote the following:

During the past few years, all the free territory of the globe, with the exception of China, has been occupied by the powers of Europe and North America. This has already brought about several conflicts and shifts of spheres of influence, and these foreshadow more terrible upheavals in the near future. For it is necessary to make haste. The nations which have not yet made provision for themselves run the risk of never receiving their share and never participating in the tremendous exploitation of the globe which will be one of the most essential features of the next century (i.e., the twentieth). That is why all Europe and America have lately been afflicted with the fever of colonial expansion, of 'imperialism', that most noteworthy feature of the end of the nineteenth century.

And the author added:

In this partition of the world, in this furious hunt for the treasures and the big markets of the globe, the relative strength of the empires founded in this nineteenth century is totally out of proportion to the place occupied in Europe by the nations which founded them. The dominant powers in Europe, the arbiters of her destiny, are *not* equally preponderant in the whole world. And, as colonial might, the hope of controlling as yet unassessed wealth, will evidently react upon the relative strength of the European powers, the colonial question – 'imperialism', if you will – which has already modified the political conditions of Europe itself, will modify them more and more.[93]

VII. Imperialism as a Special Stage of Capitalism

We must now try to sum up, to draw together the threads of what has been said above on the subject of imperialism. Imperialism emerged as the development and direct continuation of the fundamental characteristics of capitalism in general. But capitalism only became capitalist imperialism at a definite and very high stage of its development, when certain of its fundamental characteristics began to change into their opposites, when the features of the epoch of transition from capitalism to a higher social and economic system had taken shape and revealed themselves in all spheres. Economically, the main thing in this process is the displacement of capitalist free competition by capitalist monopoly. Free competition is the basic feature of capitalism, and of commodity production generally; monopoly is the exact opposite of free competition, but we have seen the latter being transformed into monopoly before our eyes, creating large-scale industry and forcing out small industry, replacing large-scale by still larger-scale industry, and carrying concentration of production and capital to the point where out of it has grown and is growing monopoly: cartels, syndicates and trusts, and merging with them, the capital of a dozen or so banks, which manipulate thousands of millions. At the same time the monopolies, which have grown out of free competition, do not eliminate the latter, but exist above it and alongside it, and thereby give rise to a number of very acute, intense antagonisms, frictions and conflicts. Monopoly is the transition from capitalism to a higher system.

If it were necessary to give the briefest possible definition of imperialism, we should have to say that imperialism is the monopoly stage of capitalism. Such a definition would include what is most important, for, on the one hand, finance capital is the bank capital of a few very big monopolist banks, merged with the capital of the monopolist associations of industrialists; and, on the other hand, the division of the world is the transition from a colonial policy which has extended without hindrance to territories unseized by any capitalist power, to a colonial policy of monopolist possession of the territory of the world, which has been completely divided up.

But very brief definitions, although convenient, for they sum up the main points, are nevertheless inadequate, since we have to deduce from them some especially important features of the phenomenon that has to be defined. And so, without forgetting the conditional and relative value of all definitions in general, which can never embrace all the concatenations of a phenomenon in its full development, we must give a definition of imperialism that will include the following five of its basic features:

(1) the concentration of production and capital has developed to such a high stage that it has created monopolies which play a decisive role in economic life; (2) the merging of bank capital with industrial capital, and the creation, on the basis of this 'finance capital', of a financial oligarchy; (3) the export of capital as distinguished from the export of commodities acquires exceptional importance; (4) the formation of international monopolist capitalist associations which share the world among themselves and (5) the territorial division of the whole world among the biggest capitalist powers is completed. Imperialism is capitalism at that stage of development at which the dominance of monopolies and finance capital is established; in which the export of capital has acquired pronounced importance; in which the division of the world among the international trusts has begun, in which the division of all territories of the globe among the biggest capitalist powers has been completed.

We shall see later that imperialism can and must be defined differently if we bear in mind not only the basic, purely economic concepts – to which the above definition is limited – but also the historical place of this stage of capitalism in relation to capitalism in general, or the relation between imperialism and the two main trends in the working-class movement. The thing to be noted at this point is that imperialism, as interpreted above, undoubtedly represents a special stage in the development of capitalism. To enable the reader to obtain the most well-grounded idea of imperialism, I deliberately tried to quote as extensively as possible *bourgeois* economists who have to admit the particularly incontrovertible facts concerning the latest stage of capitalist economy. With the same object in view, I have quoted detailed statistics which enable one to see to what degree bank capital, etc., has grown, in what precisely the transformation of quantity into quality, of developed capitalism into imperialism, was expressed. Needless to say, of course, all boundaries in nature and in society are conventional and changeable, and it would be absurd to argue, for example, about the particular year or decade in which imperialism 'definitely' became established.

In the matter of defining imperialism, however, we have to enter into controversy, primarily, with Karl Kautsky, the principal Marxist theoretician of the epoch of the so-called Second International – that is, of the twenty-five years between 1889 and 1914. The fundamental ideas expressed in our definition of imperialism were very resolutely attacked by Kautsky in 1915, and even in November 1914, when he said that imperialism must not be regarded as a 'phase' or stage of economy, but as a policy, a definite policy 'preferred' by finance capital; that imperialism must not be 'identified' with 'present-day capitalism'; that if imperialism is to be understood to mean 'all the phenomena of present-day capitalism' – cartels, protection, the domination of the financiers, and colonial policy – then the question as to whether imperialism is necessary to capitalism becomes reduced to the 'flattest tautology', because, in that case, 'imperialism is naturally a vital necessity for capitalism', and so on. The best way to present Kautsky's idea is to quote his own definition of imperialism, which is diametrically opposed to the substance of the ideas which I have set forth (for the objections coming from the camp of the German Marxists, who have been advocating similar ideas for many years already, have been long known to Kautsky as the objections of a definite trend in Marxism).

Kautsky's definition is as follows:

> Imperialism is a product of highly developed industrial capitalism. It consists in the striving of every industrial capitalist nation to bring under its control or to annex all large areas of *agrarian* [Kautsky's italics] territory, irrespective of what nations inhabit it.[94]

This definition is of no use at all because it one-sidedly, i.e., arbitrarily, singles out only the national question (although the latter is extremely important in itself as well as in its relation to imperialism), it arbitrarily and *inaccurately* connects this question *only* with industrial capital in the countries which annex other nations, and in an equally arbitrary and inaccurate manner pushes into the forefront the annexation of agrarian regions.

Imperialism is a striving for annexations – this is what the *political* part of Kautsky's definition amounts to. It is correct, but very incomplete, for politically, imperialism is, in general, a striving towards violence and reaction. For the moment, however, we are interested in the *economic* aspect of the question, which Kautsky *himself* introduced into his definition. The inaccuracies in Kautsky's definition are glaring. The characteristic feature of imperialism is not industrial *but* finance capital. It is not an accident that in France it was precisely the extraordinarily rapid development of *finance* capital, and the weakening of industrial capital, that from the eighties onwards gave rise to the extreme intensification of annexationist (colonial) policy. The characteristic feature of imperialism is precisely that it strives to annex *not only* agrarian territories, but even most highly industrialised regions (German appetite for Belgium; French appetite for Lorraine), because (1) the fact that the world is already partitioned obliges those contemplating a *redivision* to reach out for *every kind* of territory, and (2) an essential feature of imperialism is the rivalry between several great powers in the striving for hegemony, i.e., for the conquest of territory, not so much directly for themselves as to weaken the adversary and undermine *his* hegemony. (Belgium is particularly important for Germany as a base for operations against Britain; Britain needs Baghdad as a base for operations against Germany, etc.)

Kautsky refers especially – and repeatedly – to English writers who, he alleges, have given a purely political meaning to the word 'imperialism' in the sense that he, Kautsky, understands it. We take up the work by the English writer Hobson, *Imperialism*, which appeared in 1902, and there we read:

> The new imperialism differs from the older, first, in substituting for the ambition of a single growing empire the theory and the practice of competing empires, each motivated by similar lusts of political aggrandisement and commercial gain; secondly, in the dominance of financial or investing over mercantile interests.[95]

We see that Kautsky is absolutely wrong in referring to English writers generally (unless he meant the vulgar English imperialists, or the avowed apologists for imperialism). We see that Kautsky, while claiming that he continues to advocate Marxism, as a matter of fact takes a step backward compared with the *social-liberal* Hobson, who *more correctly* takes into account two 'historically concrete' (Kautsky's definition is a mockery of historical concreteness!) features of modern imperialism: (1) the competition between *several* imperialisms, and (2) the predominance of the financier over the merchant. If it is chiefly a question of the annexation of agrarian countries by industrial countries, then the role of the merchant is put in the forefront.

Kautsky's definition is not only wrong and un-Marxist. It serves as a basis for a whole system of views which signify a rupture with Marxist theory and Marxist practice all along the line. I shall refer to this later. The argument about words which Kautsky raises as to whether the latest stage of capitalism should be called imperialism or the stage of finance capital is not worth serious attention. Call it what you will, it makes no difference. The essence of the matter is that Kautsky detaches the politics of imperialism from its economics, speaks of annexations as being a policy 'preferred' by finance capital, and opposes to it another bourgeois policy which, he alleges, is possible on this very same basis of finance capital. It follows, then, that monopolies in the economy are compatible with non-monopolistic, non-violent, non-annexationist methods in politics. It follows, then, that the territorial division of the world, which was completed during this very epoch of finance capital, and which constitutes the basis of the present peculiar forms of rivalry between the biggest capitalist states, is compatible with a non-imperialist policy. The result is a slurring over and a blunting of the most profound contradictions of the latest stage of capitalism, instead of an exposure of their depth; the result is bourgeois reformism instead of Marxism.

Kautsky enters into controversy with the German apologist of imperialism and annexations, Cunow, who clumsily and cynically argues that imperialism is present-day capitalism; the development of capitalism is inevitable and progressive; therefore, imperialism is progressive; therefore, we should grovel before it and glorify it! This is something like the caricature of the Russian Marxists which the Narodniks drew in 1894–5. They argued: if the Marxists believe that capitalism is inevitable in Russia, that it is progressive, then they ought to open a tavern and begin to implant capitalism! Kautsky's reply to Cunow is as follows: imperialism is not present-day capitalism; it is only one of the forms of the policy of present-day capitalism. This policy we can and should fight, fight imperialism, annexations, etc.

The reply seems quite plausible, but in effect it is a more subtle and more disguised (and therefore more dangerous) advocacy of conciliation with imperialism, because a 'fight' against the policy of the trusts and banks that does not affect the economic basis of the trusts and banks is mere bourgeois reformism and pacifism, the benevolent and innocent expression of pious wishes. Evasion of existing contradictions, forgetting the most important of them, instead of revealing their full depth – such is Kautsky's theory, which has nothing in common with Marxism. Naturally, such a 'theory' can only serve the purpose of advocating unity with the Cunows!

'From the purely economic point of view', writes Kautsky, 'it is not impossible that capitalism will yet go through a new phase, that of the extension of the policy of the cartels to foreign policy, the phase of ultra-imperialism,'[96] i.e., of a super-imperialism, of a union of the imperialisms of the whole world and not struggles among them, a phase when wars shall cease under capitalism, a phase of 'the joint exploitation of the world by internationally united finance capital.'[97]

We shall have to deal with this 'theory of ultra-imperialism' later on in order to show in detail how decisively and completely it breaks with Marxism. At present, in keeping with the general plan of the present work, we must examine the exact economic data on this question. 'From the purely economic point of view', is 'ultra-imperialism' possible, or is it ultra-nonsense?

If the purely economic point of view is meant to be a 'pure' abstraction, then all that can be said reduces itself to the following proposition: development is proceeding towards monopolies, hence, towards a single world monopoly, towards a single world trust. This is indisputable, but it is also as completely meaningless as is the statement that 'development is proceeding' towards the manufacture of foodstuffs in laboratories.

In this sense the 'theory' of ultra-imperialism is no less absurd than a 'theory of ultra-agriculture' would be.

If, however, we are discussing the 'purely economic' conditions of the epoch of finance capital as a historically concrete epoch which began at the turn of the twentieth century, then the best reply that one can make to the lifeless abstractions of 'ultra-imperialism' (which serve exclusively a most reactionary aim: that of diverting attention from the depth of *existing* antagonisms) is to contrast them with the concrete economic realities of the present-day world economy. Kautsky's utterly meaningless talk about ultra-imperialism encourages, among other things, that profoundly mistaken idea which only brings grist to the mill of the apologists of imperialism, i.e., that the rule of finance capital *lessens* the unevenness and contradictions inherent in the world economy, whereas, in reality, it increases them.

R. Calwer, in his little book, *An Introduction to the World Economy*,[98] made an attempt to summarise the main, purely economic, data that enable one to obtain a concrete picture of the internal relations of the world economy at the turn of the twentieth century. He divides the world into five 'main economic areas', as follows: (1) Central Europe (the whole of Europe with the exception of Russia and Great Britain); (2) Great Britain; (3) Russia; (4) Eastern Asia; (5) America; he includes the colonies in the 'areas' of the states to which they belong and 'leaves aside' a few countries not distributed according to areas, such as Persia, Afghanistan, and Arabia in Asia, Morocco and Abyssinia in Africa, etc.

Here is a brief summary of the economic data he quotes on these regions.

We see three areas of highly developed capitalism (high development of means of transport, of trade and of industry): the Central European, the British and the American areas. Among these are three states which dominate the world: Germany, Great Britain, and the United States. Imperialist rivalry and the struggle between these countries have become extremely keen because Germany has only an insignificant area and few colonies; the creation of 'Central Europe' is still a matter for the future, it is being born in the midst of a desperate struggle. For the moment the distinctive feature of the whole of Europe is political disunity. In the British and American areas, on the other hand, political

Table 17

Principal economic areas	Area Million sq. miles	Pop. Millions	Transport Railways (thou. km)	Transport Mercantile fleet (millions tons)	Trade Imports, exports (thous-million marks)	Industry Of coal (mill. tons)	Industry Of pig iron (mill. tons)	Industry Number of cotton spindles (millions)
1) Central Europe	27.6 (23.6)	388 (146)	204	8	41	251	15	26
2) Britain	28.9 (28.6)	398 (355)	140	11	25	249	9	51
3) Russia	22	131	63	1	3	16	3	7
4) Eastern Asia	12	389	8	1	2	8	0.02	2
5) America	30	148	379	6	14	245	14	19

NOTE: The figures in parentheses show the area and population of the colonies.

concentration is very highly developed, but there is a vast disparity between the immense colonies of the one and the insignificant colonies of the other. In the colonies, however, capitalism is only beginning to develop. The struggle for South America is becoming more and more acute.

There are two areas where capitalism is little developed: Russia and Eastern Asia. In the former, the population is extremely sparse, in the latter it is extremely dense; in the former political concentration is high, in the latter it does not exist. The partitioning of China is only just beginning, and the struggle for it between Japan, the United States, etc., is continually gaining in intensity.

Compare this reality – the vast diversity of economic and political conditions, the extreme disparity in the rate of development of the various countries, etc., and the violent struggles among the imperialist states – with Kautsky's silly little fable about 'peaceful' ultra-imperialism. Is this not the reactionary attempt of a frightened philistine to hide from stern reality? Are not the international cartels which Kautsky imagines are the embryos of 'ultra-imperialism' (in the same way as one 'can' describe the manufacture of tablets in a laboratory as ultra-agriculture in embryo) an example of the division *and the redivision* of the world, the transition from peaceful division to non-peaceful division and vice versa? Is not American and other finance capital, which divided the whole world peacefully with Germany's participation in, for example, the international rail syndicate, or in the international mercantile shipping trust, now engaged in *redividing* the world on the basis of a new relation of forces that is being changed by methods *anything but* peaceful?

Finance capital and the trusts do not diminish but increase the differences in the rate of growth of the various parts of the world economy. Once the relation of forces is changed, what other solution of the contradictions can be found *under capitalism* than that of *force*? Railway statistics[99] provide remarkably exact data on the different rates of growth of capitalism and finance capital in world economy. In the last decades of imperialist development, the total length of railways has changed as follows:

Table 18

	Railways (000 kilometers)					
	1890		1913		+	
Europe	224		346		+122	
U.S.	268		411		+143	
All colonies	82	125	210	347	+128	+222
Independent and semi-independent states of Asia and America	43		137		+94	
Total	617		1,104			

Thus, the development of railways has been most rapid in the colonies and in the independent (and semi-independent) states of Asia and America. Here, as we know, the finance capital of the four or five biggest capitalist states holds undisputed sway. Two hundred thousand kilometres of new railways in the colonies and in the other countries of Asia and America represent a capital of more than 40,000 million marks newly invested on particularly advantageous terms, with special guarantees of a good return and with profitable orders for steel works, etc., etc.

Capitalism is growing with the greatest rapidity in the colonies and in overseas countries. Among the latter, new imperialist powers are emerging (e.g., Japan). The struggle among the world imperialisms is becoming more acute. The tribute levied by finance capital on the most profitable colonial and overseas enterprises is increasing. In the division of this 'booty', an exceptionally large part goes to countries which do not always stand at the top of the list in the rapidity of the development of their productive forces. In the case of the biggest countries, together with their colonies, the total length of railways was as follows:

Table 19. (000 kilometres)

	1890	1913	
U.S.	268	413	+145
British Empire	107	208	+101
Russia	32	78	+46
Germany	43	68	+25
France	41	63	+22
Total	491	830	+339

Thus, about 80 per cent of the total existing railways are concentrated in the hands of the five biggest powers. But the concentration of the *ownership* of these railways, the concentration of finance capital, is immeasurably greater since the French and British millionaires, for example, own an enormous amount of shares and bonds in American, Russian and other railways.

Thanks to her colonies, Great Britain has increased the length of 'her' railways by 100,000 kilometres, four times as much as Germany. And yet, it is well known that the development of productive forces in Germany, and especially the development of the coal and iron industries, has been incomparably more rapid during this period than in Britain – not to speak of France and Russia. In 1892, Germany produced 4,900,000 tons of pig-iron and Great Britain produced 6,800,000 tons; in 1912, Germany produced 17,600,000 tons and Great Britain, 9,000,000 tons. Germany, therefore, had an overwhelming superiority over Britain in this respect.[100] The question is: what means other than war could there be *under capitalism* to overcome the disparity between the development of productive forces and the accumulation of capital on the one side, and the division of colonies and spheres of influence for finance capital on the other?

VIII. Parasitism and Decay of Capitalism

We now have to examine yet another significant aspect of imperialism to which most of the discussions on the subject usually attach insufficient importance. One of the shortcomings of the Marxist Hilferding is that on this point he has taken a step backward compared with the non-Marxist Hobson. I refer to parasitism, which is characteristic of imperialism.

As we have seen, the deepest economic foundation of imperialism is monopoly. This is capitalist monopoly, i.e., monopoly which has grown out of capitalism and which exists in the general environment of capitalism, commodity production and competition, in permanent and insoluble contradiction to this general environment. Nevertheless, like all monopoly, it inevitably engenders a tendency of stagnation and decay. Since monopoly prices are established, even temporarily, the motive cause of technical and, consequently, of all other progress disappears to a certain extent and, further, the economic possibility arises of deliberately retarding technical progress. For instance, in America, a certain Owens invented a machine which revolutionised the manufacture of bottles. The German bottle-manufacturing cartel purchased Owens's patent, but pigeon-holed it, refrained from utilising it. Certainly, monopoly under capitalism can never completely, and for a very long period of time, eliminate competition in the world market (and this, by the by, is one of the reasons why the theory of ultra-imperialism is so absurd). Certainly, the possibility of reducing the cost of production and increasing profits by introducing technical improvements operates in the direction of change. But the tendency to stagnation and decay, which is characteristic of monopoly, continues to operate, and in some branches of industry, in some countries, for certain periods of time, it gains the upper hand.

The monopoly ownership of very extensive, rich or well-situated colonies operates in the same direction.

Further, imperialism is an immense accumulation of money capital in a few countries, amounting, as we have seen, to 100,000–150,000 million francs in securities. Hence the extraordinary growth of a class, or rather, of a stratum of rentiers, i.e., people who live by 'clipping coupons', who take no part in any enterprise whatever, whose profession is idleness. The export of capital, one of the most essential economic bases of imperialism, still more completely isolates the rentiers from production and sets the seal of parasitism on the whole country that lives by exploiting the labour of several overseas countries and colonies.

'In 1893', writes Hobson, 'the British capital invested abroad represented about 15 per cent of the total wealth of the United Kingdom.'[101] Let me remind the reader that by 1915 this capital had increased about two and a half times. 'Aggressive imperialism', says Hobson further on,

which costs the tax-payer so dear, which is of so little value to the manufacturer and trader ... is a source of great gain to the investor ... The annual income Great Britain derives from commissions in her whole foreign and colonial trade, import and export, is estimated by Sir

R. Giffen at £18,000,000 (nearly 170 million roubles) for 1899, taken at
2 1/2 per cent, upon a turnover of £800,000,000.

Great as this sum is, it cannot explain the aggressive imperialism of
Great Britain, which is explained by the income of £90 million to £100
million from 'invested' capital, the income of the rentiers.

The income of the rentiers is five *times* greater than the income
obtained from the foreign trade of the biggest 'trading' country in the
world! This is the essence of imperialism and imperialist parasitism.

For that reason, the term 'rentier state' (*Rentnerstaat*), or usurer
state, is coming into common use in the economic literature that deals
with imperialism. The world has become divided into a handful of
usurer states and a vast majority of debtor states. 'At the top of the list
of foreign investments', says Schulze-Gaevernitz,

> are those placed in politically dependent or allied countries: Great Britain
> grants loans to Egypt, Japan, China and South America. Her navy plays
> here the part of bailiff in case of necessity. Great Britain's political power
> protects her from the indignation of her debtors.[102]

Sartorius von Waltershausen in his book, *The National Economic
System of Capital Investments Abroad,* cites Holland as the model
'rentier state' and points out that Great Britain and France are now
becoming such.[103] Schilder is of the opinion that five industrial states
have become 'definitely pronounced creditor countries': Great Britain,
France, Germany, Belgium and Switzerland. He does not include
Holland in this list simply because she is 'industrially little developed'.[104]
The United States is a creditor only of the American countries.

'Great Britain', says Schulze-Gaevernitz,

> is gradually becoming transformed from an industrial into a creditor
> state. Notwithstanding the absolute increase in industrial output and
> the export of manufactured goods, there is an increase in the relative
> importance of income from interest and dividends, issues of securities,
> commissions and speculation in the whole of the national economy. In
> my opinion it is precisely this that forms the economic basis of imperialist

ascendancy. The creditor is more firmly attached to the debtor than the seller is to the buyer.[105]

In regard to Germany, A. Lansburgh, the publisher of the Berlin *Die Bank*, in 1911, in an article entitled 'Germany – a Rentier State', wrote the following: 'People in Germany are ready to sneer at the yearning to become rentiers that is observed in France. But they forget that as far as the bourgeoisie is concerned the situation in Germany is becoming more and more like that in France.'[106]

The rentier state is a state of parasitic, decaying capitalism, and this circumstance cannot fail to influence all the socio-political conditions of the countries concerned, in general, and the two fundamental trends in the working-class movement, in particular. To demonstrate this in the clearest possible manner let me quote Hobson, who is a most reliable witness, since he cannot be suspected of leaning towards Marxist orthodoxy; on the other hand, he is an Englishman who is very well acquainted with the situation in the country which is richest in colonies, in finance capital, and in imperialist experience.

With the Anglo-Boer War fresh in his mind, Hobson describes the connection between imperialism and the interests of the 'financiers', their growing profits from contracts, supplies, etc., and writes:

> While the directors of this definitely parasitic policy are capitalists, the same motives appeal to special classes of the workers. In many towns most important trades are dependent upon government employment or contracts; the imperialism of the metal and shipbuilding centres is attributable in no small degree to this fact.

Two sets of circumstances, in this writer's opinion, have weakened the old empires: (1) 'economic parasitism,' and (2) the formation of armies recruited from subject peoples. 'There is first the habit of economic parasitism, by which the ruling state has used its provinces, colonies, and dependencies in order to enrich its ruling class and to bribe its lower classes into acquiescence.' And I shall add that the economic possibility of such bribery, whatever its form may be, requires high monopolist profits.

As for the second circumstance, Hobson writes:

One of the strangest symptoms of the blindness of imperialism is the reckless indifference with which Great Britain, France and other imperial nations are embarking on this perilous dependence. Great Britain has gone farthest. Most of the fighting by which we have won our Indian Empire has been done by natives; in India, as more recently in Egypt, great standing armies are placed under British commanders; almost all the fighting associated with our African dominions, except in the southern part, has been done for us by natives.

Hobson gives the following economic appraisal of the prospect of the partitioning of China:

The greater part of Western Europe might then assume the appearance and character already exhibited by tracts of country in the South of England, in the Riviera and in the tourist-ridden or residential parts of Italy and Switzerland, little clusters of wealthy aristocrats drawing dividends and pensions from the Far East, with a somewhat larger group of professional retainers and tradesmen and a larger body of personal servants and workers in the transport trade and in the final stages of production of the more perishable goods; all the main arterial industries would have disappeared, the staple foods and manufactures flowing in as tribute from Asia and Africa ... We have foreshadowed the possibility of even a larger alliance of Western states, a European federation of great powers which, so far from forwarding the cause of world civilisation, might introduce the gigantic peril of a Western parasitism, a group of advanced industrial nations, whose upper classes drew vast tribute from Asia and Africa, with which they supported great tame masses of retainers, no longer engaged in the staple industries of agriculture and manufacture, but kept in the performance of personal or minor indus-trial services under the control of a new financial aristocracy. Let those who would scout such a theory (it would be better to say: prospect) as undeserving of consideration examine the economic and social condition of districts in Southern England today which are already reduced to this condition, and reflect upon the vast extension of such a system which might be rendered feasible by the subjection of China to the economic control of similar groups of financiers, investors, and political and business officials, draining the greatest potential reservoir of profit the world has ever known, in order to consume it in Europe. The situation is far too complex, the play of world forces far too incalculable, to render this or any other single interpretation of the future very probable; but the influences which govern the imperialism of Western Europe today are moving in this direction, and, unless counteracted or diverted, make towards some such consummation.[107]

The author is quite right: if the forces of imperialism had not been counteracted they would have led precisely to what he has described. The significance of a 'United States of Europe' in the present imperialist situation is correctly appraised. He should have added, however, that, also *within* the working-class movement, the opportunists, who are for the moment victorious in most countries, are 'working' systematically and undeviatingly in this very direction. Imperialism, which means the partitioning of the world, and the exploitation of other countries besides China, which means high monopoly profits for a handful of very rich countries, makes it economically possible to bribe the upper strata of the proletariat, and thereby fosters, gives shape to, and strengthens opportunism. We must not, however, lose sight of the forces which counteract imperialism in general, and opportunism in particular, and which, naturally, the social-liberal Hobson is unable to perceive.

The German opportunist, Gerhard Hildebrand, who was once expelled from the Party for defending imperialism, and who could today be a leader of the so-called 'Social-Democratic' Party of Germany, supplements Hobson well by his advocacy of a 'United States of Western Europe' (without Russia) for the purpose of 'joint' action ... against the African Negroes, against the 'great Islamic movement', for the maintenance of a 'powerful army and navy', against a 'Sino-Japanese coalition',[108] etc.

The description of 'British imperialism' in Schulze-Gaevernitz's book reveals the same parasitical traits. The national income of Great Britain approximately doubled from 1865 to 1898, while the income 'from abroad' increased *nine-fold* in the same period. While the 'merit' of imperialism is that it 'trains the Negro to habits of industry' (you cannot manage without coercion …), the 'danger' of imperialism lies in that

> Europe will shift the burden of physical toil – first agricultural and mining, then the rougher work in industry – on to the coloured races, and itself be content with the role of rentier, and in this way, perhaps, pave the way for the economic, and later, the political emancipation of the coloured races.

An increasing proportion of land in England is being taken out of cultivation and used for sport, for the diversion of the rich. As far as Scotland – the most aristocratic place for hunting and other sports – is concerned, it is said that 'it lives on its past and on Mr. Carnegie' (the American multimillionaire). On horse racing and fox hunting alone England annually spends £14,000,000 (nearly 130 million roubles). The number of rentiers in England is about one million. The percentage of the productively employed population to the total population is declining:

Table 20

	Population England and Wales (000,000)	Workers in basic industries (000,000)	Per cent of total population
1851	17.9	4.1	23
1901	32.5	4.9	15

And in speaking of the British working class, the bourgeois student of 'British imperialism at the beginning of the twentieth century' is obliged to distinguish systematically between the *'upper stratum'* of the workers and the *'lower stratum of the proletariat proper'*. The upper stratum furnishes the bulk of the membership of co-operatives, of trade unions, of sporting clubs and of numerous religious sects. To this level is adapted the electoral system, which in Great Britain is still *'sufficiently restricted to exclude the lower stratum of the proletariat proper'*! In order to present the condition of the British working class in a rosy light, only this upper stratum – which constitutes a *minority of* the proletariat – is usually spoken of. For instance, 'the problem of unemployment is mainly a London problem and that of the lower proletarian stratum, *to which the politicians attach little importance ...*'[109] He should have said: to which the bourgeois politicians and the 'socialist' opportunists attach little importance.

One of the special features of imperialism connected with the facts I am describing, is the decline in emigration from imperialist countries and the increase in immigration into these countries from the more backward countries where lower wages are paid. As Hobson observes, emigration from Great Britain has been declining since 1884. In that year the number of emigrants was 242,000, while in 1900, the number was 169,000. Emigration from Germany reached the highest point between 1881 and 1890, with a total of 1,453,000 emigrants. In the course of the following two decades, it fell to 544,000 and to 341,000. On the other hand, there was an increase in the number of workers entering Germany from Austria, Italy, Russia and other countries. According to the 1907 census, there were 1,342,294 foreigners in Germany, of whom 440,800 were industrial workers and 257,329 agricultural workers.[110] In France, the workers employed in the mining industry are, 'in great part', foreigners: Poles, Italians and Spaniards.[111] In the United States, immigrants from Eastern and Southern Europe are engaged in the most poorly paid jobs, while American workers provide the highest percentage of overseers or of the better-paid workers.[112] Imperialism has the tendency to create privileged sections also among the workers, and to detach them from the broad masses of the proletariat.

It must be observed that in Great Britain the tendency of imperialism to split the workers, to strengthen opportunism among them and to cause temporary decay in the working-class movement, revealed itself much earlier than the end of the nineteenth and the beginning of the twentieth centuries; for two important distinguishing features of imperialism were already observed in Great Britain in the middle of the nineteenth century – vast colonial possessions and a monopolist position in the world market. Marx and Engels traced this connection between opportunism in the working-class movement and the imperialist features of British capitalism systematically, during the course of several decades. For example, on 7 October 1858, Engels wrote to Marx:

The English proletariat is actually becoming more and more bourgeois, so that this most bourgeois of all nations is apparently aiming ultimately at the possession of a bourgeois aristocracy and a bourgeois proletariat *alongside* the bourgeoisie. For a nation which exploits the whole world this is of course to a certain extent justifiable.[13]

Almost a quarter of a century later, in a letter dated 11 August 1881, Engels speaks of the 'worst English trade unions which allow themselves to be led by men sold to, or at least paid by, the middle class'. In a letter to Kautsky, dated 12 September 1882, Engels wrote:

You ask me what the English workers think about colonial policy. Well, exactly the same as they think about politics in general. There is no workers' party here, there are only Conservatives and Liberal-Radicals, and the workers gaily share the feast of England's monopoly of the world market and the colonies.[113]

(Engels expressed similar ideas in the press in his preface to the second edition of *The Condition of the Working Class in England*, which appeared in 1892.)

This clearly shows the causes and effects. The causes are: (1) exploitation of the whole world by this country; (2) its monopolist position in the world market; (3) its colonial monopoly. The effects are: (1) a section of the British proletariat becomes bourgeois; (2) a section of the proletariat allows itself to be led by men bought by, or at least paid by, the bourgeoisie. The imperialism of the beginning of the twentieth century completed the division of the world among a handful of states, each of which today exploits (in the sense of drawing superprofits from) a part of the 'whole world' only a little smaller than that which England exploited in 1858; each of them occupies a monopolist position in the world market thanks to trusts, cartels, finance capital and creditor and debtor relations; each of them enjoys to some degree a colonial monopoly (we have seen that out of the total of *75,000,000* sq. km., which comprise the *whole* colonial world, *65,000,000* sq. km., or 86 per cent, belong to six powers; *61,000,000* sq. km., or 81 per cent, belong to three powers).

The distinctive feature of the present situation is the prevalence of such economic and political conditions that are bound to increase the irreconcilability between opportunism and the general and vital interests of the working-class movement: imperialism has grown from an embryo into the predominant system; capitalist monopolies occupy first place in economics and politics; the division of the world has been completed; on the other hand, instead of the undivided monopoly of Great Britain, we see a few imperialist powers contending for the right to share in this monopoly, and this struggle is characteristic of the whole period of the early twentieth century. Opportunism cannot now be completely triumphant in the working-class movement of one country for decades as it was in Britain in the second half of the nineteenth century; but in a number of countries, it has grown ripe, overripe, and rotten, and has become completely merged with bourgeois policy in the form of 'social-chauvinism'.[114]

IX. Critique of Imperialism

By the critique of imperialism, in the broad sense of the term, we mean the attitude of the different classes of society towards imperialist policy in connection with their general ideology.

The enormous dimensions of finance capital concentrated in a few hands and creating an extraordinarily dense and widespread network of relationships and connections which subordinates not only the small and medium, but also the very small capitalists and small masters, on the one hand, and the increasingly intense struggle waged against other national state groups of financiers for the division of the world and domination over other countries, on the other hand, cause the propertied classes to go over entirely to the side of imperialism. 'General' enthusiasm over the prospects of imperialism, furious defence of it and painting it in the brightest colours – such are the signs of the times. Imperialist ideology also penetrates the working class. No Chinese Wall separates it from the other classes. The leaders of the present-day, so-called, 'Social-Democratic' Party of Germany are justly called 'social-imperialists', that is, socialists in words and imperialists in deeds;

but as early as 1902, Hobson noted the existence in Britain of 'Fabian imperialists' who belonged to the opportunist Fabian Society.

Bourgeois scholars and publicists usually come out in defence of imperialism in a somewhat veiled form; they obscure its complete domination and its deep-going roots, strive to push specific and secondary details into the forefront and do their very best to distract attention from essentials by means of absolutely ridiculous schemes for 'reform', such as police supervision of the trusts or banks, etc. Cynical and frank imperialists who are bold enough to admit the absurdity of the idea of reforming the fundamental characteristics of imperialism are a rarer phenomenon.

Here is an example. The German imperialists attempt, in the magazine *Archives of World Economy*, to follow the national emancipation movements in the colonies, particularly, of course, in colonies other than those belonging to Germany. They note the unrest and the protest movements in India, the movement in Natal (South Africa), in the Dutch East Indies, etc. One of them, commenting on an English report of a conference held on 28–30 June 1910, of representatives of various subject nations and races, of peoples of Asia, Africa and Europe who are under foreign rule, writes as follows in appraising the speeches delivered at this conference:

> We are told that we must fight imperialism; that the ruling states should recognise the right of subject peoples to independence; that an international tribunal should supervise the fulfilment of treaties concluded between the great powers and weak peoples. Further than the expression of these pious wishes they do not go. We see no trace of understanding of the fact that imperialism is inseparably bound up with capitalism in its present form and that, therefore [!!], an open struggle against imperialism would be hopeless, unless, perhaps, the fight were to be confined to protests against certain of its especially abhorrent excesses.[115]

Since the reform of the basis of imperialism is a deception, a 'pious wish', since the bourgeois representatives of the oppressed nations go no 'further' forward, the bourgeois representative of an oppressing nation goes 'further' *backward*, to servility towards imperialism under cover of the claim to be 'scientific'. That is also 'logic'!

The questions as to whether it is possible to reform the basis of imperialism, whether to go forward to the further intensification and deepening of the antagonisms which it engenders, or backward, towards allaying these antagonisms, are fundamental questions in the critique of imperialism. Since the specific political features of imperialism are reaction everywhere and increased national oppression due to the oppression of the financial oligarchy and the elimination of free competition, a petty-bourgeois-democratic opposition to imperialism arose at the beginning of the twentieth century in nearly all imperialist countries. Kautsky not only did not trouble to oppose, was not only unable to oppose this petty-bourgeois reformist opposition, which is really reactionary in its economic basis, but became merged with it in practice, and this is precisely where Kautsky and the broad international Kautskian trend deserted Marxism.

In the United States, the imperialist war waged against Spain in 1898 stirred up the opposition of the 'anti-imperialists', the last of the Mohicans of bourgeois democracy who declared this war to be 'criminal', regarded the annexation of foreign territories as a violation of the Constitution, declared that the treatment of Aguinaldo, leader of the Filipinos (the Americans promised him the independence of his country, but later landed troops and annexed it), was 'jingo treachery', and quoted the words of Lincoln: 'When the white man governs himself, that is self-government; but when he governs himself and also governs others, it is no longer self-government; it is despotism.'[116] But as long as all this criticism shrank from recognising the inseverable bond between imperialism and the trusts, and, therefore, between imperialism and the foundations of capitalism, while it shrank from joining the forces engendered by large-scale capitalism and its development, it remained a 'pious wish'.

This is also the main attitude taken by Hobson in his critique of imperialism. Hobson anticipated Kautsky in protesting against the 'inevitability of imperialism' argument, and in urging the necessity of 'increasing the consuming capacity' of the people (under capitalism!). The petty-bourgeois point of view in the critique of imperialism, the omnipotence of the banks, the financial oligarchy, etc., is adopted by the authors I have often quoted, such as Agahd, A. Lansburgh, L. Eschwege, and among the French writers Victor Berard, author of a superficial book entitled *England and Imperialism* which appeared in 1900. All these authors, who make no claim to be Marxists, contrast imperialism with free competition and democracy, condemn the Baghdad railway scheme, which is leading to conflicts and war, utter 'pious wishes' for peace, etc. This applies also to the compiler of international stock and share issue statistics, A. Neymarck, who, after calculating the thousands of millions of francs representing 'international' securities, exclaimed in 1912: 'Is it possible to believe that peace may be disturbed ... that, in the face of these enormous figures, anyone would risk starting a war?'[117]

Such simple-mindedness on the part of the bourgeois economists is not surprising; moreover, *it is in their interest* to pretend to be so naive and to talk 'seriously' about peace under imperialism. But what remains of Kautsky's Marxism, when, in 1914, 1915 and 1916, he takes up the same bourgeois-reformist point of view and affirms that 'everybody is agreed' (imperialists, pseudo-socialists and social-pacifists) on the matter of peace? Instead of an analysis of imperialism and an exposure of the depths of its contradictions, we have nothing but a reformist 'pious wish' to wave them aside, to evade them.

Here is a sample of Kautsky's economic criticism of imperialism. He takes the statistics of the British export and import trade with Egypt for 1872 and 1912; it seems that this export and import trade has grown more slowly than British foreign trade as a whole. From this Kautsky concludes that 'we have no reason to suppose that without military occupation the growth of British trade with Egypt would have been less, simply as a result of the mere operation of economic factors.' 'The urge of capital to expand ... can be best promoted, not by the violent methods of imperialism, but by peaceful democracy.'[118]

This argument of Kautsky's, which is repeated in every key by his Russian armour-bearer (and Russian shielder of the social-chauvinists), Mr. Spectator, constitutes the basis of Kautskian critique of imperialism, and that is why we must deal with it in greater detail. We will begin with a quotation from Hilferding, whose conclusions Kautsky on many occasions, and notably in April 1915, has declared to have been 'unanimously adopted by all socialist theoreticians'.

'It is not the business of the proletariat', writes Hilferding,

> to contrast the more progressive capitalist policy with that of the now bygone era of free trade and of hostility towards the state. The reply of the proletariat to the economic policy of finance capital, to imperialism, cannot be free trade, but socialism. The aim of proletarian policy cannot today be the ideal of restoring free competition – which has now become a reactionary ideal – but the complete elimination of competition by the abolition of capitalism.[119]

Kautsky broke with Marxism by advocating in the epoch of finance capital a 'reactionary ideal', 'peaceful democracy', 'the mere operation of economic factors', for *objectively* this ideal drags us back from monopoly to non-monopoly capitalism, and is a reformist swindle.

Trade with Egypt (or with any other colony or semi-colony) 'would have grown more' *without* military occupation, without imperialism, and without finance capital. What does this mean? That capitalism would have developed more rapidly if free competition had not been restricted by monopolies in general, or by the 'connections', yoke (i.e., also the monopoly) of finance capital, or by the monopolist possession of colonies by certain countries?

Kautsky's argument can have no other meaning; and *this* 'meaning' is meaningless. Let us assume that free competition, without any sort of monopoly, would have developed capitalism and trade more rapidly. But the more rapidly trade and capitalism develop, the greater is the concentration of production and capital which *gives rise* to monopoly. And monopolies have *already* arisen – precisely out of free competition! Even if monopolies have now begun to retard progress, it is not an argument in favour of free competition, which has become impossible after it has given rise to monopoly.

Whichever way one turns Kautsky's argument, one will find nothing in it except reaction and bourgeois reformism.

Even if we correct this argument and say, as Spectator says, that the trade of the colonies with Britain is now developing more slowly than their trade with other countries, it does not save Kautsky; for it *is also* monopoly, *also* imperialism that is beating Great Britain, only it is the monopoly and imperialism of another country (America, Germany). It is known that the cartels have given rise to a new and peculiar form of protective tariffs, i.e., goods suitable for export are protected (Engels noted this in Vol. III of *Capital*).[120] It is known, too, that the cartels add finance capital have a system peculiar to themselves, that of 'exporting goods at cut-rate prices', or 'dumping', as the English call it: within a given country the cartel sells its goods at high monopoly prices, but sells them abroad at a much lower price to undercut the competitor, to enlarge its own production to the utmost, etc. If Germany's trade with the British colonies is developing more rapidly than Great Britain's, it only proves that German imperialism is younger, stronger and better organised than British imperialism, is superior to it; but it by no means proves the 'superiority' of free trade, for it is not a fight between free trade and protection and colonial dependence, but between two rival imperialisms, two monopolies, two groups of finance capital. The superiority of German imperialism over British imperialism is more potent than the wall of colonial frontiers or of protective tariffs: to use this as an 'argument' in *favour* of free trade and 'peaceful democracy' is banal, it means forgetting the essential features and characteristics of imperialism, substituting petty-bourgeois reformism for Marxism.

It is interesting to note that even the bourgeois economist, A. Lansburgh, whose criticism of imperialism is as petty-bourgeois as Kautsky's, nevertheless got closer to a more scientific study of trade statistics. He did not compare one single country, chosen at random, and one single colony with the other countries; he examined the export trade of an imperialist country: (1) with countries which are financially dependent upon it, and borrow money from it; and (2) with countries which are financially independent. He obtained the following results [see Table 21].

Lansburgh did not draw *conclusions* and therefore, strangely enough, failed to observe that if the figures prove anything at all, they prove that *he is wrong*, for the exports to countries financially dependent on Germany have grown *more rapidly*, if only slightly, than exports to the countries which are financially independent. (I emphasise the 'if', for Lansburgh's figures are far from complete.)

Table 21. Export Trade of Germany (000,000 marks)

To countries financially dependent on Germany	1889	1908	Per cent increase
Romania	48.2	70.8	47
Portugal	19.0	32.8	73
Argentina	60.7	147.0	143
Brazil	48.7	84.5	73
Chile	28.3	64.0	114
Total	234.8	451.5	92
To countries financially dependent of Germany			
Great Britain	651.8	997.4	53
France	210.2	437.9	108
Belgium	137.2	322.8	135
Switzerland	177.4	401.1	127
Australia	21.2	64.5	205
Dutch East Indies	8.8	40.7	363
Total	1,206.6	2,264.4	87

Tracing the connection between exports and loans, Lansburgh writes:

In 1890–91, a Romanian loan was floated through the German banks, which had already in previous years made advances on this loan. It was used chiefly to purchase railway materials in Germany. In 1891, German exports to Romania amounted to 55 million marks. The following year they dropped to 39.4 million marks and, with fluctuations, to 25.4 million in 1900. Only in very recent years have they regained the level of 1891, thanks to two new loans.

German exports to Portugal rose, following the loans of 1888 – to 21,100,000 (1890); then, in the two following years, they dropped to 16,200,000 and 7,400,000, and regained their former level only in 1903.

The figures of German trade with Argentina are still more striking. Loans were floated in 1888 and 1890; German exports to Argentina reached 60,700,000 marks (1889). Two years later they amounted to only 18,600,000 marks, less than one-third of the previous figure. It was not until 1901 that they regained and surpassed the level of 1889, and then only as a result of new loans floated by the state and by municipalities, with advances to build power stations, and with other credit operations.

Exports to Chile, as a consequence of the loan of 1889, rose to 45,200,000 marks (in 1892), and a year later dropped to 22,500,000 marks. A new Chilean loan floated by the German banks in 1906 was followed by a rise of exports to 84,700,000 marks in 1907, only to fall again to 52,400,000 marks in 1908.[121]

From these facts Lansburgh draws the amusing petty-bourgeois moral of how unstable and irregular export trade is when it is bound up with loans, how bad it is to invest capital abroad instead of 'naturally' and 'harmoniously' developing home industry, how 'costly' are the millions in bakshish that Krupp has to pay in floating foreign loans, etc. But the facts tell us clearly: the increase in exports is connected with just *these* swindling tricks of finance capital, which is not concerned with bourgeois morality, but with skinning the ox twice – first, it pockets the profits from the loan; then it pockets other profits from the *same* loan which the borrower uses to make purchases from Krupp, or to purchase railway material from the Steel Syndicate, etc.

I repeat that I do not by any means consider Lansburgh's figures to be perfect; but I had to quote them because they are more scientific than Kautsky's and Spectator's and because Lansburgh showed the correct way to approach the question. In discussing the significance of finance capital in regard to exports, etc., one must be able to single out the connection of exports especially and solely with the tricks of the financiers, especially and solely with the sale of goods by cartels, etc. Simply to compare colonies with non-colonies, one imperialism with another imperialism, one semi-colony or colony (Egypt) with all other countries, is to evade and to obscure the very *essence* of the question.

Kautsky's theoretical critique of imperialism has nothing in common with Marxism and serves only as a preamble to propaganda for peace and unity with the opportunists and the social-chauvinists, precisely for the reason that it evades and obscures the very profound and fundamental contradictions of imperialism: the contradictions between monopoly and free competition which exists side by side with it, between the gigantic 'operations' (and gigantic profits) of finance capital and 'honest' trade in the free market, the contradiction between cartels and trusts, on the one hand, and non-cartelised industry, on the other, etc.

The notorious theory of 'ultra-imperialism', invented by Kautsky, is just as reactionary. Compare his arguments on this subject in 1915, with Hobson's arguments in 1902.

Kautsky: '... Cannot the present imperialist policy be supplanted by a new, ultra-imperialist policy, which will introduce the joint exploitation of the world by internationally united finance capital in place of the mutual rivalries of national finance capitals? Such a new phase of capitalism is at any rate conceivable. Can it be achieved? Sufficient premises are still lacking to enable us to answer this question.'[122]

Hobson: 'Christendom thus laid out in a few great federal empires, each with a retinue of uncivilised dependencies, seems to many the most legitimate development of present tendencies, and one which would offer the best hope of permanent peace on an assured basis of inter-imperialism.'

Kautsky called ultra-imperialism or super-imperialism what Hobson, thirteen years earlier, described as inter-imperialism. Except for coining a new and clever catchword, replacing one Latin prefix by another, the only progress Kautsky has made in the sphere of 'scientific' thought is that he gave out as Marxism what Hobson, in effect, described as the cant of English parsons. After the Anglo-Boer War it was quite natural for this highly honourable caste to exert their main efforts to *console* the British middle class and the workers who had lost many of their relatives on the battlefields of South Africa and who were obliged to pay higher taxes in order to guarantee still higher profits for the British financiers. And what better consolation could there be than the theory that imperialism is not so bad; that it stands close to inter- (or ultra-) imperialism, which can ensure permanent peace? No matter what the good intentions of the English parsons, or of sentimental Kautsky, may have been, the only objective, i.e., real, social significance of Kautsky's 'theory' is this: it is a most reactionary method of consoling the masses with hopes of permanent peace being possible under capitalism, by distracting their attention from the sharp antagonisms and acute problems of the present times, and directing it towards illusory prospects of an imaginary 'ultraimperialism' of the future. Deception of the masses – that is all there is in Kautsky's 'Marxist' theory.

Indeed, it is enough to compare well-known and indisputable facts to become convinced of the utter falsity of the prospects which Kautsky tries to conjure up before the German workers (and the workers of all lands). Let us consider India, Indo-China and China. It is known that these three colonial and semi-colonial countries, with a population of six to seven hundred million, are subjected to the exploitation of the finance capital of several imperialist powers: Great Britain, France, Japan, the USA, etc. Let us assume that these imperialist countries form alliances against one another in order to protect or enlarge their possessions, their interests and their spheres of influence in these Asiatic states; these alliances will be 'inter-imperialist', or 'ultra-imperialist' alliances. Let us assume that *all* the imperialist countries conclude an alliance for the 'peaceful' division of these parts of Asia; this alliance would be an alliance of 'internationally united finance capital'. There are actual examples of alliances of this kind in the history of the twentieth century – the attitude of the powers to China, for instance. We ask, is it 'conceivable', assuming that the capitalist system remains intact – and this is precisely the assumption that Kautsky does make – that such alliances would be more than temporary, that they would eliminate friction, conflicts and struggle in every possible form?

The question has only to be presented clearly for any other than a negative answer to be impossible. This is because the only conceivable basis under capitalism for the division of spheres of influence, interests, colonies, etc., is a calculation of the *strength* of those participating, their general economic, financial, military strength, etc. And the strength of these participants in the division does not change to an equal degree, for the *even* development of different undertakings, trusts, branches of industry, or countries is impossible under capitalism. Half a century ago Germany was a miserable, insignificant country, if her capitalist strength is compared with that of the Britain of that time; Japan compared with Russia in the same way. Is it 'conceivable' that in ten or twenty years' time the relative strength of the imperialist powers will have remained unchanged? It is out of the question.

Therefore, in the realities of the capitalist system, and not in the banal philistine fantasies of English parsons, or of the German 'Marxist', Kautsky, 'inter-imperialist' or 'ultra-imperialist' alliances, no matter what form they may assume, whether of one imperialist coalition against another, or of a general alliance embracing *all* the imperialist powers, are *inevitably nothing* more than a 'truce' in periods between wars. Peaceful alliances prepare the ground for wars, and in their turn grow out of wars; the one conditions the other, producing alternating forms of peaceful and non-peaceful struggle on *one and the same* basis of imperialist connections and relations within world economics and world politics. But in order to pacify the workers and reconcile them with the social-chauvinists who have deserted to the side of the bourgeoisie, over-wise Kautsky *separates* one link of a single chain from another, separates the present peaceful (and ultra-imperialist, nay, ultra-ultra-imperialist) alliance of *all* the powers for the 'pacification' of China (remember the suppression of the Boxer Rebellion) from the non-peaceful conflict of tomorrow, which will prepare the ground for another 'peaceful' general alliance for the partition, say, of Turkey, on the day after tomorrow, *etc., etc.* Instead of showing the living connection between periods of imperialist peace and periods of imperialist war, Kautsky presents the workers with a lifeless abstraction in order to reconcile them to their lifeless leaders.

An American writer, Hill, in his *A History of the Diplomacy in the International Development of Europe* refers in his preface to the following periods in the recent history of diplomacy: (1) the era of revolution; (2) the constitutional movement; (3) the present era of 'commercial imperialism'.[123] Another writer divides the history of Great Britain's 'world policy' since 1870 into four periods: (1) the first Asiatic period (that of the struggle against Russia's advance in Central Asia towards India); (2) the African period (approximately 1885–1902): that of the struggle against France for the partition of Africa (the 'Fashoda incident' of 1898 which brought her within a hair's breadth of war with France); (3) the second Asiatic period (alliance with Japan against Russia); and (4) the 'European' period, chiefly anti-German.[124] 'The political patrol clashes take place on the financial field,' wrote the banker Riesser in 1905, in showing how French finance capital operating in Italy was preparing the way for a political alliance of these countries, and how a conflict was developing between Germany and Great Britain over Persia, between all the European capitalists over Chinese loans, etc. Behold, the living reality of peaceful 'ultra-imperialist' alliances in their inseverable connection with ordinary imperialist conflicts!

Kautsky's obscuring of the deepest contradictions of imperialism, which inevitably boils down to painting imperialism in bright colours, leaves its traces in this writer's criticism of the political features of imperialism. Imperialism is the epoch of finance capital and of monopolies, which introduce everywhere the striving for domination, not for freedom. Whatever the political system, the result of these tendencies is everywhere reaction and an extreme intensification of antagonisms in this field. Particularly intensified become the yoke of national oppression and the striving for annexations, i.e., the violation of national independence (for annexation is nothing but the violation of the right of nations to self-determination). Hilferding rightly notes the connection between imperialism and the intensification of national oppression. 'In the newly opened-up countries', he writes,

> the capital imported into them intensifies antagonisms and excites against the intruders the constantly growing resistance of the peoples who are awakening to national consciousness; this resistance can easily develop into dangerous measures against foreign capital. The old social relations become completely revolutionised, the age-long agrarian isolation of 'nations without history' is destroyed and they are drawn into the capitalist whirlpool. Capitalism itself gradually provides the subjugated with the means and resources for their emancipation and they set out to achieve the goal which once seemed highest to the European nations: the creation of a united national state as a means to economic and cultural freedom. This movement for national independence threatens European capital in its most valuable and most promising fields of exploitation, and European capital can maintain its domination only by continually increasing its military forces.[125]

To this must be added that it is not only in newly opened-up countries, but also in the old, that imperialism is leading to annexation, to increased national oppression, and, consequently, also to increasing

resistance. While objecting to the intensification of political reaction by imperialism, Kautsky leaves in the shade a question that has
become particularly urgent, viz., the impossibility of unity with the
opportunists in the epoch of imperialism. While objecting to annexations, he presents his objections in a form that is most acceptable and
least offensive to the opportunists. He addresses himself to a German
audience, yet he obscures the most topical and important point, for
instance, the annexation of Alsace-Lorraine by Germany. In order to
appraise this 'mental aberration' of Kautsky's I shall take the following
example. Let us suppose that a Japanese condemns the annexation of
the Philippines by the Americans. The question is: will many believe
that he does so because he has a horror of annexations as such, and
not because he himself has a desire to annex the Philippines? And shall
we not be constrained to admit that the 'fight' the Japanese is waging
against annexations can be regarded as being sincere and politically
honest only if he fights against the annexation of Korea by Japan, and
urges freedom for Korea to secede from Japan?

Kautsky's theoretical analysis of imperialism, as well as his economic
and political critique of imperialism, are permeated *through and through*
with a spirit, absolutely irreconcilable with Marxism, of obscuring and
glossing over the fundamental contradictions of imperialism and with
a striving to preserve at all costs the crumbling unity with opportunism
in the European working-class movement.

X. The Place of Imperialism in History

We have seen that in its economic essence imperialism is monopoly
capitalism. This in itself determines its place in history, for monopoly
that grows out of the soil of free competition, and precisely out of free
competition, is the transition from the capitalist system to a higher
socio-economic order. We must take special note of the four principal
types of monopoly, or principal manifestations of monopoly capitalism,
which are characteristic of the epoch we are examining.

Firstly, monopoly arose out of the concentration of production at
a very high stage. This refers to the monopolist capitalist associations,

cartels, syndicates, and trusts. We have seen the important part these play in present-day economic life. At the beginning of the twentieth century, monopolies had acquired complete supremacy in the advanced countries, and although the first steps towards the formation of the cartels were taken by countries enjoying the protection of high tariffs (Germany, America), Great Britain, with her system of free trade, revealed the same basic phenomenon, only a little later, namely, the birth of monopoly out of the concentration of production.

Secondly, monopolies have stimulated the seizure of the most important sources of raw materials, especially for the basic and most highly cartelised industries in capitalist society: the coal and iron industries. The monopoly of the most important sources of raw materials has enormously increased the power of big capital, and has sharpened the antagonism between cartelised and non-cartelised industry.

Thirdly, monopoly has sprung from the banks. The banks have developed from modest middleman enterprises into the monopolists of finance capital. Some three to five of the biggest banks in each of the foremost capitalist countries have achieved the 'personal link-up' between industrial and bank capital, and have concentrated in their hands the control of thousands upon thousands of millions which form the greater part of the capital and income of entire countries. A financial oligarchy, which throws a close network of dependence relationships over all the economic and political institutions of present-day bourgeois society without exception – such is the most striking manifestation of this monopoly.

Fourthly, monopoly has grown out of colonial policy. To the numerous 'old' motives of colonial policy, finance capital has added the struggle for the sources of raw materials, for the export of capital, for spheres of influence, i.e., for spheres for profitable deals, concessions, monopoly profits and so on, economic territory in general. When the colonies of the European powers, for instance, comprised only one-tenth of the territory of Africa (as was the case in 1876), colonial policy was able to develop – by methods other than those of monopoly – by the 'free grabbing' of territories, so to speak. But when nine-tenths of Africa had been seized (by 1900), when the whole world had been divided up, there was inevitably ushered in the era of monopoly possession of colonies and, consequently, of particularly intense struggle for the division and the redivision of the world.

The extent to which monopolist capital has intensified all the contradictions of capitalism is generally known. It is sufficient to mention the high cost of living and the tyranny of the cartels. This intensification of contradictions constitutes the most powerful driving force of the transitional period of history, which began from the time of the final victory of world finance capital.

Monopolies, oligarchy, the striving for domination and not for freedom, the exploitation of an increasing number of small or weak nations by a handful of the richest or most powerful nations – all these have given birth to those distinctive characteristics of imperialism which compel us to define it as parasitic or decaying capitalism. More and more prominently there emerges, as one of the tendencies of imperialism, the creation of the 'rentier state', the usurer state, in which the bourgeoisie to an ever-increasing degree lives on the proceeds of capital exports and by 'clipping coupons'. It would be a mistake to believe that this tendency to decay precludes the rapid growth of capitalism. It does not. In the epoch of imperialism, certain branches of industry, certain strata of the bourgeoisie and certain countries betray, to a greater or lesser degree, now one and now another of these tendencies. On the whole, capitalism is growing far more rapidly than before; but this growth is not only becoming more and more uneven in general, its unevenness also manifests itself, in particular, in the decay of the countries which are richest in capital (Britain).

In regard to the rapidity of Germany's economic development, Riesser, the author of the book on the big German banks, states:

> The progress of the preceding period (1848–70), which had not been exactly slow, compares with the rapidity with which the whole of Germany's national economy, and with it German banking, progressed during this period (1870–1905) in about the same way as the speed of the mail coach in the good old days compares with the speed of the present-day automobile ... which is whizzing past so fast that it endangers not only innocent pedestrians in its path, but also the occupants of the car.

In its turn, this finance capital which has grown with such extraordinary rapidity is not unwilling, precisely because it has grown so quickly, to pass on to a more 'tranquil' possession of colonies which have to be seized – and not only by peaceful methods – from richer nations. In the United States, economic development in the last decades has been even more rapid than in Germany, *and for this very reason*, the parasitic features of modern American capitalism have stood out with particular prominence. On the other hand, a comparison of, say, the republican American bourgeoisie with the monarchist Japanese or German bourgeoisie shows that the most pronounced political distinction diminishes to an extreme degree in the epoch of imperialism – not because it is unimportant in general, but because in all these cases we are talking about a bourgeoisie which has definite features of parasitism.

The receipt of high monopoly profits by the capitalists in one of the numerous branches of industry, in one of the numerous countries, etc., makes it economically possible for them to bribe certain sections of the workers, and for a time a fairly considerable minority of them, and win them to the side of the bourgeoisie of a given industry or given nation against all the others. The intensification of antagonisms between imperialist nations for the division of the world increases this urge. And so there is created that bond between imperialism and opportunism, which revealed itself first and most clearly in Great Britain, owing to the fact that certain features of imperialist development were observable there much earlier than in other countries. Some writers, L. Martov, for example, are prone to wave aside the connection between imperialism and opportunism in the working-class movement – a particularly glaring fact at the present time – by resorting to 'official optimism' (à la Kautsky and Huysmans) like the following: the cause of the opponents of capitalism would be hopeless if it were progressive capitalism that led to the increase of opportunism, or, if it were the best-paid workers who were inclined towards opportunism, etc. We must have no illusions about 'optimism' of this kind. It is optimism in respect of opportunism; it is optimism which serves to conceal opportunism. As a matter of fact, the extraordinary rapidity and the particularly revolting character of the development of opportunism is by no means a guarantee that its victory will be durable: the rapid growth of a painful abscess on a healthy body can only cause it to burst more quickly and thus relieve the body of it. The most dangerous of all in this respect are those who do not wish to understand that the fight against imperialism is a sham and humbug unless it is inseparably bound up with the fight against opportunism.

From all that has been said in this book on the economic essence of imperialism, it follows that we must define it as capitalism in transition, or, more precisely, as moribund capitalism. It is very instructive in this respect to note that bourgeois economists, in describing modern capitalism, frequently employ catchwords and phrases like 'interlocking', 'absence of isolation', etc.; 'in conformity with their functions and course of development', banks are 'not purely private business enterprises: they are more and more outgrowing the sphere of purely private business regulation'. And this very Riesser, whose words I have just quoted, declares with all seriousness that the 'prophecy' of the Marxists concerning 'socialisation' has 'not come true'!

What then does this catchword 'interlocking' express? It merely expresses the most striking feature of the process going on before our eyes. It shows that the observer counts the separate trees, but cannot see the wood. It slavishly copies the superficial, the fortuitous, the chaotic. It reveals the observer as one who is overwhelmed by the mass of raw material and is utterly incapable of appreciating its meaning and importance. Ownership of shares, the relations between owners of private property 'interlock in a haphazard way'. But underlying this interlocking, its very base, are the changing social relations of production. When a big enterprise assumes gigantic proportions, and, on the basis of an exact computation of mass data, organises according to plan the supply of primary raw materials to the extent of two-thirds, or three-fourths, of all that is necessary for tens of millions of people; when the raw materials are transported in a systematic and organised manner to the most suitable places of production, sometimes situated hundreds or thousands of miles from each other; when a single centre directs all the consecutive stages of processing the material right up to the manufacture of numerous varieties of finished articles; when these products are distributed according to a single plan among tens and hundreds of millions of consumers (the marketing of oil in America and Germany by the American oil trust) – then it becomes evident

230 of Imperialism and the National Question

that we have socialisation of production, and not mere 'interlocking', that private economic and private property relations constitute a shell which no longer fits its contents, a shell which must inevitably decay if its removal is artificially delayed, a shell which may remain in a state of decay for a fairly long period (if, at the worst, the cure of the opportunist abscess is protracted), but which will inevitably be removed.

The enthusiastic admirer of German imperialism, Schulze-Gaevernitz, exclaims:

> Once the supreme management of the German banks has been entrusted to the hands of a dozen persons, their activity is even today more significant for the public good than that of the majority of the Ministers of State … (The 'interlocking' of bankers, ministers, magnates of industry and rentiers is here conveniently forgotten.) If we imagine the development of those tendencies we have noted carried to their logical conclusion we will have: the money capital of the nation united in the banks; the banks themselves combined into cartels; the investment capital of the nation cast in the shape of securities. Then the forecast of that genius Saint-Simon will be fulfilled: 'The present anarchy of production, which corresponds to the fact that economic relations are developing without uniform regulation, must make way for organisation in production. Production will no longer be directed by isolated manufacturers, independent of each other and ignorant of man's economic needs; that will be done by a certain public institution. A central committee of management, being able to survey the large field of social economy from a more elevated point of view, will regulate it for the benefit of the whole of society, will put the means of production into suitable hands, and above all will take care that there be constant harmony between production and consumption. Institutions already exist which have assumed as part of their functions a certain organisation of economic labour, the banks.' We are still a long way from the fulfilment of Saint-Simon's forecast, but we are on the way towards it: Marxism, different from what Marx imagined, but different only in form.[126]

A crushing 'refutation' of Marx indeed, which retreats a step from Marx's precise, scientific analysis to Saint-Simon's guesswork, the guesswork of a genius, but guesswork all the same.

The Discussion on Self-Determination Summed Up[1]

Issue No. 2 of the *Herald* (*Vorbote* No. 2, April 1916), the Marxist journal of the Zimmerwald Left, published theses for and against the self-determination of nations, signed by the Editorial Board of our Central Organ, *Sotsial-Demokrat,* and by the Editorial Board of the organ of the Polish Social-Democratic opposition, *Gazeta Robotnicza.* Above the reader will find a reprint of the former[2] and a translation of the latter theses.[3] This is practically the first time that the question has been presented so extensively in the international field: it was raised only in respect of Poland in the discussion carried on in the German Marxist journal *Neue Zeit* twenty years ago, 1895–6, before the London International Socialist Congress of 1896, by Rosa Luxemburg, Karl Kautsky and the Polish 'independents' (champions of the independence of Poland, the Polish Socialist Party), who represented three different views.[4] [see The Rights of Nations to Self-Determination] Since then, as far as we know, the question of self-determination has been discussed at all systematically only by the Dutch and the Poles. Let us hope that the *Herald* will succeed in promoting the discussion of this question, so urgent today, among the British, Americans, French, Germans and Italians. Official socialism, represented both by direct supporters of 'their own' governments, the Plekhanovs, Davids and Co., and the undercover defenders of opportunism, the Kautskyites (among them Axelrod, Martov, Chkheidze and others), has told so many lies on this question that for a long time there will inevitably be efforts, on the one hand, to maintain silence and evade the issue, and, on the other, workers' demands for 'direct answers' to these 'accursed questions'.

We shall try to keep our readers informed of the struggle between the trends: among socialists abroad.

This question is of specific importance to us Russian Social-Democrats; the present discussion is a continuation of the one that took place in 1903 and 1913;[5] during the war this question has been the cause of some wavering in the thinking of Party members: it has been made more acute by the trickery of such prominent leaders of the Gvozdyov or chauvinist workers' party as Martov and Chkheidze, in their efforts to evade the substance of the problem. It is essential, therefore, to sum up at least the initial results of the discussion that has been started in the international field.

It will be seen from the theses that our Polish comrades provide us with a direct answer to some of our arguments, for example, on Marxism and Proudhonism. In most cases, however, they do not answer us directly but indirectly, by opposing *their* assertions to ours. Let us examine both their direct and indirect answers.

1. Socialism and the Self-Determination of Nations

We have affirmed that it would be a betrayal of socialism to refuse to implement the self-determination of nations under socialism. We are told in reply that 'the right of self-determination is not applicable to a socialist society'. The difference is a radical one. Where does it stem from?

'We know', runs our opponents' reasoning, 'that socialism will abolish every kind of national oppression since it abolishes the class interests that lead to it ...' What has this argument about the *economic* prerequisites for the abolition of national oppression, which are very well known and undisputed, to do with a discussion of *one* of the forms of *political* oppression, namely, the forcible retention of one nation within the state frontiers of another? This is nothing but an attempt to evade political questions! And subsequent arguments further convince us *that* our judgement is right:

We have no reason to believe that in a socialist society, the nation will exist as an economic and political unit. It will in all probability assume the character of a cultural and linguistic unit only, because the territorial division of a socialist cultural zone, if practised at all, can be made only according to the needs of production and, furthermore, the question of such a division will naturally not be decided by individual nations alone and in possession of full sovereignty [as is required by 'the right to self-determination'], but will be *determined jointly* by all the citizens concerned ...

Our Polish comrades like this last argument, on *joint* determination instead of *self-determination,* so much that they repeat it *three times* in their theses! Frequency of repetition, however, does not turn this Octobrist and reactionary argument into a Social-Democratic argument. All reactionaries and bourgeois grant to nations forcibly retained within the frontiers of a given state the right to 'determine jointly' their fate in a common parliament. Wilhelm II also gives the Belgians the right to 'determine jointly' the fate of the German Empire in a common German parliament.

Our opponents try to evade precisely the point at issue. the only one that is up for discussion – the right to secede. This would be funny if it were not so tragic!

Our very first thesis said that the liberation of oppressed nations implies a dual transformation in the political sphere: (1) the full equality of nations. This is not disputed and applies only to what takes place within the state; (2) freedom of political separation. This refers to the demarcation of state frontiers. This *only* is disputed. But it is precisely this that our opponents remain silent about. They do not want to think either about state frontiers or even about the state as such. This is a sort of 'imperialist Economism' like the old Economism of 1894–1902, which argued in this way: capitalism is victorious, *therefore* political questions are a waste of time. Imperialism is victorious, *therefore* political questions are a waste of time! Such an apolitical theory is extremely harmful to Marxism.

In his *Critique of the Gotha Programme, Marx* wrote: 'Between capitalist and communist society lies the period of the revolutionary transformation of the one into the other. There corresponds to this also a political transition period in which the state can be nothing but the revolutionary dictatorship of the proletariat.'[6] Up to now this truth has been indisputable for socialists and it includes the recognition of the fact that the *state* will exist until victorious socialism develops into full communism. Engels's dictum about the *withering away* of the state is well known. We deliberately stressed, in the first thesis, that democracy is a form of state that will also wither away when the state withers away. And until our opponents replace Marxism by some sort of 'non-state' viewpoint their arguments will constitute one big mistake.

Instead of speaking about the state (which *means*, about the demarcation of its *frontiers*!), they speak of a 'socialist cultural zone', i.e., they deliberately choose an expression that is indefinite in the sense that all state questions are obliterated! Thus, we get a ridiculous tautology: if there is no state there can, of course, be no question of frontiers. In that case the *whole* democratic-political programme is unnecessary. Nor will there be any republic when the state 'withers away'.

The German chauvinist Lensch, in the articles we mentioned in Thesis 5 (footnote), quoted an interesting passage from Engels's article 'The Po and the Rhine'. Amongst other things, Engels says in this article that in the course of historical development, which swallowed up a number of small and non-viable nations, the 'frontiers of great and viable European nations' were being increasingly determined by the 'language and sympathies' of the population. Engels calls these frontiers 'natural'.[7] Such was the case in the period of progressive capitalism in Europe, roughly from 1848 to 1871. Today, these democratically determined frontiers are more and more often being *broken down* by reactionary, imperialist capitalism. There is every sign that imperialism will leave its successor, socialism, a heritage of *less* democratic frontiers, a number of annexations in Europe and in other parts of the world. Is it to be supposed that victorious socialism, restoring and implementing full democracy all along the line, will refrain from *democratically* demarcating state frontiers and ignore the 'sympathies' of the population? Those questions need only be stated to make it quite clear that our Polish colleagues are sliding down from Marxism towards imperialist Economism.

The old Economists, who made a caricature of Marxism, told the workers that 'only the economic' was of importance to Marxists. The new Economists seem to think either that the democratic state of victorious socialism will exist without frontiers (like a 'complex of sensations' without matter) or that frontiers will be delineated 'only' in accordance with the needs of production. In actual fact its frontiers will be delineated *democratically*, i.e., in accordance with the will and 'sympathies' of the population. Capitalism rides roughshod over these sympathies, adding more obstacles to the rapprochement of nations. Socialism, by organising production *without* class oppression, by ensuring the well-being of *all* members of the state, gives *full play* to the 'sympathies' of the population, thereby promoting and greatly accelerating the drawing together and fusion of the nations.

To give the reader a rest from the heavy and clumsy Economism let us quote the reasoning of a socialist writer who is outside our dispute. That writer is Otto Bauer, who also has his own 'pet little point' – 'cultural and national autonomy' – but who argues quite correctly on a large number of most important questions. For example, in Chapter 29 of his book *The National Question and Social-Democracy*, he was doubly right in noting the use of national ideology to cover up *imperialist* policies. In Chapter 30, 'Socialism and the Principle of Nationality', he says:

> The socialist community will never be able to include whole nations within its make-up by the use of force. Imagine the masses of the people, enjoying the blessings of national culture, taking a full and active part in legislation and government, and, finally, supplied with arms – would it be possible to subordinate such a nation to the rule of an alien social organism by force? All state power rests on the force of arms. The present-day people's army, thanks to an ingenious mechanism, still constitutes a tool in the hands of a definite person, family or class exactly like the knightly and mercenary armies of the past. The army of the democratic community of a socialist society is nothing but the people armed, since it consists of highly cultured persons, working without compulsion in socialised workshops and taking full part in all spheres of political life. In such conditions any possibility of alien rule disappears.

This is true. It is *impossible* to abolish national (or any other political) oppression under capitalism, since this *requires* the abolition of classes, i.e., the introduction of socialism. But while being based on economics, socialism cannot be reduced to economics alone. A foundation – socialist production – is essential for the abolition of national oppression, but this foundation must *also* carry a democratically organised state, a democratic army, etc. By transforming capitalism into socialism the proletariat creates the *possibility* of abolishing national oppression; the possibility becomes *reality* 'only' – 'only'! – with the establishment of full democracy in all spheres, including the delineation of state frontiers in accordance with the 'sympathies' of the population, including complete freedom to secede. And this, in turn, will serve as a basis for developing the *practical* elimination of even the slightest national friction and the least national mistrust, for an accelerated drawing together and fusion of nations that will be completed when the state *withers away*. This is the Marxist theory, the theory from which our Polish colleagues have mistakenly departed.

2. Is Democracy 'Practicable' Under Imperialism

The old polemic conducted by Polish Social-Democrats against the self-determination of nations is based entirely on the argument that it is 'impracticable' under capitalism. As long ago as 1903 we, the *Iskra* supporters, laughed at this argument in the Programme Commission of the Second Congress of the RSDLP and said that it was repetition of the distortion of Marxism preached by the (late lamented) Economists. In our theses we dealt with this error in particular detail and it is precisely on this point, which contains the theoretical kernel of the whole dispute, that the Polish comrades did not wish to (or could not?) answer *any* of our arguments.

To prove the economic impossibility of self-determination would require an economic analysis such as that used to prove the impracticability of prohibiting machines or introducing labour-money, etc. No one has even attempted to make such an analysis. No one will maintain that it has been possible to introduce 'labour-money' under capitalism 'by way of exception' in even one country, in the way it was possible for one small country to realise this impracticable self-determination, even without war or revolution, 'by way of exception', in the era of the most rabid imperialism (Norway, 1905).

In general, political democracy is merely one of the possible *forms* of superstructure *above* capitalism (although it is theoretically the normal one for 'pure' capitalism). The facts show that both capitalism and imperialism develop within the framework of *any* political form and subordinate them *all*. It is, therefore, a basic theoretical error to speak of the 'impracticability' of *one* of the forms and of *one* of the demands of democracy.

The absence of an answer to these arguments from our Polish colleagues compels us to consider the discussion closed on this point. To make it graphic, so to say, we made the very concrete assertion that it would be 'ridiculous' to deny the 'practicability' of the restoration of Poland today, making it dependent on the strategic and other aspects of the present war. No reply was forthcoming!

The Polish comrades simply *repeated* an obviously incorrect assertion (§ II, 1), saying that 'in questions of the annexation of foreign territories, forms of political democracy are pushed aside; sheer force is decisive … Capital will never allow the people to decide the question of their state frontiers …' As though 'capital' could 'allow the people' to select *its* civil servants, the servants of imperialism! Or as though weighty decisions on important democratic questions, such as the *establishment* of a republic in place of a monarchy, or a militia in place of a regular army, were, *in general*, conceivable without 'sheer force'. Subjectively, the Polish comrades want to make Marxism 'more profound', but they are doing it altogether unsuccessfully. *Objectively*, their phrases about impracticability are opportunism, because their tacit assumption is: this is 'impracticable' *without* a series of revolutions, in the same way as democracy *as a whole*, *all* its demands taken together, is impracticable under imperialism.

Once only, at the very end of § II,1, in the discussion on Alsace, our Polish colleagues abandoned the position of imperialist Economism and approached the question of one of the forms of democracy with a concrete answer and not with general references to the 'economic'. And it was precisely this approach that was wrong! It would, they wrote, be 'particularist, undemocratic' if *some* Algatians, without asking the French, were to 'impose' on them a union with Alsace, although part of Alsace was German-oriented and this threatened war!!! The confusion is amusing: self-determination presumes (this is in itself clear, and we have given it special emphasis in our theses) freedom to *separate* from the oppressor state; but the fact that *union* with a state presumes the consent of *that state* is something that is 'not customarily' mentioned in politics any more than the 'consent' of a capitalist to receive profit or of a worker to receive wages is mentioned in economics! It is ridiculous even to speak of such a thing.

If one wants to be a Marxist politician, one should, in speaking of Alsace, attack the German socialist scoundrels for not fighting for Alsace's freedom to secede and attack the French socialist scoundrels for making their peace with the French bourgeoisie who want to annex the whole of Alsace by force – and both of them for serving the imperialism of 'their own' country and for fearing a separate state, even if only a little one – the thing is to show *how* the socialists who recognise self-determination would solve the problem in a few weeks without going against the will of the Alsatians. To argue, instead, about the horrible danger of the French Alsatians 'forcing' themselves on France is a real pearl.

3. What Is Annexation?

We raised this question in a most definite manner in our theses (Section 7). The Polish comrades did *not* reply to it: they evaded it, insisting (1) that they are against annexations and explaining (2) why they are against them. It is true that these are very important questions. But they are questions of *another kind*. If we want our principles to be theoretically sound at all, if we want them to be clearly and precisely formulated, we cannot *evade* the question of what an annexation is, since this concept is used in our political propaganda and agitation. The evasion of the question in a discussion between colleagues cannot be interpreted as anything but desertion of one's position.

Why have we raised this question? We explained this when we raised it. It is because 'a protest against annexations is nothing but recognition of the right to Self-determination'. The concept of annexation usually includes: (1) the concept of force (joining by means of force); (2) the concept of oppression by another nation (the joining of '*alien*' regions, etc.), and, sometimes, (3) the concept of violation of the *status quo*. We pointed this out in the theses and this did not meet with any criticism.

Can Social-Democrats be against the use of force in general, it may be asked? Obviously not. This means that we are against annexations not because they constitute force, but for some other reason. Nor can the Social-Democrats be for the *status quo*. However you may twist and turn, annexation is *violation of the self-determination* of a nation, it is the establishment of state *frontiers contrary to the will of the population*.

To be against annexations *means* to be in favour of the right to self-determination. To be 'against the forcible retention of any nation within the frontiers of a given state' (we deliberately employed this slightly changed formulation of the same idea in Section 4 of our theses, and the Polish comrades *answered* us with *complete* clarity at the beginning of their § I, 4, *that* they 'are against the forcible retention of oppressed nations within the frontiers of the annexing state') – is *the same* as being in favour of the self-determination of nations.

We do not want to haggle over words. If there is a party that says in its programme (or in a resolution binding on all the form does not matter) that it is against annexations,[8] against the forcible retention of oppressed nations within the frontiers of *its* state, we declare our complete agreement in principle with that party. It would be absurd to insist on the *word* 'self-determination'. And if there are people in our Party who want to change *words* in this spirit, who want to amend Clause 9 of our Party Programme, we should consider our differences with *such* comrades to be anything but a matter of principle!

The only things that matter are political clarity and the theoretical soundness of our slogans.

In verbal discussions on this question – the importance of which nobody will deny, especially now, in view of the war – we have met the following argument (we have not come across it in the press): *a protest against* a known evil does not necessarily mean recognition of a positive concept that precludes the evil. This is obviously an unfounded argument and, apparently, as such has not been reproduced in the press. If a socialist party declares that it is 'against the forcible retention of an oppressed nation within the frontiers of the annexing state', it is *thereby committed to renounce retention by force* when it comes to power.

We do not for one moment doubt that if Hindenburg were to accomplish the semi-conquest of Russia tomorrow and this semi-conquest were to be expressed by the appearance of a now Polish state (in connection with the desire of Britain and France to weaken tsarism somewhat), something that is quite 'practicable' from the standpoint of the economic laws of capitalism and imperialism, and if, the day after tomorrow, the socialist revolution were to be victorious in Petrograd, Berlin and Warsaw, the Polish socialist government, like the Russian and German socialist governments, would renounce the 'forcible retention' of, say, the Ukrainians, 'within the frontiers of the Polish state'. If there were members of the *Gazeta Robotnicza* Editorial Board in that government they would no doubt sacrifice their 'theses', thereby disproving the 'theory' that 'the right of self-determination is not applicable to a socialist society'. If we thought otherwise, we should not put a comradely discussion with the Polish Social-Democrats on the agenda but would rather conduct a ruthless struggle against them as chauvinists.

Suppose I were to go out into the streets of any European city and make a public 'protest', which I then published in the press, against my not being permitted to purchase a man as a slave. There is no doubt that people would have the right to regard me as a slave-owner, a champion of the principle, or system, if you like of slavery. No one would be fooled by the fact that my sympathies with slavery were expressed in the negative form of a protest and not in a positive form ('I am for slavery'). A political 'protest' is *quite* the equivalent of a political programme; this is so obvious that one feels rather awkward at having to explain it. In any case, we are firmly convinced that on the part of the Zimmerwald Left, at any rate – we do not speak of the Zimmerwald group as a whole since it contains Martov and other Kautskyites – we shall not meet with any 'protest' if we say that in the Third International there will be no place for people capable of separating a political protest from a political programme, of counterposing the one to the other, etc.

Not wishing to haggle over words, we take the liberty of expressing the sincere hope that the Polish Social-Democrats will try soon to formulate, officially, their proposal to delete Clause 9 from our Party Programme (which is also *theirs*) and also from the Programme of the International (the resolution of the 1896 London Congress), as well as *their own* definition of the relevant political concepts of 'old and new annexations' and of 'the forcible retention of an oppressed nation within the frontiers of the annexing state'.

Let us now turn to the next question.

4. For or Against Annexations?

In § 3 of Part One of their theses the Polish comrades declare very definitely that they are against any kind of annexation. Unfortunately, in § 4 of the same part we find an assertion that must be considered annexationist. It opens with the following ... how can it be put more delicately? ... the following strange phrase

> The starting-point of Social-Democracy's struggle against annexations, against the forcible retention of oppressed nations within the frontiers of the annexing state is *renunciation of any defence of the fatherland* [the authors' italics], which, in the era of imperialism, is defence of the rights of one's own bourgeoisie to oppress and plunder foreign peoples ...

What's this? How is it put?

'The starting-point of the struggle against annexations is renunciation of *any* defence of the fatherland ...' But any national war and any national revolt can be called 'defence of the fatherland' and, until now, has been *generally* recognised as such! We are against annotations, *but* ... we mean by this that we are against the annexed waging a war *for* their liberation from those who have annexed them, that we are against the annexed revolting to liberate themselves from those who have annexed them! Isn't that an annexationist declaration?

The authors of the theses motivate their ... strange assertion by saying that 'in the era of imperialism' defence of the fatherland amounts to defence of the right of one's own bourgeoisie to oppress foreign peoples. This, however, is true *only* in respect of all imperialist war, i.e., in respect of a war *between* imperialist powers or groups of powers, when *both* belligerents not only oppress 'foreign peoples' but are fighting a war to *decide* who shall have a *greater share* in oppressing foreign peoples!

The authors seem to present the question of 'defence of the fatherland' very differently from the way it is presented by our Party. We renounce 'defence of the fatherland' in an *imperialist* war. This is said as clearly as it can be in the Manifesto of our Party's Central Committee and in the Berne resolutions reprinted in the pamphlet *Socialism and War*, which has been published both in German and French.[9] We stressed this twice in our theses (footnotes to Sections 4 and 6). The authors of the Polish theses seem to renounce defence of the fatherland *in general,* i.e., *for a national war as well,* believing, perhaps, that in the 'era of imperialism' national wars *are impossible.* We say 'perhaps' because the Polish comrades have *not* expressed this view in their theses.

Such a view is clearly expressed in the theses of the German *Internationale* group and in the Junius pamphlet which is dealt with in a special article. In addition to what is said there, let us note that the national revolt of an annexed region or country against the annexing country may be called precisely a revolt and not a war (we have heard this objection made and, therefore, cite it here, although we do not think this terminological dispute a serious one). In any case, hardly anybody would risk denying that annexed Belgium, Serbia, Galicia and Armenia would call their 'revolt' against those who annexed them 'defence of the fatherland' *and would do so in all justice.* It looks as if the Polish comrades are *against* this type of revolt on the grounds that there is *also* a bourgeoisie in these annexed countries which *also* oppresses foreign peoples or, more exactly, could oppress them, since the question is one of the '*right* to oppress'. Consequently, the given war or revolt is not assessed on the strength of its *real* social content (the struggle of an oppressed nation for its liberation from the oppressor nation) but the possible exercise of the '*right* to oppress' by a bourgeoisie which is at present itself oppressed. If Belgium, let us say, is annexed by Germany in 1917, and in 1918 revolts to secure her liberation, the Polish comrades will be against her revolt on the grounds that the Belgian bourgeoisie possess 'the right to oppress foreign peoples'!

There is nothing Marxist or even revolutionary in this argument. If we do not want to betray socialism we *must* support *every* revolt against our chief enemy, the bourgeoisie of the big states, provided it is not the revolt of a reactionary class. By refusing to support the revolt of annexed regions we become, objectively, annexationists. It is precisely in the 'era of imperialism', which is the era of nascent social revolution, that the proletariat will today give especially vigorous support to any revolt of the annexed regions so that tomorrow, or simultaneously, it may attack the bourgeoisie of the 'great' power that is weakened by the revolt.

The Polish comrades, however, go further in their annexationism. They are not only against any revolt by the annexed regions; they are against *any* restoration of their independence, even a peaceful one! Listen to this:

> Social-Democracy, rejecting all responsibility for the consequences of the policy of oppression pursued by imperialism, and conducting the sharpest struggle against them, *does not by any means favour the erection of new frontier posts in Europe or the re-erection of those swept away by imperialism*' [the authors' italics].

Today 'imperialism has swept away the frontier posts' between Germany and Belgium and between Russia and Galicia. International Social-Democracy, if you please, ought to be against their re-erection in general, whatever the means. In 1905, 'in the era of imperialism', when Norway's autonomous Diet proclaimed her secession from Sweden, and Sweden's war against Norway, as preached by the Swedish reactionaries, did not take place, what with the resistance of the Swedish workers and the international imperialist situation – Social-Democracy ought to have been against Norway's secession, since it undoubtedly meant 'the erection of new frontier posts in Europe'!!

This is downright annexationism. There is no need to refute it because it refutes itself. No socialist party would risk taking this stand: 'We oppose annexations in general but we sanction annexations for Europe or tolerate them once they have been made' …

We need deal only with the theoretical sources of the error that has led our Polish comrades to such a patent … 'impossibility'. We shall say further on why there is no reason to make exceptions for 'Europe'. The following two phrases from the theses will explain the other sources of the error: 'Wherever the wheel of imperialism has rolled over and crushed an already formed capitalist state, the political and economic concentration of the capitalist world, paving the way for socialism, takes place in the brutal form of imperialist oppression …'

This justification of annexations is not Marxism but Struveism. Russian Social-Democrats who remember the 1890s in Russia have a good knowledge of this manner of distorting Marxism, which is common to Struve, Cunow, Legien and Co. In another of the theses (II, 3) of the Polish comrades we read the following, specifically about the German Struveists, the so-called 'social-imperialists':

(The slogan of self-determination) 'provides the social-imperialists with an opportunity, by demonstrating the illusory nature of that slogan, to represent our struggle against national oppression as historically unfounded sentimentality, thereby undermining the faith of the proletariat in the scientific validity of the Social-Democratic programme …'

This means that the authors consider the position of the German Struveists 'scientific'! Our congratulations.

One 'trifle', however, brings down this amazing argument which threatens to show that the Lensches, Cunows and Parvuses are *right* in comparison to us: it is that the Lensches are consistent people in their own way and in issue No. 8–9 of the chauvinist German *Glocke* – we deliberately quoted it in our theses – Lensch demonstrates *simultaneously* both the 'scientific invalidity' of the self-determination slogan (the Polish Social-Democrats apparently believe that *this* argument of Lensch's is irrefutable, as can be seen from their arguments in the theses we have quoted) and the 'scientific invalidity' of the slogan against annexations!!

For Lensch had an excellent understanding of that simple truth which we pointed out to those Polish colleagues who showed no desire to reply to our statement: there is no difference 'either political or economic', or even logical, between the 'recognition' of self-determination and the 'protest' against annexations. If the Polish comrades regard the arguments of the Lensches against self-determination to be irrefutable, there is one *fact* that has to be accepted: the Lensches also use *all* these arguments to oppose the struggle against annexations.

The theoretical error that underlies all the arguments of our Polish colleagues has led them to the point of becoming *inconsistent annexationists*.

5. Why Are Social-Democrats Against Annexations?

In our view the answer is obvious: because annexation violates the self-determination of nations, or, in other words, is a form of national oppression.

In the view of the Polish Social-Democrats there have to be *special* explanations of why we are against annexations, and it is these (I, 3 in the theses) that inevitably enmesh the authors in a further series of contradictions.

They produce two reasons to 'justify' our opposition to annexations (the 'scientifically valid' arguments of the Lensches notwithstanding):

First: 'To the assertion that annexations in Europe are essential for the military security of a victorious imperialist state, the Social-Democrats counterpose the fact that annexations only serve to sharpen antagonisms, thereby increasing the danger of war ...'

This is an inadequate reply to the Lensches because their chief argument is not that annexations are a military necessity but that they are *economically* progressive and under imperialism mean concentration. Where is the logic if the Polish Social-Democrats in the same breath recognise the progressive nature of such a concentration, refusing to re-erect frontier posts in Europe that have been swept away by imperialism, and protest *against* annexations?

Furthermore, the danger of *what* wars is increased by annexations? Not imperialist wars, because they have other causes: the chief antagonisms in the present imperialist war are undoubtedly those between Germany and Britain, and between Germany and Russia. These antagonisms have nothing to do with annexations. It is the danger of *national* wars and national revolts that is increased. But how can one declare national wars to be *impossible* in 'the era of imperialism', on the one hand, and then speak of the 'danger' of national wars, on the other? This is not logical.

The second argument:

> [Annexations] create a gulf between the proletariat of the ruling nation and that of the oppressed nation. . . the proletariat of the oppressed nation would unite with its bourgeoisie and regard the proletariat of the ruling nation as its enemy. Instead of the proletariat waging an international class struggle against the international bourgeoisie it would be split and ideologically corrupted ...

We fully agree with these arguments. But is it logical to put forward simultaneously two arguments on the same question which cancel each other out. In § 3 of the first part of the theses we find the above arguments that regard annexations as causing a *split* in the proletariat, and next to it, in § 4, we are told that we must oppose the annulment of annexations already effected in Europe and favour 'the education of the working masses of the oppressed and the oppressor nations in a spirit of solidarity in struggle'. If the annulment of annexations is reactionary 'sentimentality', annexations *must not* be said to create a 'gulf' between sections of the 'proletariat' and cause a 'split', but should, on the contrary, be regarded as a condition for the *bringing together* of the proletariat of different nations.

We say: In order that we may have the strength to accomplish the socialist revolution and overthrow the bourgeoisie, the workers must unite more closely, and this close union is promoted by the struggle for self-determination, i.e., the struggle against annexations. We are consistent. But the Polish comrades who say that European annexations are 'non-annullable' and national wars, 'impossible', defeat themselves by contending 'against' annexations with the use of arguments *about* national wars! These arguments are to the effect that annexations *hamper* the drawing together and fusion of workers of different nations!

In other words, the Polish Social-Democrats, in order to contend against annexations, have to draw for arguments on the theoretical stock *they themselves* reject in principle.

The question of colonies makes this even more obvious.

6. Is it Right to Contrast 'Europe' With the Colonies in the Present Question?

Our theses say that the demand for the immediate liberation of the colonies is as 'impracticable' (that is, it cannot be effected without a number of revolutions and is not stable without socialism) under capitalism as the self-determination of nations, the election of civil servants by the people, the democratic republic, and so on – and, furthermore, that the demand for the liberation of the colonies is nothing more than 'the recognition of the right of nations to self-determination'.

The Polish comrades have not answered a single one of these arguments. They have tried to differentiate between 'Europe' and the colonies. For Europe alone they become inconsistent annexationists by refusing to annul any annexations once these have been made. As for the colonies, they demand unconditionally: 'Get out of the colonies!'

Russian socialists must put forward the demand: 'Get out of Turkestan, Khiva, Bukhara, etc.', but, it is alleged, they would be guilty of 'utopianism', 'unscientific sentimentality' and so on if they demanded a similar freedom of secession for Poland, Finland, the Ukraine, etc. British socialists must demand: 'Get out of Africa, India, Australia', but not out of Ireland. What are the theoretical grounds for a distinction that is so patently false? This question cannot be evaded.

The chief 'ground' of those opposed to self-determination is its 'impracticability'. The same idea, with a nuance, is expressed in the reference to 'economic and political concentration'.

Obviously, concentration *also* comes about with the annexation of colonies. There was formerly an economic distinction between the colonies and the European peoples – at least, the majority of the latter – the colonies having been drawn into *commodity* exchange but not into capitalist *production*. Imperialism changed this. Imperialism is, among other things, the export of *capital*. Capitalist production is being transplanted to the colonies at an ever-increasing rate. They cannot be extricated from dependence on European finance capital. From the military standpoint, as well as from the standpoint of expansion, the separation of the colonies is practicable, as a general rule, only under socialism; under capitalism it is practicable only by way of exception or at the cost of a series of revolts and revolutions both in the colonies and the metropolitan countries.

The greater part of the dependent nations in Europe are capitalistically more developed than the colonies (though not all, the exceptions being the Albanians and many non-Russian peoples in Russia). But it is just this that generates greater resistance to national oppression and annexations! Precisely because of this, the development of capitalism is *more secure* in Europe under any political conditions, including those of separation, than in the colonies … 'There', the Polish comrades say about the colonies (I, 4), 'capitalism is still confronted with the task of developing the productive forces independently …' This is even *more* noticeable in Europe: capitalism is undoubtedly developing the productive forces more vigorously, rapidly and independently in Poland, Finland, the Ukraine and Alsace than in India, Turkestan, Egypt and other straightforward colonies. In a commodity producing society, no independent development, or development of any sort whatsoever, is possible without capital. In Europe the dependent nations have both *their own* capital and easy access to it on a wide range of terms. The colonies have no capital of *their own,* or none to speak of, and under finance capital no colony can obtain any except on terms of political submission. What then, in face of all this, is the significance of the demand to liberate the colonies immediately and unconditionally? Is it not clear that it is more 'utopian' in the vulgar, caricature-'Marxist' sense of the word, 'utopian', in the sense in which it is used by the Struves, Lenches, Cunows, with the Polish comrades unfortunately following in their footsteps? Any deviation from the ordinary, the commonplace, as well as everything that is revolutionary, is here labeled 'utopianism'. But revolutionary movements of *all* kinds – including national movements – are more possible, more practicable, more stubborn, more conscious and more difficult to defeat in Europe than they are in the colonies.

Socialism, say the Polish comrades (I, 3), 'will be able to give the underdeveloped peoples of the colonies *unselfish, cultural aid without ruling* over them'. This is perfectly true. But what grounds are there for supposing that a great nation, a great state that goes over to socialism, will not be able to attract a small, oppressed European *nation* by means of 'unselfish cultural aid'? It is the freedom to secede '*granted*' to the colonies by the Polish Social-Democrats that will attract the small but cultured and politically *exacting* oppressed nations of Europe to union with great socialist states, because under socialism a great state will mean so many hours *less* work a day and so much more *pay* a day. The masses of working people, as they liberate themselves from the bourgeois yoke, *will gravitate* irresistibly towards union and integration with the great, advanced socialist nations for the sake of that 'cultural aid', provided yesterday's oppressors do not infringe on the long-oppressed nations' highly developed democratic feeling of self-respect, and provided they are granted equality in everything, including state construction, that of, experience in organising 'their own' state. Under capitalism this 'experience' means war, isolation, seclusion, and the narrow egoism of the small, privileged nations (Holland, Switzerland). Under socialism the working people themselves will nowhere consent to seclusion merely for the above-mentioned purely economic motives, while the variety of political forms, freedom to secede, and experience in state organisation – there will be all this until the state in all its forms withers away – will be the basis of a prosperous cultured life and an earnest that the nations will draw closer together and integrate at an ever faster pace.

By setting the colonies aside and contrasting them to Europe, the Polish comrades step into a contradiction which immediately brings down the whole of their fallacious argument.

7. Marxism or Proudhonism?

By way of an exception, our Polish comrades parry our reference to Marx's attitude towards the separation of Ireland directly and not indirectly. What is their objection? References to Marx's position from 1848 to 1871, they say, are 'not of the slightest value'. The argument advanced in support of this unusually irate and peremptory assertion is that 'at one and the same time' Marx opposed the strivings for independence of the 'Czechs, South Slavs. etc.[10]

The argument is so very irate because it is so very unsound. According to the Polish Marxists, Marx was simply a muddlehead who 'in one breath' said contradictory things! This is altogether untrue, and it is certainly not Marxism. It is precisely the demand for 'concrete' analysis, which our Polish comrades insist on, *but do not themselves apply*, that makes it necessary for us to investigate whether Marx's different attitudes towards different concrete 'national' movements did not spring from *one and the same* socialist outlook.

Marx is known to have favoured Polish independence in the interests of *European* democracy in its struggle against the power and influence – or, it might be said, against the omnipotence and predominating reactionary influence – of tsarism. That this attitude was correct was most clearly and practically demonstrated in 1849, when the Russian serf army crushed the national liberation and revolutionary-democratic rebellion in Hungary. From that time until Marx's death, and even later, until 1890, when there was a danger that tsarism, allied with France, would wage a reactionary war against a *non-imperialist* and nationally independent Germany, Engels stood first and foremost for a struggle against tsarism. It was for this reason, and exclusively for this reason, that Marx and Engels were opposed to the national movement of the Czechs and South Slavs. A simple reference to what Marx and Engels wrote in 1841 and 1848 will prove to anyone who is interested in Marxism in real earnest and not merely for the purpose of brushing Marxism aside, that Marx and Engels at that time drew a clear and definite *distinction* between 'whole reactionary nations' serving as 'Russian outposts' in Europe, and 'revolutionary nations' namely, the Germans, Poles and Magyars. This is a fact. And it was indicated *at the time with incontrovertible* truth: in 1848 revolutionary nations fought for liberty, whose principal enemy was tsarism, whereas the Czechs, etc., were in fact reactionary nations, and outposts of tsarism.

What is the lesson to be *drawn* from this concrete example which must be analysed *concretely* if there is any desire to be true to Marxism? Only this: (1) that the interests of the liberation of a number of big and very big nations in Europe rate higher than the interests of the movement for liberation of small nations; (2) that the demand for democracy must not be considered in isolation but on a European – today we should say a world – scale.

That is all there is to it. There is no hint of any repudiation of that elementary socialist principle which the Poles forget but to which Marx was *always* faithful – that no nation can be free if it oppresses other nations. If the concrete situation which confronted Marx when tsarism dominated international politics were to repeat itself, for instance, in the form of a few nations starting a socialist revolution (as a bourgeois-democratic revolution was started in Europe in 1848), and *other* nations serving as the chief bulwarks of bourgeois reaction – then I too would have to be in favour of a revolutionary war against the latter, in favour of 'crushing' them, in favour of destroying all their outposts, no matter what small-nation movements arose in them. Consequently, instead of rejecting any examples of Marx's tactics – this would mean professing Marxism while abandoning it in practice – we must analyse them concretely and draw invaluable lessons for the future. The several demands of democracy, including self-determination, are not an absolute, but only a *small part* of the general-democratic (now: general-socialist) *world* movement. In individual concrete casts, the part *may* contradict the whole; if so, it must be rejected. It is possible that the republican movement in one country may be merely an instrument of the clerical or financial-monarchist intrigues of other countries; if so, we must *not* support this particular, concrete movement, but it would be ridiculous to delete the demand for a republic from the programme of international Social-Democracy on these grounds.

In what way has the concrete situation changed between the periods of 1848–71 and 1898–1916 (I take the most important landmarks of imperialism as a period: from the Spanish-American imperialist war to the European imperialist war)? Tsarism has manifestly and indisputably ceased to be the chief mainstay of reaction, first, because it is supported by international finance capital, particularly French, and, secondly, because of 1905. At that time the system of big national states – the democracies of Europe – was bringing democracy and socialism to the world in spite of tsarism.[11] Marx and Engels did not live to see the period of imperialism. The system now is a handful of imperialist 'Great' Powers (five or six in number), each oppressing other *nations:* and this oppression is a source for artificially retarding the collapse of capitalism, and artificially supporting opportunism and social-chauvinism in the imperialist nations which dominate the world. At that time, West-European democracy, liberating the big nations, was opposed to tsarism, which used certain small-nation movements for reactionary ends. Today, the socialist proletariat, split into chauvinists, 'social-imperialists', on the one hand, and revolutionaries, on the other, is confronted by an *alliance* of tsarist imperialism and advanced capitalist, European, imperialism, which is based on their common oppression of a number of nations.

Such are the concrete changes that have taken place in the situation, and it is just these that; the Polish Social-Democrats ignore, in spite of their promise to be concrete! Hence the concrete change in the *application* of the same socialist principles: *formerly* the main thing was to fight 'against tsarism' (and against certain small-nation movements that *it* was using for undemocratic ends), and for the greater revolutionary peoples of the West; the main thing *today* is to stand against the united, aligned front of the imperialist powers, the imperialist bourgeoisie and the social-imperialists, and *for* the utilisation of *all* national movements against imperialism for the purposes of the socialist revolution. The *more purely* proletarian the struggle against the general imperialist front now is, the more vital, obviously, is the internationalist principle: 'No nation can be free if it oppresses other nations.'

In the name of their doctrinaire concept of social revolution, the Proudhonists ignored the international role of Poland and brushed aside the national movements. Equally doctrinaire is the attitude of the Polish Social-Democrats, who *break up* the international front of struggle against the social-imperialists, and (objectively) help the latter by their vacillations on the question of annexations. For it is precisely the international front of proletarian struggle that has changed in relation to the concrete position of the small nations: at that time (1848–71) the small nations were important as the potential allies either of 'Western democracy' and the revolutionary nations, or of tsarism; now (1898–1914) that is no longer so; today they are important as one of the nutritive media of the parasitism and, consequently, the social-imperialism of the 'dominant nations'. The important thing is not whether one-fiftieth or one-hundredth of the small nations are liberated before the socialist revolution, but the fact that in the epoch of imperialism, owing to objective causes, the proletariat has been split into two international camps, one of which has been corrupted by the crumbs that fall from the table of the dominant-nation bourgeoisie – obtained, among other things, from the double or triple exploitation of small nations – while the other cannot liberate itself without liberating the small nations, without educating the masses in an anti-chauvinist, i.e., anti-annexationist, i.e., 'self-determinationist', spirit.

This, the most important aspect of the question, is ignored by our Polish comrades, who do *not* view things from the key position in the epoch of imperialism, the standpoint of the division of the international proletariat into two camps.

Here are some other concrete examples of their Proudhonism: (1) their attitude to the Irish rebellion of 1916, of which later: (2) the declaration in the theses (11, 3, end of § 3) that the slogan of socialist revolution 'must not be overshadowed by anything'. The idea that the slogan of socialist revolution can be 'overshadowed' by *linking* it up with a consistently revolutionary position on all questions, including the national question, is certainly profoundly anti-Marxist.

The Polish Social-Democrats consider our programme 'national-reformist'. Compare these two practical proposals: (1) for autonomy (Polish theses, III, 4), and (2) for freedom to secede. It is in this, and in this alone, that our programmes differ! And is it not clear that it is precisely the first programme that is reformist and not the second? A reformist change is one which leaves intact the foundations of the power of the ruling class and is merely a concession leaving its power unimpaired. A revolutionary change undermines the foundations of power. A reformist national programme does *not* abolish *all* the privileges of the ruling nation; it does *not* establish complete equality; it does *not* abolish national oppression *in all its forms*. An 'autonomous' nation does not enjoy rights equal to those of the 'ruling' nation; our Polish comrades could not have failed to notice this had they not (like our old Economists) obstinately avoided making an analysis of *political* concepts and categories. Until 1905 autonomous Norway, as a part of Sweden, enjoyed the widest autonomy, but she was not Sweden's equal. Only by her free secession was her equality manifested *in practice* and proved (and let us add in parenthesis that: it was this free secession that created the basis for a more intimate and more democratic association, founded on equality of rights). As long as Norway was merely autonomous, the Swedish aristocracy had one additional privilege; and secession did not 'mitigate' this privilege (the essence of reformism lies in *mitigating* an evil and not in destroying it), but *eliminated* it *altogether* (the principal criterion of the revolutionary character of a programme).

Incidentally, autonomy, as a reform, differs in principle from freedom to secede, as a revolutionary measure. This is unquestionable. But as everyone knows, in practice a reform is often merely a step towards revolution. It is autonomy that enables a nation forcibly retained within the boundaries of a given state to crystallise into a nation, to gather, assess and organise its forces, and to select the most opportune moment for a *declaration* ... in the 'Norwegian' spirit: We, the autonomous diet of such-and-such a nation, or of such-and-such a *territory,* declare that the Emperor of all the Russias has ceased to be King of Poland, etc. The usual 'objection' to this is that such questions are decided by wars and not by declarations. True: in the vast majority of cases they are decided by wars (just as questions of the form of government of big states are decided, in the vast majority of cases, only by wars and revolutions). However, it would do no harm to reflect whether *such* an 'objection' to the political programme of a revolutionary party is logical. Are we opposed to wars and revolutions *for* what is just and beneficial to the proletariat, *for* democracy and socialism?

'But we cannot be in favour of a war between great nations, in favour of the slaughter of twenty million people for the sake of the problematical liberation of a small nation with a population of perhaps ten or twenty million!' Of course not! And it does not mean that we throw complete national equality out of our Programme; it means that the democratic interests of *one* country must be subordinated to the democratic interests of *several and all* countries. Let us assume that between two great monarchies there is a little monarchy whose kinglet is 'bound' by blood and other ties to the monarchs of both neighbouring countries. Let us further assume that the declaration of a republic in the little country and the expulsion of *its* monarch would in practice lead to a war between the two neighbouring big countries for the restoration of that or another monarch in the little country. There is no doubt that all international Social-Democracy, as well as the really internationalist section of Social-Democracy in the little country, *would be against substituting a republic for the monarchy* in this case. The substitution of a republic for a monarchy is not an absolute, but one of the democratic demands, subordinate to the interests of democracy (and still more, of course, to those of the socialist proletariat) as a whole. A case like this would in all probability not give rise to the slightest disagreement among Social-Democrats in any country. But if any Social-Democrat were to propose on *these* grounds that the demand for a republic be deleted altogether from the programme of international Social-Democracy, he would certainly be regarded as quite mad. He would be told that after all one must not forget the elementary logical difference between the *general* and the *particular*.

This example brings us, from a somewhat different angle, to the question of the *internationalist* education of the working class. Can such education – on the necessity and urgent importance of which differences of opinion among the Zimmerwald Left are inconceivable – be *concretely identical* in great, oppressor nations and in small, oppressed nations, in annexing nations and in annexed nations?

Obviously not. The way to the common goal-complete equality, the closest association and the eventual *amalgamation of all* nations – obviously runs along different routes in each concrete case, as, let us say, the way to a paint in the centre of this page runs left from one edge and right, from the opposite edge. If a Social-Democrat from a great, oppressing, annexing nation, while advocating the amalgamation of nations in general, were for one moment to forget that 'his' Nicholas II, 'his' Wilhelm, George, Poincaré, etc., *also stand* for *amalgamation* with small nations (by means of annexations) – Nicholas II for 'amalgamation' with Galicia, Wilhelm II for 'amalgamation' with Belgium, etc. – such a Social-Democrat would be a ridiculous doctrinaire in theory and an abettor of imperialism in practice.

In the internationalist education of the workers of the oppressor countries, emphasis must necessarily be laid on their advocating freedom for the oppressed countries to secede and their fighting for it. Without this there can be *no* internationalism. It is our right and duty to treat every Social-Democrat of an oppressor nation who *fails* to conduct such propaganda as a scoundrel and an imperialist. This is an absolute demand, even where the *chance* of secession being possible and 'practicable' before the introduction of socialism is only one in a thousand.

It is our duty to teach the workers to be 'indifferent' to national distinctions. There is no doubt about that. But it must not be the indifference of the *annexationists*. A member of an oppressor nation must be 'indifferent' to whether small nations belong to *his* state *or to a neighbouring* state, or to themselves, according to where their sympathies lie: without such 'indifference' he is *not* a Social-Democrat. To be an internationalist Social-Democrat one must *not* think only of one's own nation, but place *above it* the interests of all nations, their common liberty and equality. Everyone accepts this in 'theory' but displays an annexationist indifference in practice. There is the root of the evil.

On the other hand, a Social-Democrat from a small nation must emphasise in his agitation the *second* word of our general formula: 'voluntary *integration*' of nations. He may, without failing in his duties as an internationalist, be in favour of *both* the political independence of his nation and its integration with the neighbouring state of X, Y, Z, etc. But in all cases, he must fight *against* small-nation narrow-mindedness, seclusion and isolation, consider the whole and the general, subordinate the particular to the general interest.

People who have not gone into the question thoroughly think that it is 'contradictory' for the Social-Democrats of oppressor nations to insist on the 'freedom to *secede*', while Social-Democrats of oppressed nations insist on the 'freedom to *integrate*'. However, a little reflection will show that there is not, and cannot be, any *other* road to internationalism and the amalgamation of nations, any other road *from the given* situation to this goal.

And now we come to the *specific* position of Dutch and Polish Social-Democrats.

8. The Specific and the General in the Position of the Dutch and Polish Social-Democrat Internationalists

There is not the slightest doubt that the Dutch and Polish Marxists who oppose self-determination are among the best revolutionary and internationalist elements in international Social-Democracy. How *can* it be then that their theoretical arguments as we have seen, are a mass of errors? There is not a single correct general argument, nothing but imperialist Economism!

It is not at all due to the especially bad subjective qualities of the Dutch and Polish comrades but to the *specific* objective conditions in their countries. Both countries are: (1) small and helpless in the present-day 'system' of great powers; (2) both are geographically situated between tremendously powerful imperialist plunderers engaged in the most bitter rivalry with each other (Britain and Germany; Germany and Russia); (3) in both there are terribly strong memories and traditions of the times when they *themselves* were great powers: Holland was once a colonial power greater than England, Poland was more cultured and was a stronger great power than Russia and Prussia; (4) to this day both retain their privileges consisting in the oppression of other peoples: the Dutch bourgeois owns the very wealthy Dutch East Indies; the Polish landed proprietor oppresses the Ukrainian and Byelorussian peasant; the Polish bourgeois, the Jew, etc.

The particularity comprised in the combination of these four points is not to be found in Ireland, Portugal (she was at one time annexed to Spain), Alsace, Norway, Finland, the Ukraine, the Lettish and Byelorussian territories or many others. And it is this very peculiarity that is the *real essence* of the matter! When the Dutch and Polish Social-Democrats reason against self-determination, using *general* arguments, i.e., those that concern imperialism in general, socialism in general, democracy in general, national oppression in general, we may truly say that they wallow in mistakes. But one has only to discard this obviously erroneous *shell* of general arguments and examine the *essence* of the question from the standpoint of the *specific* conditions obtaining in Holland and Poland for their particular position to become *comprehensible* and quite legitimate. It may be said, without any fear of sounding paradoxical, that when the Dutch and Polish Marxists battle against self-determination they do not say quite what they mean, or, to put it another way, mean quite what they say.[12]

We have already quoted one example in our theses. Gorter is against the self-determination of *his own* country but *in favour* of self-determination for the Dutch East Indies, oppressed as they are by 'his' nation! Is it any wonder that we see in him a more sincere internationalist and a fellow-thinker who is closer to us than those who recognise self-determination as verbally and hypocritically as Kautsky in Germany, and Trotsky and Martov in Russia? The general and fundamental principles of Marxism undoubtedly imply the duty to struggle for the freedom to secede for nations that are oppressed by 'one's own' nation, but they certainty do not require the independence specifically of Holland to be made a matter of paramount importance – Holland, which suffers most from her narrow, callous, selfish and stultifying seclusion: let the whole world burn, we stand aside from it all, 'we' are satisfied with our old spoils and the rich 'left-overs', the Indies, 'we' are not concerned with anything else!

Here is another example. Karl Radek, a Polish Social-Democrat, who has done particularly great service by his determined struggle for internationalism in German Social-Democracy since the outbreak of war, made a furious attack on self-determination in an article entitled 'The Right of Nations to Self-Determination' (*Lichtstrahlen*).[13] He quotes, incidentally, *only* Dutch and Polish authorities in his support and propounds, amongst others, the argument that self-determination fosters the idea that 'it is allegedly the duty of Social-Democrats to support any struggle for independence'.

From the standpoint of *general* theory this argument is outrageous, because it is clearly illogical: first, no democratic demand can fail to give rise to abuses, unless the specific is subordinated to the general; we are not obliged to support either 'any' struggle for independence or 'any' republican or anti-clerical movement. Secondly, *no* formula for the struggle against national oppression can fail to suffer from the *same* 'shortcoming'. Radek himself in *Berner Tagwacht* used the formula (1915, Issue 253): 'Against old and new annexations.' Any

Polish nationalist will legitimately 'deduce' from this formula: 'Poland is an annexment, I am against annexations, i.e., I am for the independence of Poland.' Or I recall Rosa Luxemburg saying in an article written in 1908,[14] that the formula: 'against national oppression' was quite adequate. But any Polish nationalist would say – *and quite justly* – that annexation is *one* of the forms of national oppression, *consequently,* etc.

However, take Poland's *specific* conditions in place of these general arguments: her independence *today* is 'impracticable' without wars or revolutions. To be in favour of an all-European war merely for the sake of restoring Poland is to be a nationalist of the worst sort, and to place the interests of a small number of Poles above those of the hundreds of millions of people who suffer from war. Such, indeed, are the 'Fracy' (the Right wing of the PSP)[15] who are socialists only in word, and compared with whom the Polish Social-Democrats are a thousand times right. To raise the question of Poland's independence *today,* with the *existing* alignment of the *neighbouring* imperialist powers, is really to run after a will-o'-the-wisp, plunge into narrow-minded nationalism and forget the necessary premise of an all-European or at least a Russian and a German revolution. To have put forward in 1908–14 freedom of coalition in Russia as an independent slogan would also have meant running after a will-o'-the-wisp, and would, objectively, have helped the Stolypin labour party (now the Potresov-Gvozdyov party, which, incidentally, is the same thing). But it would be madness to remove freedom of coalition in general from the programme of Social-Democracy!

A third and, perhaps, the most important example. We read in the Polish theses (III, end of 82) that the idea of an independent Polish buffer state is opposed on the grounds that it is an

> inane utopia of small impotent groups. Put into effect, it would mean the creation of a tiny fragment of a Polish state that would be a military colony of one or another group of Great Powers, a plaything of their military or economic interests, an area exploited by foreign capital, and a battlefield in future war.

This is all very *true* when used as an argument *against* the slogan of Polish independence *today*, because even a revolution in Poland alone would change nothing and would only divert the attention of the masses in Poland from *the main thing* – the connection between their struggle and that of the Russian and German proletariat. It is not a paradox but a fact that today the Polish proletariat as such can help the cause of socialism and freedom, *including the freedom of Poland*, only by *joint* struggle with the proletariat of the neighbouring countries, against the *narrow Polish* nationalists. The great historical service rendered by the Polish Social-Democrats in the struggle against the nationalists cannot possibly be denied.

But these same arguments, which are true from the standpoint of Poland's *specific* conditions in the *present* epoch, are manifestly untrue in the *general* form in which they are presented. So long as there are wars, Poland will always remain a battlefield in wars *between* Germany and Russia, but this is no argument against greater political liberty (and, therefore, against political independence) in the periods between wars. The same applies to the arguments about exploitation by foreign capital and Poland's role as a plaything of foreign interests. The Polish Social-Democrats cannot, at the moment, raise the slogan of Poland's independence, for the Poles, as proletarian internationalists, can do *nothing* about it without stooping, like the 'Fracy', to humble servitude to *one* of the imperialist monarchies. But it is *not* indifferent to the Russian and German workers whether Poland is independent, they take part in annexing her (and that would mean educating the Russian and German workers and peasants in the basest turpitude and their consent to play the part of executioner of other peoples).

The situation is, indeed, bewildering, but there is a way out in which *all* participants would remain internationalists: the Russian and German Social-Democrats by demanding for Poland unconditional '*freedom* to secede'; the Polish Social-Democrats by working for the unity of the proletarian struggle in both small and big countries without putting forward the slogan of Polish independence for the given epoch or the given period.

9. Engels's Letter to Kautsky

In his pamphlet *Socialism and Colonial Politics* (Berlin, 1907), Kautsky, who was then still a Marxist, published a letter written to him by Engels, dated 12 September 1882, which is extremely interesting in relation to the question under discussion. Here is the principal part of the letter:

> In my opinion the colonies proper, i.e., the countries occupied by a European population-Canada, the Cape, Australia - will all become independent; on the other hand, the countries inhabited by a native population, which are simply subjugated-India, Algeria, the Dutch, Portuguese and Spanish possessions-must be taken over for the time being by the proletariat and led as rapidly as possible towards independence. How this process will develop is difficult to say. India will perhaps, indeed very probably, make a revolution, and as a proletariat in process of self-emancipation cannot conduct any colonial wars, it would have to be allowed to run its course; it would not pass off without all sorts of destruction, of course, but that sort of thing is inseparable from all revolutions. The same might also take place elsewhere, e.g., in Algeria and Egypt, and would certainly be the best thing *for us*. We shall have enough to do at home. Once Europe is reorganised, and North America, that will furnish such colossal power and such an example that the semi-civilised countries will of themselves follow in their wake; economic needs, if anything, will see to that. But as to what social and political phases these countries will then have to pass through before they likewise arrive at socialist organisation, I think we today can advance only rather idle hypotheses. One thing alone is certain: *the victorious proletariat can force no blessings of any kind upon any foreign nation without undermining its own victory by so doing.* Which of course by no means excludes defensive wars of various kinds ...[16]

Engels does not at all suppose that the 'economic' alone will directly remove all difficulties. An economic revolution will be a stimulus to *all* peoples to *strive* for socialism; but at the same time revolutions - against the socialist state - and wars are possible. Politics will inevitably adapt themselves to the economy, but not immediately or smoothly, not simply, not directly. Engels mentions as 'certain' only one, absolutely internationalist, principle, and this he applies *to all* 'foreign nations', i.e., not to colonial nations only: to force blessings upon them would mean to undermine the victory of the proletariat.

Just because the proletariat has carried out a social revolution it will not become holy and immune from errors and weaknesses. But it will be inevitably led to realise this truth by possible errors (and selfish interest – attempts to saddle *others*).

We of the Zimmerwald Left all hold the same conviction as Kautsky, for example, held before his desertion of Marxism for the defence of chauvinism in 1914, namely, that the socialist revolution is quite possible *in the very near* future – 'any day', as Kautsky himself once put it. National antipathies will not disappear so quickly: the hatred – and perfectly legitimate hatred – of an oppressed nation for its oppressor *will last* for a while; it will evaporate only *after* the victory of socialism and *after* the final establishment of completely democratic relations between nations. If we are to be faithful to socialism, we must even now educate the masses in the spirit of internationalism, which is impossible in oppressor nations without advocating freedom of secession for oppressed nations.

10. The Irish Rebellion of 1916

Our theses were written before the outbreak of this rebellion, which must be the touchstone of our theoretical views.

The views of the opponents of self-determination lead to the conclusion that the vitality of small nations oppressed by imperialism has already been sapped, that they cannot play any role against imperialism, that support of their purely national aspirations will lead to nothing, etc. The imperialist war of 1914–16 has provided *facts* which refute such conclusions.

The war proved to be an epoch of crisis for the West-European nations, and for *imperialism* as a whole. Every crisis discards the conventionalities, tears away the outer wrappings, sweeps away the obsolete and reveals the underlying springs and forces. What has it revealed from the standpoint of the movement of oppressed nations? In the colonies there have been a number of attempts at rebellion, which the oppressor nations, naturally did all they could to hide by means of a military censorship. Nevertheless, it is known that in Singapore the British brutally suppressed a mutiny among their Indian troops; that there were attempts at rebellion in French Annam (see *Nashe Slovo*) and in the German Cameroons (see the Junius pamphlet); that in Europe, on the one hand, there was a rebellion in Ireland, which the 'freedom-loving' English, who did not dare to extend conscription to Ireland, suppressed by executions, and, on the other, the Austrian Government passed the death sentence on the deputies of the Czech Diet 'for treason', and shot whole Czech regiments for the same 'crime'.

This list is, of course, far from complete. Nevertheless, it proves that, *owing* to the crisis of imperialism, the flames of national revolt have flared up *both* in the colonies and in Europe, and that national sympathies and antipathies have manifested themselves in spite of the Draconian threats and measures of repression. All this before the crisis of imperialism hit its peak; the power of the imperialist bourgeoisie was yet to be undermined (this may be brought about by a war of 'attrition' but has not yet happened) and the proletarian movements in the imperialist countries were still very feeble. What will happen when the war has caused complete exhaustion, or when, in one state at least, the power of the bourgeoisie has been shaken under the blows of proletarian struggle, as that of tsarism in 1905?

On 9 May 1916, there appeared in *Berner Tagwacht* the organ of the Zimmerwald group, including some of the Leftists, an article on the Irish rebellion entitled 'Their Song Is Over' and signed with the initials K. R. [Karl Radek]. It described the Irish rebellion as being nothing more nor less than a 'putsch', for, as the author argued, 'the Irish question was an agrarian one', the peasants had been pacified by reforms, and the nationalist movement remained only a 'purely urban, petty-bourgeois movement, which, notwithstanding the sensation it caused, had not much social backing'.

It is not surprising that this monstrously doctrinaire and pedantic assessment coincided with that of a Russian national-liberal Cadet,

Mr. A. Kulisher (*Rech*[17] No. 102, April 15, 1916), who also labelled the rebellion 'the Dublin putsch'.

It is to be hoped that, in accordance with the adage, 'it's an ill wind that blows nobody any good', many comrades, who were not aware of the morass they were sinking into by repudiating 'self-determination' and by treating the national movements of small nations with disdain, will have their eyes opened by the 'accidental' coincidence of opinion held by a Social-Democrat and a representative of the imperialist bourgeoisie!!

The term 'putsch', in its scientific sense, may be employed only when the attempt at insurrection has revealed nothing but a circle of conspirators or stupid maniacs, and has aroused no sympathy among the masses. The centuries-old Irish national movement, having passed through various stages and combinations of class interest, manifested itself, in particular, in a mass Irish National Congress in America (*Vorworts* 20 March 1916) which called for Irish independence; it also manifested itself in street fighting conducted by a section of the urban petty bourgeoisie *and a section of the workers* after a long period of mass agitation, demonstrations, suppression of newspapers, etc. Whoever calls such a rebellion a 'putsch' is either a hardened reactionary, or a doctrinaire hopelessly incapable of envisaging a social revolution as a living phenomenon.

To imagine that social revolution is *conceivable* without revolts by small nations in the colonies and in Europe, without revolutionary outbursts by a section of the petty bourgeoisie *with all its prejudices*, without a movement of the politically non-conscious proletarian and semi-proletarian masses against oppression by the landowners, the church, and the monarchy, against national oppression, etc. – to imagine all this is to *repudiate social revolution*. So, one army lines up in one place and says, 'We are for socialism', and another, somewhere else and says, 'We are for imperialism', and that will be a social revolution! Only those who hold such a ridiculously pedantic view could vilify the Irish rebellion by calling it a 'putsch'.

Whoever expects a 'pure' social revolution will *never* live to see it. Such a person pays lip-service to revolution without understanding what revolution is.

The Russian Revolution of 1905 was a bourgeois-democratic revolution. It consisted of a series of battles in which *all* the discontented classes, groups and elements of the population participated. Among these there were masses imbued with the crudest *prejudices*, with the vaguest and most fantastic aims of struggle; there were small groups which accepted Japanese money, there were speculators and adventurers, etc. But *objectively*, the mass movement was breaking the hack of tsarism and paving the way for democracy; for this reason the class-conscious workers led it.

The socialist revolution in Europe *cannot* be anything other than an outburst of mass struggle on the part of all and sundry oppressed and discontented elements. Inevitably, sections of the petty bourgeoisie and of the backward workers will participate in it – without such participation, *mass* struggle is *impossible*, without it *no* revolution is possible – and just as inevitably will they bring into the movement their prejudices, their reactionary fantasies, their weaknesses and errors. But *objectively* they will attack *capital*, and the class-conscious vanguard of the revolution, the advanced proletariat, expressing this objective truth of a variegated and discordant, motley and outwardly fragmented, mass struggle, will be able to unite and direct it, capture power, seize the banks, expropriate the trusts which all hate (though for difficult reasons!), and introduce other dictatorial measures which in their totality will amount to the overthrow of the bourgeoisie and the victory of socialism, which, however, will by no means immediately 'purge' itself of petty-bourgeois slag.

Social-Democracy, we read in the Polish theses (I, 4), 'must utilise the struggle of the young colonial bourgeoisie against European imperialism *in order to sharpen the revolutionary crisis in Europe*'. (Authors' italics.)

Is it not clear that it is least of all permissible to contrast Europe to the colonies in *this* respect? The struggle of the oppressed nations *in Europe*, a struggle capable of going all the way to insurrection and street fighting, capable of breaking down the iron discipline of the army and martial law, will 'sharpen the revolutionary crisis in Europe' to an infinitely greater degree than a much more developed rebellion in a remote colony. A blow delivered against the power of the English imperialist bourgeoisie by a rebellion in Ireland is a hundred times more significant politically than a blow of equal force delivered in Asia or in Africa.

The French chauvinist press recently reported the publication in Belgium of the eightieth issue of an illegal journal, *Free Belgium*.[18] Of course, the chauvinist press of France very often lies, but this piece of news seems to be true. Whereas chauvinist and Kautskyite German Social-Democracy has failed to establish a free press for itself during the two years of war, and has meekly borne the yoke of military censorship (only the Left Radical elements, to their credit be it said, have published pamphlets and manifestos, in spite of the censorship) – an oppressed civilised nation has reacted to a military oppression unparalleled in ferocity by establishing an organ of revolutionary protest! The dialectics of history are such that small nations, powerless as an *independent* factor in the struggle against imperialism, play a part as one of the ferments, one of the bacilli, which help the *real* anti-imperialist force, the socialist proletariat, to make its appearance on the scene.

The general staffs in the current war are doing their utmost to utilise any national and revolutionary movement in the enemy camp: the Germans utilise the Irish rebellion, the French – the Czech movement, etc. They are acting quite correctly from their own point of view. A serious war would not be treated seriously if advantage were not taken of the enemy's slightest weakness and if every opportunity that presented itself were not seized upon, the more, so since it is impossible to know beforehand at what moment, where, and with what force some powder magazine will 'explode'. We would be very poor revolutionaries if, in the proletariat's great war of liberation for socialism, we did not know how to utilise *every* popular movement against *every single* disaster imperialism brings in order to intensify and extend the crisis. If we were, on the one hand, to repeat in a thousand keys the declaration that we are 'opposed' to all national oppression and, on the other, to describe the heroic revolt of the most mobile and enlightened section of certain classes in an oppressed nation against its oppressors as a 'putsch', we should be sinking to the same level of stupidity as the Kautskyites.

It is the misfortune of the Irish that they rose prematurely, before the European revolt of the proletariat had *had time* to mature. Capitalism is not so harmoniously built that the various sources of rebellion can immediately merge of their own accord, without reverses and defeats. On the other hand, the very fact that revolts do break out at different times, in different places, and are of different kinds, guarantees wide scope and depth to the general movement; but it is only in premature, individual, sporadic and therefore unsuccessful, revolutionary movements that the masses gain experience, acquire knowledge, gather strength, and get to know their real leaders, the socialist proletarians, and in this way prepare for the general onslaught, just as certain strikes, demonstrations, local and national, mutinies in the army, outbreaks among the peasantry, etc., prepared the way for the general onslaught in 1905.

11. Conclusion

Contrary to the erroneous assertions of the Polish Social-Democrats, the demand for the self-determination of nations has played no less a role in our Party agitation than, for example, the arming of the people, the separation of the church from the state, the election of civil servants by the gene pie and other points the philistines have called 'utopian'. On the contrary, the strengthening of the national movements after 1905 naturally prompted more vigorous agitation by our Party, including a number of articles in 1912–13, and the resolution of our Party in 1913 giving a precise 'anti-Kautskian' definition (i.e., one that does not tolerate purely verbal 'recognition') of the *content* of the point.

It will not do to overlook a fact which was revealed at that early date: opportunists of various nationalities, the Ukrainian Yorkevich, the Bundist Liebman, Scrnkovsky, the Russian myrmidon of Potresov and Co., all spoke *in favour* of Rosa Luxemburg's arguments *against* self-determination! What for Rosa Luxemburg, the Polish Social-Democrat, had been merely an incorrect theoretical generalisation of the *specific* conditions of the movement in Poland, became *objective* opportunist support for Great-Russian imperialism when actually applied to more extensive circumstances, to conditions obtaining in a big state instead of a small one, when applied on an international scale instead of the narrow Polish scale. The history of *trends* in political thought (as distinct from the views of individuals) has proved the correctness of our programme.

Outspoken social-imperialists, such as Lensch, still rail against both self-determination and the renunciation of annexations. As for the Kautskyites, they hypocritically recognise self-determination – Trotsky and Martov are going the same way here in Russia. *Both of them*, like Kautsky, say they favour self-determination. What happens in practice? Take Trotsky's articles 'The Nation and the Economy' in *Nashe Slovo,* and you will find his usual eclecticism: on the one hand, the economy unites nations and, on the other, national oppression divides them. The conclusion? The conclusion is that the prevailing hypocrisy remains unexposed, agitation is dull and does not touch upon what is most important, basic, significant and closely connected with practice – one's attitude to the nation that is oppressed by 'one's own' nation. Martov and other secretaries abroad simply preferred to forget – a profitable lapse of memory! – the struggle of their colleague and fellow-member Semkovsky against self-determination. In the legal press of the Gvozdyovites (*Nash Golos*) Martov spoke *in favour* of self-determination, pointing out the indisputable truth that during the imperialist war it does not *yet* imply participation, etc., but evading the main thing – he also evades it in the illegal, free press! – which is that *even in peace time* Russia set a world record for the oppression of nations with an imperialism that is much more crude, medieval, economically backward and militarily bureaucratic. The Russian Social-Democrat who 'recognises' the self-determination of nations more or less as it is recognised by Messrs. Plekhanov, Potresov and Co., that is, without bothering to fight for the freedom of secession for nations oppressed by tsarism, is *in fact* an imperialist and a lackey of tsarism.

No matter what the subjective 'good' intentions of Trotsky and Martov may be, their evasiveness objectively supports Russian social-imperialism. The epoch of imperialism has turned all the 'great' powers into the oppressors of a number of nations, and the development of imperialism will inevitably lead to a more definite division of trends in this question in international Social-Democracy as well.

Draft Theses on National and Colonial Questions for the Second Congress of the Communist International[1]

In submitting for discussion by the Second Congress of the Communist International the following draft theses on the national and the colonial questions I would request all comrades, especially those who possess concrete information on any of these very complex problems, to let me have their opinions, amendments, addenda and concrete remarks *in the most concise form* (*no more than two or three pages*), particularly on the following points:

Austrian experience;

Polish-Jewish and Ukrainian experience;

Alsace-Lorraine and Belgium;

Ireland;

Danish-German, Italo-French and Italo-Slav relations;

Balkan experience;

Eastern peoples;

The struggle against Pan-Islamism;

Relations in the Caucasus;

The Bashkir and Tatar Republics;

Kirghizia; Turkestan, its experience;

Negroes in America;

Colonies;

China-Korea-Japan.

N. Lenin
5 June 1920

1) An abstract or formal posing of the problem of equality in general and national equality in particular is in the very nature of bourgeois democracy. Under the guise of the equality of the individual in general, bourgeois democracy proclaims the formal or legal equality of the property-owner and the proletarian, the exploiter and the exploited, thereby grossly deceiving the oppressed classes. On the plea that all men are absolutely equal, the bourgeoisie is transforming the idea of equality, which is itself a reflection of relations in commodity production, into a weapon in its struggle against the abolition of classes. The real meaning of the demand for equality consists in its being a demand for the abolition of classes.

2) In conformity with its fundamental task of combating bourgeois democracy and exposing its falseness and hypocrisy, the Communist Party, as the avowed champion of the proletarian struggle to overthrow the bourgeois yoke, must base its policy, in the national question too, not on abstract and formal principles but, first, on a precise appraisal of the specific historical situation and, primarily, of economic conditions; second, on a clear distinction between the interests of the oppressed classes, of working and exploited people, and the general concept of national interests as a whole, which implies the interests of the ruling class; third, on an equally clear distinction between the oppressed, dependent and subject nations and the oppressing, exploiting and sovereign nations, in order to counter the bourgeois-democratic lies that play down this colonial and financial enslavement of the vast majority of the world's population by an insignificant minority of the richest and advanced capitalist countries, a feature characteristic of the era of finance capital and imperialism.

3) The imperialist war of 1914–18 has very clearly revealed to all nations and to the oppressed classes of the whole world the falseness of bourgeois-democratic phrases, by practically demonstrating that the Treaty of Versailles of the celebrated 'Western democracies' is an even more brutal and foul act of violence against weak nations than was the Treaty of Brest-Litovsk of the German Junkers and the Kaiser. The League of Nations and the entire post war policy of the Entente reveal this truth with even greater clarity and distinctness. They are everywhere intensifying the revolutionary struggle both of the proletariat in the

advanced countries and of the toiling masses in the colonial and dependent countries. They are hastening the collapse of the petty-bourgeois nationalist illusions that nations can live together in peace and equality under capitalism.

4) From these fundamental premises it follows that the Communist International's entire policy on the national and the colonial questions should rest primarily on a closer union of the proletarians and the working masses of all nations and countries for a joint revolutionary struggle to overthrow the landowners and the bourgeoisie. This union alone will guarantee victory over capitalism, without which the abolition of national oppression and inequality is impossible.

5) The world political situation has now placed the dictatorship of the proletariat on the order of the day. World political developments are of necessity concentrated on a single focus – the struggle of the world bourgeoisie against the Soviet Russian Republic, around which are inevitably grouped, on the one hand, the Soviet movements of the advanced workers in all countries, and, on the other, all the national liberation movements in the colonies and among the oppressed nationalities, who are learning from bitter experience that their only salvation lies in the Soviet system's victory over world imperialism.

6) Consequently, one cannot at present confine oneself to a bare recognition or proclamation of the need for closer union between the working people of the various nations; a policy must be pursued that will achieve the closest alliance, with Soviet Russia, of all the national and colonial liberation movements. The form of this alliance should be determined by the degree of development of the communist movement in the proletariat of each country, or of the bourgeois-democratic liberation movement of the workers and peasants in backward countries or among backward nationalities.

7) Federation is a transitional form to the complete unity of the working people of different nations. The feasibility of federation has already been demonstrated in practice both by the relations between the RSFSR and other Soviet Republics (the Hungarian, Finnish[2] and Latvian[3] in the past, and the Azerbaijan and Ukrainian at present), and by the relations within the RSFSR in respect of nationalities which formerly enjoyed neither statehood nor autonomy (e.g., the Bashkir and Tatar autonomous

republics in the RSFSR, founded in 1919 and 1920 respectively).

8) In this respect, it is the task of the Communist International to further develop and also to study and test by experience these new federations, which are arising on the basis of the Soviet system and the Soviet movement. In recognising that federation is a transitional form to complete unity, it is necessary to strive for ever closer federal unity, bearing in mind, first, that the Soviet republics, surrounded as they are by the imperialist powers of the whole world – which from the military standpoint are immeasurably stronger – cannot possibly continue to exist without the closest alliance; second, that a close economic alliance between the Soviet republics is necessary, otherwise the productive forces which have been ruined by imperialism cannot be restored and the well-being of the working people cannot be ensured; third, that there is a tendency towards the creation of a single world economy, regulated by the proletariat of all nations as an integral whole and according to a common plan. This tendency has already revealed itself quite clearly under capitalism and is bound to be further developed and consummated under socialism.

9) The Communist International's national policy in the sphere of relations within the state cannot be restricted to the bare, formal, purely declaratory and actually non-committal recognition of the equality of nations to which the bourgeois democrats confine themselves – both those who frankly admit being such, and those who assume the name of socialists (such as the socialists of the Second International).

In all their propaganda and agitation – both within parliament and outside it – the Communist parties must consistently expose that constant violation of the equality of nations and of the guaranteed rights of national minorities which is to be seen in all capitalist countries, despite their 'democratic' constitutions. It is also necessary, first, constantly to explain that only the Soviet system is capable of ensuring genuine equality of nations, by uniting first the proletarians and then the whole mass of the working population in the struggle against the bourgeoisie; and, second, that all Communist parties should render direct aid to the revolutionary movements among the dependent and underprivileged nations (for example, Ireland, the American Negroes, etc.) and in the colonies.

Without the latter condition, which is particularly important, the struggle against the oppression of dependent nations and colonies, as well as recognition of their right to secede are but a false signboard, as is evidenced by the parties of the Second International.

10) Recognition of internationalism in word, and its replacement in deed by petty-bourgeois nationalism and pacifism, in all propaganda, agitation and practical work, is very common, not only among the parties of the Second International, but also among those which have withdrawn from it, and often even among parties which now call themselves communist. The urgency of the struggle against this evil, against the most deep-rooted petty-bourgeois national prejudices, looms ever larger with the mounting exigency of the task of converting the dictatorship of the proletariat from a national dictatorship (i.e., existing in a single country and incapable of determining world politics) into an international one (i.e., a dictatorship of the proletariat involving at least several advanced countries, and capable of exercising a decisive influence upon world politics as a whole). Petty-bourgeois nationalism proclaims as internationalism the mere recognition of the equality of nations, and nothing more. Quite apart from the fact that this recognition is purely verbal, petty-bourgeois nationalism preserves national self-interest intact, whereas proletarian internationalism demands, first, that the interests of the proletarian struggle in any one country should be subordinated to the interests of that struggle on a world-wide scale, and, second, that a nation which is achieving victory over the bourgeoisie should be able and willing to make the greatest national sacrifices for the overthrow of international capital.

Thus, in countries that are already fully capitalist and have workers' parties that really act as the vanguard of the proletariat, the struggle against opportunist and petty-bourgeois pacifist distortions of the concept and policy of internationalism is a primary and cardinal task.

11) With regard to the more backward states and nations, in which feudal or patriarchal and patriarchal-peasant relations predominate, it is particularly important to bear in mind:

First, that all Communist parties must assist the bourgeois-democratic liberation movement in these countries, and that the duty of rendering the most active assistance rests primarily with the workers of the country the backward nation is colonially or financially dependent on;

Second, the need for a struggle against the clergy and other influential reactionary and medieval elements in backward countries;

Third, the need to combat Pan-Islamism and similar trends, which strive to combine the liberation movement against European and American imperialism with an attempt to strengthen the positions of the khans, landowners, mullahs, etc.;

Fourth, the need, in backward countries, to give special support to the peasant movement against the landowners, against landed proprietorship, and against all manifestations or survivals of feudalism, and to strive to lend the peasant movement the most revolutionary character by establishing the closest possible alliance between the West European communist proletariat and the revolutionary peasant movement in the East, in the colonies, and in the backward countries generally. It is particularly necessary to exert every effort to apply the basic principles of the Soviet system in countries where pre-capitalist relations predominate – by setting up 'working people's Soviets', etc.;

Fifth, the need for a determined struggle against attempts to give a communist colouring to bourgeois-democratic liberation trends in the backward countries; the Communist International should support bourgeois-democratic national movements in colonial and backward countries only on condition that, in these countries, the elements of future proletarian parties, which will be communist not only in name, are brought together and trained to understand their special tasks, i.e., those of the struggle against the bourgeois-democratic movements within their own nations. The Communist International must enter into a temporary alliance with bourgeois democracy in the colonial and backward countries, but should not merge with it, and should under all circumstances uphold the independence of the proletarian movement even if it is in its most embryonic form;

Sixth, the need constantly to explain and expose among the broadest working masses of all countries, and particularly of the backward countries, the deception systematically practised by the imperialist powers, which, under the guise of politically independent states, set up states that are wholly dependent upon them economically, financially and militarily. Under present-day international conditions there is no salvation for dependent and weak nations except in a union of Soviet republics.

12) The age-old oppression of colonial and weak nationalities by the imperialist powers has not only filled the working masses of the oppressed countries with animosity towards the oppressor nations, but has also aroused distrust in these nations in general, even in their proletariat. The despicable betrayal of socialism by the majority of the official leaders of this proletariat in 1914–19, when 'defence of country' was used as a social-chauvinist cloak to conceal the defence of the 'right' of their 'own' bourgeoisie to oppress colonies and fleece financially dependent countries, was certain to enhance this perfectly legitimate distrust. On the other hand, the more backward the country, the stronger is the hold of small-scale agricultural production, patriarchalism and isolation, which inevitably lend particular strength and tenacity to the deepest of petty-bourgeois prejudices, i.e., to national egoism and national narrow-mindedness. These prejudices are bound to die out very slowly, for they can disappear only after imperialism and capitalism have disappeared in the advanced countries, and after the entire foundation of the backward countries' economic life has radically changed. It is therefore the duty of the class-conscious communist proletariat of all countries to regard with particular caution and attention the survivals of national sentiments in the countries and among nationalities which have been oppressed the longest; it is equally necessary to make certain concessions with a view to more rapidly overcoming this distrust and these prejudices. Complete victory over capitalism cannot be won unless the proletariat and, following it, the mass of working people in all countries and nations throughout the world voluntarily strive for alliance and unity.

Memo Combatting Dominant Nation Chauvinism[1]

I declare war to the death on dominant nation chauvinism. I shall eat it with all my healthy teeth as soon as I get rid of this accursed bad tooth.

It must be *absolutely* insisted that the Union Central Executive Committee should be *presided over* in turn by a:

Russian,

Ukrainian,

Georgian, etc.

Absolutely!

Yours,

Lenin

The Question of Nationalities
or 'Autonomisation'

I suppose I have been very remiss with respect to the workers of Russia for not having intervened energetically and decisively enough in the notorious question of autonomisation, which, it appears, is officially called the question of the Soviet socialist republics.

When this question arose last summer, I was ill; and then in autumn I relied too much on my recovery and on the October and December plenary meetings giving me an opportunity of intervening in this question. However, I did not manage to attend the October Plenary Meeting (when this question came up) or the one in December, and so the question passed me by almost completely.

I have only had time for a talk with Comrade Dzerzhinsky, who came from the Caucasus and told me how this matter stood in Georgia. I have also managed to exchange a few words with Comrade Zinoviev and express my apprehensions on this matter. From what I was told by Comrade Dzerzhinsky, who was at the head of the commission sent by the C.C. to 'investigate' the Georgian incident, I could only draw the greatest apprehensions. If matters had come to such a pass that Orjonikidze could go to the extreme of applying physical violence, as Comrade Dzerzhinsky informed me, we can imagine what a mess we have got ourselves into. Obviously, the whole business of 'autonomisation' was radically wrong and badly timed.

It is said that a united apparatus was needed. Where did that assurance come from? Did it not come from that same Russian apparatus which, as I pointed out in one of the preceding sections of my diary, we took over from tsarism and slightly anointed with Soviet oil?

There is no doubt that that measure should have been delayed somewhat until we could say that we vouched for our apparatus as our own. But now, we must, in all conscience, admit the contrary; the apparatus we call ours is, in fact, still quite alien to us; it is a bourgeois and tsarist hotch-potch and there has been no possibility of getting rid of it in the course of the past five years without the help of other countries and because we have been 'busy' most of the time with military engagements and the fight against famine.

It is quite natural that in such circumstances the 'freedom to secede from the union' by which we justify ourselves will be a mere scrap of paper, unable to defend the non-Russians from the onslaught of that really Russian man, the Great-Russian chauvinist, in substance a rascal and a tyrant, such as the typical Russian bureaucrat is. There is no doubt that the infinitesimal percentage of Soviet and sovietised workers will drown in that tide of chauvinistic Great-Russian riffraff like a fly in milk.

It is said in defence of this measure that the People's Commissariats directly concerned with national psychology and national education were set up as separate bodies. But there the question arises: can these People's Commissariats be made quite independent? And secondly: were we careful enough to take measures to provide the non-Russians with a real safeguard against the truly Russian bully? I do not think we took such measures although we could and should have done so.

I think that Stalin's haste and his infatuation with pure administration, together with his spite against the notorious 'nationalist-socialism', played a fatal role here.[1] In politics spite generally plays the basest of roles.

I also fear that Comrade Dzerzhinsky, who went to the Caucasus to investigate the 'crime' of those 'nationalist-socialists', distinguished himself there by his truly Russian frame of mind (it is common knowledge that people of other nationalities who have become Russified over-do this Russian frame of mind) and that the impartiality of his whole commission was typified well enough by Orgonikidze's 'man-handling'. I think that no provocation or even insult can justify such Russian manhandling and that Comrade Dzerzhinsky was inexcusably guilty in adopting a light-hearted attitude towards it.

For all the citizens in the Caucasus, Orjonikidze was the authority.

Orjonikidze had no right to display that irritability to which he and Dzerzhinsky referred. On the contrary, Orjonikidze should have behaved with a restraint which cannot be demanded of any ordinary citizen, still less of a man accused of a 'political' crime. And, to tell the truth, those nationalist-socialists were citizens who were accused of a political crime, and the terms of the accusation were such that it could not be described otherwise.

Here we have an important question of principle: how is internationalism to be understood?

Lenin

30 December 1922

Taken down by M.V.

Continuation of the notes.

31 December 1922

In my writings on the national question, I have already said that an abstract presentation of the question of nationalism in general is of no use at all. A distinction must necessarily be made between the nationalism of an oppressor nation and that of an oppressed nation, the nationalism of a big nation and that of a small nation.

In respect of the second kind of nationalism we, nationals of a big nation, have nearly always been guilty, in historic practice, of an infinite number of cases of violence; furthermore, we commit violence and insult an infinite number of times without noticing it. It is sufficient to recall my Volga reminiscences of how non-Russians are treated; how the Poles are not called by any other name than Polyachiska, how the Tatar is nicknamed Prince, how the Ukrainians are always Khokhols and the Georgians and other Caucasian nationals always Kapkasians.

That is why internationalism on the part of oppressors or 'great' nations, as they are called (though they are great only in their violence, only great as bullies), must consist not only in the observance of the formal equality of nations but even in an inequality of the oppressor nation, the great nation, that must make up for the inequality which obtains in actual practice. Anybody who does not understand this has not grasped the real proletarian attitude to the national question, he is still essentially petty bourgeois in his point of view and is, therefore, sure to descend to the bourgeois point of view.

What is important for the proletarian? For the proletarian it is not only important, it is absolutely essential that he should be assured that the non-Russians place the greatest possible trust in the proletarian class struggle. What is needed to ensure this? Not merely formal equality. In one way or another, by one's attitude or by concessions, it is necessary to compensate the non-Russian for the lack of trust, for the suspicion and the insults to which the government of the 'dominant' nation subjected them in the past.

I think it is unnecessary to explain this to Bolsheviks, to Communists, in greater detail. And I think that in the present instance, as far as the Georgian nation is concerned, we have a typical case in which a genu-inely proletarian attitude makes profound caution, thoughtfulness and a readiness to compromise a matter of necessity for us. The Georgian [Stalin] who is neglectful of this aspect of the question, or who carelessly flings about accusations of 'nationalist-socialism' (whereas he himself is a real and true 'nationalist-socialist', and even a vulgar Great-Russian bully), violates, in substance, the interests of proletarian class solidarity, for nothing holds up the development and strengthening of proletar-ian class solidarity so much as national injustice; 'offended' nationals are not sensitive to anything so much as to the feeling of equality and the violation of this equality, if only through negligence or jest- to the violation of that equality by their proletarian comrades. That is why in this case it is better to over-do rather than under-do the concessions and leniency towards the national minorities. That is why, in this case, the fundamental interest of proletarian class struggle, requires that we never adopt a formal attitude to the national question, but always take into account the specific attitude of the proletarian of the oppressed (or small) nation towards the oppressor (or great) nation.

Lenin

Taken down by M. V.

31 December 1922

Continuation of the notes.

31 December 1922

What practical measures must be taken in the present situation?

Firstly, we must maintain and strengthen the union of socialist republics. Of this there can be no doubt. This measure is necessary for us and it is necessary for the world communist proletariat in its struggle against the world bourgeoisie and its defence against bourgeois intrigues.

Secondly, the union of socialist republics must be retained for its diplomatic apparatus. By the way, this apparatus is an exceptional component of our state apparatus. We have not allowed a single influential person from the old tsarist apparatus into it. All sections with any authority are composed of Communists. That is why it has already won for itself (this may be said boldly) the name of a reliable communist apparatus purged to an incomparably greater extent of the old tsarist, bourgeois and petty-bourgeois elements than that which we have had to make do with in other People's Commissariats.

Thirdly, exemplary punishment must be inflicted on Comrade Orjonikidze (I say this all the more regretfully as I am one of his personal friends and have worked with him abroad) and the investigation of all the material which Dzerzhinsky's commission has collected must be completed or started over again to correct the enormous mass of wrongs and biased judgments which it doubtlessly contains. The political responsibility for all this truly Great-Russian nationalist campaign must, of course, be laid on Stalin and Dzerzhinsky.

Fourthly, the strictest rules must be introduced on the use of the national language in the non-Russian republics of our union, and these rules must be checked with special care. There is no doubt that our apparatus being what it is, there is bound to be, on the pretext of unity in the railway service, unity in the fiscal service and so on, a mass of truly Russian abuses. Special ingenuity is necessary for the struggle against these abuses, not to mention special sincerity on the part of those who undertake this struggle. A detailed code will be required, and only the nationals living in the republic in question can draw it up at all successfully. And then we cannot be sure in advance that as a result of this work we shall not take a step backward at our next Congress of Soviets, i.e., retain the union of Soviet socialist republics only for military and diplomatic affairs, and in all other respects restore full independence to the individual People's Commissariats.

It must be borne in mind that the decentralisation of the People's Commissariats and the lack of co-ordination in their work as far as Moscow and other centres are concerned can be compensated sufficiently by Party authority, if it is exercised with sufficient prudence and impartiality; the harm that can result to our state from a lack of unification between the national apparatuses and the Russian apparatus is infinitely less than that which will be done not only to us, but to the whole International, and to the hundreds of millions of the peoples of Asia, which is destined to follow us on to the stage of history in the near future. It would be unpardonable opportunism if, on the eve of debut of the East, just as it is awakening, we undermined our prestige with its peoples, even if only by the slightest crudity or injustice towards our own non-Russian nationalities. The need to rally against the imperialists of the West, who are defending the capitalist world, is one thing. There can be no doubt about that and it would be superfluous for me to speak about my unconditional approval of it. It is another thing when we ourselves lapse, even if only in trifles, into imperialist attitudes towards oppressed nationalities, thus undermining all our principled sincerity, all our principled defence of the struggle against imperialism. But the morrow of world history will be a day when the awakening peoples oppressed by imperialism are finally aroused and the decisive long and hard struggle for their liberation begins.

Lenin
31 December 1922
Taken down by M. V.

Notes

Critical Remarks on the National Question (1913)

1 Published: Published in 1913, in the journal *Prosveshcheniye* Nos. 10, 11 and 12. Signed: *V. Ilyin*. Published according to the journal text.

The article 'Critical Remarks on the National Question' was written by Lenin in October–December 1913 and published the same year in the Bolshevik legal journal *Prosveshcheniye* Nos. 10, 11 and 12.

The article was preceded by lectures on the national question which Lenin delivered in a number of Swiss cities – Zurich, Geneva, Lausanne and Berne – in the summer of 1913.

In the autumn of 1913 Lenin made a report on the national question at the 'August' ('Summer') Conference of the Central Committee of the RSDLP with Party workers. A resolution on the report drafted by Lenin was adopted. After the Conference Lenin started work on his article 'Critical Remarks on the National Question'.

2 *Severnaya Pravda (Northern Truth)* – one of the names of the newspaper *Pravda*. *Pravda* – a legal Bolshevik daily published in St. Petersburg. Founded on the initiative of the St. Petersburg workers in April 1912.

Pravda was a popular working-class newspaper, published with money collected by the workers themselves. A wide circle of worker-correspondents and worker-publicists formed around the newspaper. Over eleven thousand correspondence items from workers were published in a single year. *Pravda* had an average circulation of forty thousand, with some issues running into sixty thousand copies.

Lenin directed *Pravda* from abroad, where he was living. He wrote for the paper almost daily, gave instructions to the editorial board and rallied the Party's best literary forces around the newspaper.

Pravda was subjected to constant police persecution. During the first year of its existence, it was confiscated forty-one times, and thirty-six legal actions were brought against its editors, who served prison sentences totalling forty-seven and a half months. In the course of two years and three months, *Pravda* was closed down eight times by the tsarist government, but reissued under new names: *Rabochaya Pravda*, *Severnaya Pravda*, *Pravda Truda*, *Za Pravdu*, *Proletarskaya Pravda*, *Put Pravdy*, *Rabochy*, and *Trudovaya Pravda*. On 8 (21) [parenthetical dates belong to Gregorian calendar – *Ed.*] July 1914, on the eve of the First World War, the paper was closed down.

Publication was not resumed until after the February Revolution. Beginning from 5 (18) March 1917, *Pravda* appeared as the Central Organ of the RSDLP Lenin joined the editorial board on 5 (18) April, on his return from abroad, and took over the paper's management. In July–October 1917, *Pravda* changed its name frequently owing to persecution by the Provisional Government, appearing successively as *Listok Pravdy*, *Proletary*, *Rabochy*, and *Rabochy Put*. On 27 (9 November) October the newspaper began to appear under its old name – *Pravda*.

3   See this volume, pp. 28–34.
4   *Zeit* (*Time*) – a weekly organ of the Bund, published in Yiddish in St. Petersburg from 20 December 1912 (2 January 1913) to 5 (18) May 1914.
5   *Dzvin* (*The Bell*) – a monthly legal nationalist journal of Menshevik trend, published in the Ukrainian language in Kiev from January 1913 to the middle of 1914.
6   *Pale of Settlement* – districts in tsarist Russia where Jews were permitted permanent residence.
7   *Numerus clausus* – the numerical restriction imposed in tsarist Russia on admission of Jews to the state secondary and higher educational establishments, to employment at factories and offices, and the professions.
8   *JSLP* (Jewish Socialist Labour Party) – a petty-bourgeois nationalist organisation, founded in 1906. Its programme was based on the demand for national autonomy for the Jews – the creation of extra-territorial Jewish parliaments authorised to settle questions concerning the political organisation of Jews in Russia. The JSLP stood close to the Socialist-Revolutionaries, with whom it waged a struggle against the RSDLP.
9   *The Beilis case* – a provocative trial engineered by the tsarist government in 1913 in Kiev. Beilis, a Jew, was falsely accused of having murdered a Christian boy named Yushchinsky for ritual purposes (actually, the murder was organised by the Black Hundreds). The aim of this frame-up was to fan anti-Semitism and incite pogroms so as to divert the masses from the mounting revolutionary movement. The trial excited great public feeling. Workers' protest demonstrations were held in a number of cities. Beilis was acquitted.
10 That the Bundists often vehemently deny that *all* the Jewish bourgeois parties have accepted 'cultural-national autonomy' is understandable. This fact only too glaringly exposes the actual role being played by the Bund. When Mr. Manin, a Bundist, tried, in *Luch* to repeat his denial, he

was fully exposed by N. Skop (see *Prosveshcheniye* No. 3). But when Mr. Lev Yurkevich, in *Dzvin* (1913, Nos. 7–8, p. 92), quotes from *Prosveshcheniye* (No. 3, p. 78) N. Sk's statement that 'the Bundists together with all the Jewish bourgeois parties and groups have long been advocating cultural-national autonomy' and *distorts* this statement by *dropping* the word 'Bundists', and *substituting* the words 'national rights' for the words 'cultural national autonomy', one can only raise one's hands in amazement! Mr. Lev Yurkevich is not only a nationalist, not only an astonishing ignoramus in matters concerning the history of the Social-Democrats and their programme, but a *downright falsifier of quotations* for the benefit of the Bund. The affairs of the Bund and the Yurkeviches must be in a bad way indeed! – *Lenin*

11   *Bernsteinism* – an anti-Marxist trend in international Social-Democracy. It arose towards the close of the nineteenth century in Germany and bore the name of the German opportunist Social-Democrat Eduard Bernstein. After the death of F. Engels, Bernstein publicly advocated revision of Marx's revolutionary theory in the spirit of bourgeois liberalism (see his article 'Problems of Socialism' and his book *The Premises of Socialism and the Tasks of Social-Democracy*) in an attempt to convert the Social-Democratic Party into a petty-bourgeois party of social reforms. In Russia, this trend was represented by the 'legal Marxists', the Economists, the Bundists and the Mensheviks.

12   Lenin refers to Stalin's article 'Marxism and the National Question' published in the legal Bolshevik journal *Prosveshcheniye*, Nos. 3, 4 and 5 for 1913 under the title 'The National Question and Social-Democracy'. Chapter 4 of Stalin's article quotes the text of the national programme adopted at the Brünn Congress of the Austrian Social-Democratic Party.

13   *Novaya Rabochaya Gazeta* (*New Workers' Paper*) – a legal daily of the Menshevik liquidators, published in St. Petersburg from August 1913. From 30 January (12 February) 1914 it was superceded by *Severnaya Rabochaya Gazeta* (*Northern Workers' Paper*) and subsequently by *Nasha Rabochaya Gazeta* (*Our Workers' Paper*). Lenin repeatedly referred to this newspaper as the *Novaya Likvidatorskaya Gazeta* (*New Liquidationist Paper*).

14   See René Henry: *La Suisse et la question des langues*, Berne, 1907. – *Lenin*

15   See Ed. Blocher: *Die Nationalitäten in der Schweiz*, Berlin, 1910. – *Lenin*

16   Lenin obtained these figures from the statistical handbook *One-Day Census of Elementary Schools in the Empire, Made on 18 January 1911. Issue I, Part 2, St. Petersburg Educational Area. Gubernias of Archangel, Vologda, Novgorod, Olonets, Pskov and St. Petersburg*. St. Petersburg, 1912, p. 72.

17   See p. 58 of this volume.

18   *Dragomanov, M. P.* (1841–1895) – Ukrainian historian, ethnographer and publicist. Exponent of Ukrainian bourgeois national-liberalism.

19   *Przegląd Socjaldemokratyczny* (*Social-Democratic Review*) – a journal published by the Polish Social-Democrats in close co-operation with Rosa

Luxemburg in Kraków from 1902 to 1904 and from 1908 to 1910. – *Lenin*

20   In elaborating her ideas Rosa Luxemburg goes into details, mentioning, for example – and quite rightly – divorce laws (No. 12, p. 162 of the above-mentioned journal). – *Lenin*

21   V. Medem: 'A Contribution to the Presentation of the National Question in Russia', *Vestnik Yevropy* (*Vestnik Yevropy* (*European Messenger*) – a monthly historico-political end literary magazine of a bourgeois-liberal trend. Appeared in St. Petersburg from 1866 to 1918. The magazine published articles against the revolutionary Marxists), 1912, Nos. 8 and 9. – *Lenin*

22   Interpolations in square brackets (within passages quoted by Lenin) are by Lenin, unless otherwise indicated.

23   Lenin is referring to an article he was planning on 'The Right of Nations to Self-Determination'. The article was written in February–May 1914 and published in April–June in the journal *Prosveshcheniye* Nos. 4, 5 and 6.

The Right of Nations to Self-Determination (1914)

1   *Die Neue Zeit* – theoretical journal of the German Social-Democratic Party, published in Stuttgart from 1883 to 1923. It was edited by K. Kautsky until October 1917, and then by H. Cunow. Some the writings of the founders of Marxism were first published in this journal, among them K. Marx's *Critique of the Gotha Programme* and Engels's 'Criticism of the Draft Social-Democratic Programme of 1891'. Engels often gave pointers to the editors of *Die Neue Zeit* and criticised their deviations from Marxism. Other prominent leaders of the German and international labour movement who contributed to the journal at the end of the nineteenth and beginning of the twentieth centuries were A. Bebel, W. Liebknecht, R. Luxemburg, F. Mehring, Clara Zetkin, G. V. Plekhanov and P. Lafargue. Beginning in the late 1890s, after the death of Engels, the journal regularly published articles by revisionists, including a series of articles by E. Bernstein titled 'Problems of Socialism', which launched a revisionists' campaign against Marxism. During World War I the journal took a centrist stand and supported the social-chauvinists.

2   *Nauchnaya Mysl* (*Scientific Thought*) – a journal of a Menshevik trend, published in Riga in 1908.

3   See Karl Marx, *Capital*, Vol. I, Moscow, 1959, pp. 765, 399.

4   A certain L. Vl. [L. Vladimirov (pseudonym of M. K. Sheinfinkel) – a Social-Democrat] in Paris considers this word un-Marxist. This L. Vl. is amusingly '*superklug*' (too clever by half). And 'this too-clever-by-half' L. Vl. apparently intends to write an essay on the deletion of the words 'population', 'nation', etc., from our minimum programme (having in mind the class struggle!). – *Lenin*

5   This refers to the *Second All-Ukraine Students' Congress* held in Lvov on

19–22 June (2–5 July) 1913, to coincide with anniversary celebrations in honour of Ivan Franko, the great Ukrainian writer, scholar, public figure, and revolutionary democrat. A report 'The Ukrainian Youth and the Present Status of the Nations' was made at the Congress by the Ukrainian Social-Democrat Dontsov, who supported the slogan of an 'independent' Ukraine.

6   *Shlyakhi (Paths)* – organ of the Ukrainian Students' Union (nationalistic trend), published in Lvov from April 1913 to March 1914.

7   Lenin is quoting from Griboyedov's comedy *Woe from Wit*.

8   *Naprzod* (Forward) – central organ of the Social-Democratic Party of Galicia and Silesia, published in Kraków beginning in 1892. The newspaper, which was a vehicle of petty-bourgeois nationalist ideas, was described by Lenin as 'a very bad, and not at all Marxist organ'.

9   Since the majority of the Norwegian nation was in favour of a monarchy while the proletariat wanted a republic, the Norwegian proletariat was, generally speaking, confronted with the alternative: either revolution, if conditions were ripe for it, or submission to the will of the majority and prolonged propaganda and agitation work. – *Lenin*

10   See the official German report of the London Congress: *Verhandlungen und Beschlüsse des internationalen sozialistischen Arbeiterund Gewerkschafts-Kongresses zu London, vom 27. Juli bis 1. August 1896*, Berlin, 1896, S. 18. A Russian pamphlet has been published containing the decisions of international congresses in which the word 'self-determination' is wrongly translated as 'autonomy'. – *Lenin*

11   This refers to the abolition of serfdom in Russia in 1861.

12   It would be a very interesting piece of historical research to compare the position of a noble Polish rebel in 1863 with that of the all-Russia revolutionary democrat, Chernyshevsky, who (like Marx), was able to appreciate the importance of the Polish movement, and with that of the Ukrainian petty bourgeois Dragomanov, who appeared much later and expressed the views of a peasant, so ignorant and sluggish, and so attached to his dung heap, that his legitimate hatred of the Polish gentry blinded him to the significance which their struggle had for all-Russia democracy. (Cf. Dragomanov, *Historical Poland and Great-Russian Democracy*.) Dragomanov richly deserved the fervent kisses which were subsequently bestowed on him by Mr. P. B. Struve, who by that time had become a national-liberal. – *Lenin*

13   Lenin is referring to the Polish national liberation insurrection of 1863–4 against the yoke of the tsarist autocracy. The original cause of the rising was the tsarist government's decision to carry out a special recruitment aimed at removing the revolutionary-minded youth *en masse* from the cities. At first the rising was led by a Central National Committee formed by the petty-nobles' party of the 'Reds' in 1862. Its programme demanding national independence for Poland, equal rights for all men in the land,

irrespective of religion or birth, transfer to the peasants of the land tilled by them with full right of ownership and without redemption payments, abolition of the corvée, compensation for the landlords for the alienated lands out of the state funds, etc., attracted to the uprising diverse sections of the Polish population – artisans, workers, students, intellectuals from among the gentry, part of the peasantry and the clergy.

In the course of the insurrection, elements united around the party of the 'Whites' (the party of the big, landed aristocracy and the big bourgeoisie) joined it with the intention of using it in their own interests and, with the help of Britain and France, securing a profitable deal with the tsarist government.

The attitude of the revolutionary democrats of Russia towards the rebels was one of deep sympathy, the members of *Zemlya i Volya* secret society associated with N. G. Chernyshevsky trying to give them every possible assistance. The Central Committee of *Zemlya i Volya* issued an appeal 'To the Russian Officers and Soldiers', which was distributed among the troops sent to suppress the insurrection. A. I. Herzen and N. P. Ogaryov published a number of articles in *Kolokol* devoted to the struggle of the Polish people, and rendered material aid to the rebels.

Owing to the inconsistency of the party of the 'Reds', which failed to hold the revolutionary initiative, the leadership of the uprising passed into the hands of the 'Whites', who betrayed it. By the summer of 1864, the insurrection was brutally crushed by the tsarist troops.

Marx and Engels, who regarded the Polish insurrection of 1863–4 as a progressive movement, were fully in sympathy with it and wished the Polish people victory in its struggle for national liberation. On behalf of the German emigrant colony in London, Marx wrote an appeal for aid to the Poles.

14 Lenin refers to W. Liebknecht's reminiscences of Marx. (See the symposium *Reminiscences of Marx and Engels*, Moscow, 1957, p. 98.)

15 See Marx's letter to Engels dated 5 July 1870.

16 Cf. also Marx's letter to Engels of 3 June 1867: '... I have learned with real pleasure from the Paris letters to *The Times* about the pro-Polish exclamations of the Parisians against Russia ... Mr. Proudhon and his little doctrinaire clique are not the French people.' – *Lenin*

17 *The New York Daily Tribune* – an American newspaper published from 1841 to 1924. Until the mid-1850s it was the organ of the left wing of the American Whigs, and thereafter the organ of the Republican Party. Karl Marx contributed to the paper from August 1851 to March 1862, and at his request Friedrich Engels wrote numerous articles for it. During the period of reaction that set in in Europe, Karl Marx and Friedrich Engels used this widely circulated and at that time progressive newspaper to publish concrete material exposing the evils of capitalist society. During the American Civil War, Marx's contributions to the newspaper stopped.

His break with *The New York Daily Tribune* was largely due to the growing influence on the editorial board of the advocates of compromise with the slam-owners, and the paper's departure from progressive positions. Eventually the newspaper swung still more to the right.

18 By the way, it is not difficult to see why, from a Social-Democratic point of view, the right to 'self-determination' means *neither* federation *nor* autonomy (although, speaking in the abstract, both come under the category of 'self-determination'). The right to federation is simply meaningless, since federation implies a bilateral contract. It goes without saying that Marxists cannot include the defence of federalism in general in their programme. As far as autonomy is concerned, Marxists defend, not the 'right' to autonomy, but autonomy itself, as a general universal principle of a democratic state with a mixed national composition, and a great variety of geographical and other conditions. Consequently, the recognition of the 'right of nations to autonomy' is as absurd as that of the 'right of nations to federation'.
    – *Lenin*

19 Lenin is quoting from G. V. Plekhanov's article 'The Draft Programme of the Russian Social-Democratic Party' published in *Zarya* No. 4, 1902.

    Zarya – a Marxist scientific and political journal published legally in Stuttgart in 1901–02 by the Editorial Board of *Iskra*. Altogether four numbers (three issues) of *Zarya* appeared: No. 1 in April 1901 (actually on 23 March, new style); No. 2–3 in December 1901, and No. 4 in August 1902. The aims of the publication were set forth in the 'Draft of a Declaration of the Editorial Board of *Iskra* and *Zarya*' written by Lenin in Russia. (In 1902, during the disagreement and conflicts that arose on the Editorial Board of *Iskra* and *Zarya*, Plekhanov proposed a plan for separating the newspaper from the journal (with *Zarya* remaining under his editorship), but this proposal was not accepted, and the two publications continued under a single editorial board.

    Zarya criticised international and Russian revisionism, and defended the theoretical principles of Marxism. The following articles by Lenin were published in this journal: = 'Casual Notes', 'The Persecutors of the Zemstvo and the Hannibals of Liberalism', 'The 'Critics' on the Agrarian Question' (the first four chapters of 'The Agrarian Question and the "Critics of Marx"'), 'Review of Home Affairs', and 'The Agrarian Programme of Russian Social-Democracy', as well as Plekhanov's articles 'Criticism of Our Critics. Part I. Mr. P. Struve in the Role of Critic of the Marxian Theory of Social Development', 'Cant versus Kant, or the Testament of Mr. Bernstein' and others.

20 We are informed that the Polish Marxists attended the Summer Conference of the Russian Marxists in 1913 with only a consultative voice and did not vote at all on the right to self-determination (secession), declaring their opposition to this right in general. Of course, they had a perfect right to act the way they did, and, as hitherto, to agitate in Poland against secession.

But this is not quite what Trotsky said; for the Polish Marxists did not demand the 'deletion' of § 9 'from the programme'. – *Lenin*

21   A quotation from the sketch 'Abroad' by the Russian satirist Saltykov-Shchedrin.

22   Lenin quotes an expression from *Seminary Sketches* by the Russian writer N. G. Pomyalovsky.

23   See particularly Mr. Yurkevich's preface to Mr. Levinsky's book (written in Ukrainian) *Outline of the Development of the Ukrainian Working-Class Movement in Galicia*, Kiev, 1914. – *Lenin*

24   Lenin quotes the words of a Sevastopol soldiers' song written by Leo Tolstoy. The song is about the unsuccessful operation of the Russian troops at the river Chornaya on 4 August 1855, during the Crimean War. In that action General Read commanded two divisions.

25   It is not difficult to understand that the recognition by the Marxists of the whole of Russia, and first and foremost by the Great Russians, of the right of nations to secede in no way precludes agitation against secession by Marxists of a particular oppressed nation, just as the recognition of the right to divorce does not preclude agitation against divorce in a particular case. We think, therefore, that there will, be an inevitable increase in the number of Polish Marxists who laugh at the non-existent 'contradiction' now being 'encouraged' by Semkovsky and Trotsky. – *Lenin*

26   It would be interesting to trace the changes that take place in Polish nationalism, for example, in the process of its transformation from gentry nationalism into bourgeois nationalism, and then into peasant nationalism. In his book *Das polnische Gemeinwesen im preussischen Staat* (The Polish Community in the Prussian State; there is a Russian translation), Ludwig Bernhard, who shares the view of a German Kokoshkin, describes a very typical phenomenon: the formation of a sort of 'peasant republic' by the Poles in Germany in the form of a close alliance of the various co-operatives and other associations of Polish peasants in their struggle for nationality, religion, and 'Polish' land. German oppression has welded the Poles together and segregated them, after first awakening the nationalism of the gentry, then of the bourgeoisie, and finally of the peasant masses (especially after the campaign the Germans launched in 1873 against the use of the Polish language in schools). Things are moving in the same direction in Russia, and not only with regard to Poland. – *Lenin*

The Revolutionary Proletariat and the Right of Nations to Self-Determination (1915)

1   Written in German not earlier than 16 (29) October 16 1915. First published in 1927 in *Lenin Miscellany VI*. Published according to the translation from the German made by N. K. Krupskaya, with corrections by V. I.

Lenin. Source: *Lenin Collected Works*, Progress Publishers [1974], Moscow, Volume 21, pp. 407–14.

2   Parabellum – K. Radek.

3   See Marx's letters to Engels of 7 and 20 June 1866 and of 2 November 1867.

4   'Comprehensively[!] and unreservedly[?] respecting and demanding the independence of nations'. – *Lenin*

5   The Executive of the German Social-Democratic Party. – *Lenin*

Imperialism, the Highest Stage of Capitalism: A Popular Outline (1916)

1   This Manifesto is not given as an appendix to this edition. Manifesto can be found here: marxists.org/history/international/social-democracy/1912/basel-manifesto.

2   Figures taken from *Annalen des deutschen Reichs*, 1911, Zahn. – *Lenin*

3   Statistical Abstract of the United States, 1912, p. 202. – *Lenin*

4   *Finance Capital*, Russ. ed., pp. 286–7. – *Lenin*

5   Hans Gideon Heymann, *Die gemischten Werke im deutschen Grosseiseu-gewerbe*, Stuttgart, 1904, (§ 256, 278). – *Lenin*

6   Hermann Levy, *Monopole, Kartelle und Trusts*, Jena, 1909, § 286, 290. – *Lenin*

7   Th. Vogelstein, 'Die finanzielle Organisation der kapitalistischen Industrie und die Monopolbildungen' in *Grundriss der Sozialökonomik*, VI. Abt., Tubingen, 1914. Cf., also by the same author: *Organisationsformen der Eisenindustrie und Textilindustrie in England und Amerika*, Bd. 1, Lpz., 1910. – *Lenin*

8   Dr. Riesser, *Die deutschen Grossbanken und ihre Konzentration im Zusam-menhange mit der Entwicklung der Gesamtwirtschaft in Deutschland*, 4. Aufl., 1912, § 149; Robert Liefmann, *Kartelle und Trusts und die Weiter-bildung der volkswirtschaftlichen Organisation*, 2. Aufl., 1910, § 25. – *Lenin*

9   Dr. Fritz Kestner, *Der Organisationszwang. Eine Untersuchung über die Kämpfe zwischen Kartellen und Aussenseitern*, Berlin, 1912, § 11. – *Lenin*

10 R. Liefmann, *Beteiligungs- und Finanzierungsgesellschaften. Eine Studie über den modernen Kapitalismus und das Effektenwesen*, 1. Aufl., Jena, 1909, § 212, 218. – *Lenin*

11 Dr. S. Tschierschky, *Kartell und Trust*, Göttingen, 1903, § 13. – *Lenin*

12 Tr. Vogelstein, *Organisationsformen*, § 275. – *Lenin*

13 Report of the Commissioner of Corporations on the Tobacco Industry, Washington, 1909, p. 266, cited according to Dr. Paul Tafel, *Die nordamer-ikanischen Trusts und ihre Wirkungen auf den Fortschritt der Technik*, Stuttgart, 1913, § 48, 49. – *Lenin*

14 Riesser, op. cit., third edition, p. 547 et seq. The newspapers (June 1916) report the formation of a new gigantic trust which combines the chemical industry of Germany. – *Lenin*

15   Kestner, op. cit., § 254. – *Lenin*

16   L. Eschwege, 'Zement' in *Die Bank*, 1909, § 115 et. seq. – *Lenin*

17   Jeidels, *Das Verhältnis der deutschen Grossbanken zur Industrie mit besonderer Berüchsichtigung der Eisenindustrie*, Leipzig, 1905, § 271. – *Lenin*

18   Liefmann, *Beteiligungs- und Finanzierungsgesellschaften*, § 434. – *Lenin*

19   Ibid., § 465–66. – *Lenin*

20   Jeidels, op. cit., § 108. – *Lenin*

21   Alfred Lansburgh, 'Fünf Jahre deutsches Bankwesen' in *Die Bank*, 1913, No. 8. – *Lenin*

22   Schulze-Gaevernitz, 'Die deutsche Kreditbank' in *Grundriss der Sozialökonomik*, Tübingen, 1915, p. 137. – *Lenin*

23   R. Liefmann, *Beteilgungs- und Finanzierungsgesellschaften. Eine Studie über den modernen Kapitalismus und das Effektenwesen*, I., Jena, 1909, p. 212. – *Lenin*

24   Alfred Lansburgh, 'Das Beteilgungssystem im deutschen Bankwesen', in *Die Bank*, 1910, p. 500. – *Lenin*

25   Eugen Kaufmann, *Das französische Bankwesen*, Tübingen, 1911, pp. 356 and 362. – *Lenin*

26   Jean Lescure, *L'épargne en France*, Paris, 1914, p. 52. – *Lenin*

27   A. Lansburgh, '*Die Bank* mit den 300 Millionen' in *Die Bank*, 1914, p. 426. – *Lenin*

28   S. Tschierschky, op. cit., p. 128. – *Lenin*

29   Karl Marx, *Capital*, Vol. III, Moscow, 1959, p. 593.

30   Statistics of the National Monetary Commission, quoted in *Die Bank*, 1910, § 1200. – *Lenin*

31   *Die Bank*, 1913, § 811. – *Lenin*

32   *Die Bank*, 1914, § 316. – *Lenin*

33   Dr. Oscar Stillich, *Geld- und Bankwesen*, Berlin, 1907, § 169. – *Lenin*

34   These occurred during the widespread establishment of jointstock companies in the early seventies, which was accompanied by all manner of fraudulent operations by bourgeois businessmen, who were making a great deal of money, and by wild speculation in real estate and securities.

35   Schulze-Gaevernitz, 'Die deutsche Kreditbank' in *Grundriss der Sozialökonomik*, Tübingen, 1915, § 101. – *Lenin*

36   Riesser, op. cit., 4th ed., § 629. – *Lenin*

37   Schulze-Gaevernitz, 'Die deutsche Kreditbank' in *Grundriss der Sozialökonomik*, Tübingen, 1915, § 151. – *Lenin*

38   *Die Bank*, 1912, § 435. – *Lenin*

39   *Frankfurter Zeitung* (Frankfort Newspaper) – a German bourgeois newspaper published in Frankfort-on-Main from 1856.

40   Quoted by Schulze-Gaevernitz, op. cit., § 155. – *Lenin*

41   Jeidels, op. cit.; Riesser, op. cit. – *Lenin*

42   Jeidels, op. cit., § 156–7. – *Lenin*

43   An article by Eug. Kaufmann on French banks in *Die Bank*, 1909, 2, § 851 et. seq. – *Lenin*

44   Dr. Oscar Stillich, *Geld- und Bankwesen*, Berlin, 1907, § 147. – *Lenin*
45   Jeidels, op. cit., § 183–4. – *Lenin*
46   Ibid., § 181. – *Lenin*
47   R. Hilferding, *Finance Capital*, Moscow, 1912 (in Russian), pp. 338–9. – *Lenin*
48   R. Liefmann, op. cit., § 476. – *Lenin*
49   Hans Gideon Heymann, *Die gemischten Werke im deutschen Grosseisen-gewerbe*, Stuttgart, 1904, § 268–9. – *Lenin*
50   Liefmann, *Beteiligungsgesellschaften*, etc., § 258 of the first edition. – *Lenin*
51   Schulze-Gaevernitz in *Grundriss der Sozialökonomik*, V, 2, § 110. – *Lenin*
52   G. V. Plekhanov.
53   L. Eschwege, 'Tochtergesellschaften' in *Die Bank*, 1914, § 545. – *Lenin*
54   Kurt Heinig, 'Der Weg des Elecktrotrusts' in *Die Neue Zeit*, 1912, 30. § 484. – *Lenin*
55   E. Agahd, *Grossbanken und Weltmarkt. Die wirstschaftliche und politische Bedeutung der Grossbanken im Weltmarkt unter Berüchsichtigung ihres Einflusses auf Russlands Volkswirtscahft und die deutsche-russichen Bezie-hungen*, Berlin, 1914. – *Lenin*
56   *Produgol* – an abbreviation for the Russian Society for Trade in Mineral Fuel of the Donets Basin, founded in 1906. *Prodamet* – Society for Marketing Russian Metallurgical Goods.
57   Lysis, *Contre l'oligarchie financière en France*, 5 ed. Paris, 1908, pp. 11, 12, 26, 39, 40, 48. – *Lenin*
58   *Die Bank*, 1913, No. 7, § 630. – *Lenin*
59   Stillich, op. cit., § 143, also W. Sombart, *Die deutsche Volkswirtschaft im 19. jahrhundert*, 2. Aufl., 1909, § 526, Anlage 8. – *Lenin*
60   *Finance Capital*, p. 172. – *Lenin*
61   Stillich, op. cit., § 138 and Liefmann, op. cit., § 51. – *Lenin*
62   In *Die Bank*, 1913, § 952, L. Eschwege, *Der Sumpf*, Ibid., 1912, 1, § 223 et seq. – *Lenin*
63   'Verkehrstrust' in *Die Bank*, 1914, 1, § 89. – *Lenin*
64   The exposure in France in 1892–93 of incredible abuses, corruption of politicians, officials and the press bribed by the French Panama Canal company.
65   'Der Zug zur Bank' in *Die Bank*, 1909, 1, § 79. – *Lenin*
66   Ibid., § 301. – *Lenin*
67   Ibid., 1911, 2, § 825; 1913, 2, § 962. – *Lenin*
68   E. Agahd, op. cit., § 202. – *Lenin*
69   Bulletin de l'institut international de statistique, t. XIX, livr. II, La Haye, 1912. Data concerning small states, second column, are estimated by adding 20 per cent to the 1902 figures. – *Lenin*
70   Hobson, *Imperialism*, London, 1902, p. 58; Riesser, op. cit., § 395 and 404; P. Arndt in *Weltwirtschaftliches Archiv*, Bd. 7, 1916, § 35; Neymarck in *Bulletin*; Hilferding, *Finance Capital*, p. 492; Lloyd George, Speech in the House of Commons, May 4, 1915. Reported in the *Daily Telegraph*, 5 May 1915; B. Harms, *Probleme der Weltwirtschaft*, Jena, 1912, § 235 et seq.;

Dr. Siegmund Schilder, *Entwicklungstendenzen der Weltwirtschaft*, Berlin, 1912, Band 1, § 150; George Paish, 'Great Britain's Capital Investments, etc.', in *Journal of the Royal Statistical Society*, Vol. LXXIV, 1910–11, p. 167 et seq.; Georges Diouritch, *L'Expansion des banques allemandes a l'ètranger, ses rapports avec le développement économique de l'Allemagne*, Paris, 1909, p. 84. – *Lenin*

71 *Die Bank*, 1913, 2, § 1024–5. – *Lenin*

72 Schilder, op. cit., § 346, 350, 371. – *Lenin*

73 Riesser, op. cit., 4th ed., § 375; Diouritch, p. 283. – *Lenin*

74 *The Annals of the American Academy of Political and Social Science*, Vol. LIX, May 1915, p. 301. In the same volume on p. 331, we read that the well-known statistician Paish, in the last issue of the financial magazine *The Statist*, estimated the amount of capital exported by Britain, Germany, France, Belgium and Holland at $40,000 million, i.e., 200,000 million francs. – *Lenin*

75 Jeidels, op. cit., § 232. – *Lenin*

76 Riesser, op. cit.; Diouritch, op. cit., p. 239; Kurt Heinig, op. cit. – *Lenin*

77 Jeidels, op. cit., § 192–3. – *Lenin*

78 Diouritch, op. cit., pp. 245–46. – *Lenin*

79 *Die Bank*, 1912, 1, § 1036; 1912, 2, § 629; 1913, 1, § 388. – *Lenin*

80 Riesser, op. cit., § 125. – *Lenin*

81 Vogelstein, *Organisationsformen*, § 100. – *Lenin*

82 Liefmann, *Kartelle und Trusts*, 2. A., § 161. – *Lenin*

83 A. Supan, *Die territoriale Entwicklung der europäischen Kolonien*, 1906, § 254. – *Lenin*

84 Henry C. Morris, *The History of Colonisation*, New York, 1900, Vol. II, p. 88; Vol. 1, p. 419; Vol. 11, p. 304. – *Lenin*

85 *Die Neue Zeit*, XVI, 1, 1898, § 302. – *Lenin*

86 Ibid., § 304. – *Lenin*

87 C. P. Lucas, *Greater Rome and Greater Britain*, Oxford, 1912, or the Earl of Cromer's *Ancient and Modern Imperialism*, London, 1910. – *Lenin*

88 Schilder, op. cit., § 38–42. – *Lenin*

89 See p. 186 of this volume.

90 Wahl, *La France aux colonies* quoted by Henri Russier, *Le Partage de l'Océanie*, Paris, 1905, p. 165. – *Lenin*

91 Schulze-Gaevernitz, *Britischer Imperialismus und englischer Freihandel zu Beginn des 20-ten Jahrhunderts*, Leipzig, 1906, § 318. Sartorius v. Waltershausen says the same in *Das volkswirtschaftliche System der Kapitalanlage im Auslande*, Berlin, 1907, § 46. – *Lenin*

92 Schilder, op. cit., Vol. I, § 160–61. – *Lenin*

93 J. E. Driault, *Problèmes politiques et sociaux*, Paris, 1900, p. 299. – *Lenin*

94 *Die Neue Zeit*, 1914, 2 (B. 32), § 909, 11 Sept., 1914; cf. 1915, 2, § 107 et seq. – *Lenin*

95 Hobson, *Imperialism*, London, 1902, p. 324. – *Lenin*

96 *Die Neue Zeit*, 1914, 2 (B. 32), § 921, 11 Sept., 1914. Cf. 1915, 2, § 107 et seq. – *Lenin*

97 Ibid., 1915, 1, § 144, 30 April 1915. – *Lenin*

98 R. Calwer, *Einführung in die Weltwirtschaft*, Eerlin, 1906. – *Lenin*

99 *Statistisches Jahrbuch für das deutsche Reich*, 19⁻5; *Archiv für Eisenbahnwesen*, 1892. Minor details for the distribution of railways among the colonies of the various countries in 1890 had to be estimated approximately. – *Lenin*

100 Cf. also Edgar Crammond, 'The Economic Relations of the British and German Empires' in *The Journal of the Royal Statistical Society*, July 1914, p. 777 et seq. – *Lenin*

101 Hobson, op. cit., pp. 59, 62. – *Lenin*

102 Schulze-Gaevernitz, *Britischer Imperialismus*, § 320 et seq. – *Lenin*

103 Sartorius von Waltershausen, *Das volkswirtschaftliche System*, etc., Berlin, 1907, Buch IV. – *Lenin*

104 Schilder, op. cit., § 393. – *Lenin*

105 Schulze-Gaevernitz, op. cit., § 122. – *Lenin*

106 *Die Bank*, 1911, 1, § 10–11. – *Lenin*

107 Hobson, op. cit., pp. 103, 205, 144, 335, 386. – *Lenin*

108 Gerhard Hildebrand, *Die Erschütterung der Industrieherrschaft und des Industriesozialismus*, 1910, § 229 et seq. – *Lenin*

109 Schulze-Gaevernitz, *Britischer Imperialismus* § 301. – *Lenin*

110 *Statistik des Deutschen Reichs*, Bd. 211. – *Lenin*

111 Henger, *Die Kapitalsanlage der Franzosen*, Stuttgart, 1913. – *Lenin*

112 Hourwich, *Immigration and Labour*, New York, 1913. – *Lenin*

113 *Briefwechsel von Marx und Engels*, Bd. II, § 290; 1V, 433 – Karl Kautsky, *Sozialismus und Kolonialpolitik*, Berlin, 1907, § 79; this pamphlet was written by Kautsky in those infinitely distant days when he was still a Marxist. – *Lenin*

114 Russian social-chauvinism in its overt form, represented by the Potresovs, Chkenkelis, Maslovs, etc., and its covert form (Chkeidze, Skobelev, Axelrod, Martov, etc.) also emerged from the Russian variety of opportunism, namely, liquidationism. – *Lenin*

115 *Weltwirtschaffliches Archiv*, Bd. II, § 193. – *Lenin*

116 J. Patouillet, *L'impérialisme américain*, Dijon, 1904, p. 272. – *Lenin*

117 *Bulletin de l'Institut International de Statistique*, T. XIX, Lvr. II, p. 225. – *Lenin*

118 Kautsky, *Nationalstaat, imperialistischer Staat und Staatenbund*, Nürnberg, 1915, § 72, 70. – *Lenin*

119 *Finance Capital*, p. 567. – *Lenin*

120 Karl Marx, *Capital*, Vol. III, Moscow, 1959, pp. 117–18.

121 *Die Bank*, 1909, 2, § 819 et seq. – *Lenin*

122 *Die Neue Zeit*, 30 April 1915, § 144. – *Lenin*

123 David Jayne Hill, *History of the Diplomacy in the International Development of Europe*, Vol. I, p. X. – *Lenin*

124   Schilder, op. cit., § 178. – *Lenin*
125   *Finance Capital*, p. 487. – *Lenin*
126   *Grundriss der Sozialökonomik*, § 146. – *Lenin*

The Discussion on Self-Determination Summed Up (1916)

1   Written in July 1916. Published in October 1916 in *Sbornik Sotsial-Demokrata*, No. 1. Signed: *N. Lenin*. Published according to the *Sbornik* text. Source: *Lenin Collected Works*, Moscow, Volume 22, pp. 320–60.
2   See 'The Socialist Revolution and the Rights of Nations to Self Determination'. – *Lenin*
3   The theses were compiled by the Editorial Board of *Gazeta Robotnicza and published in Sbornik Sotsial-Demokrata* No. 1 in October 1916.
4   For an assessment of the three views on Poland's independence, see 'The Right of Nations to Self-Determination', p. 58 of this volume.
5   The 1903 discussion on the R.S.D.L.P. draft Programme, later adopted at the Party's Second Congress, and the 1913 discussion on cultural and national autonomy between the Bolsheviks on the one hand, and, the liquidators, 'Trotskyites', and Bundists on the other.
6   Marx and Engels, *Selected Works*, Vol. II, Moscow, 1955, pp. 32–3.
7   See pamphlet by Engels, *Po und Rhein*, Section IV, M/E/L, Zur deutschen Geschichte, Bd. II, 1, § 689 (no English translation available).
8   Karl Radek formulated this as 'against old and new annexations' in one of his articles in *Berner Tagwacht*. – *Lenin*
9   See 'The War and Russian Social-Democracy', 'The Conference of the RSDLP Groups Abroad' – Volume 21 of the *Collected Works*. – *Lenin*
10   Friedrich Engels, 'Der demokratische Panslawismus', in *Neue Rheinische Zeitung* Nos. 222 and 223, 15 and 16 February 1849 (no English translation available).
11   Ryazanov has published in Grunberg's *Archives of the History of Socialism* (1916, I) a very interesting article by Engels on the Polish question, written in 1866. Engels emphasises that the proletariat must recognise the political independence and 'self-determination' ('right to dispose itself' [These words are in English in the original.]) of the great, major nations of Europe, and points to the absurdity of the 'principle of nationalities' (particularly in its Bonapartist application), i.e., of placing any small nation on the same level as these big ones 'And as is to Russia,' says Engels, 'she could only be mentioned as the detainer of an immense amount of stolen property [i.e., oppressed nations] which would have been disgorged on the day of reckoning.' [27] Both Bonapartism and tsarism utilise the small-nation movements for their own benefit, against European democracy. – *Lenin*
12   Let us recall that all the Polish Social-Democrats recognised self-determination in general in their Zimmerwald declaration, although their formulation was slightly different. – *Lenin*

13 Left Radical monthly prohibited by the Prussian censor, edited by J. Borchardt – 5 December 1915, Third Year of Publication, No. 3.

14 Rosa Luxemburg's article, 'The National Question and Autonomy', in Nos. 6, 7, 8–9, 10, 12 and 14–15 of the magazine *Przeglad Socjaldemokratyczny* (Social-Democratic Review) for 1908 and 1909.

15 The Right wing of the Polish Socialist Party, a petty-bourgeois nationalist party founded in 1892.

16 Marx and Engels, *Selected Correspondence*, Moscow, 1955, p. 423.

17 *Rech* (Speech) – a daily, the Central Organ of the Cadet Party published in Petersburg from February 1906; closed down by the Petrograd Soviet's Revolutionary Military Committee on 26 October (8 November) 1917; publication continued under another title until August 1918.

18 *Libre Belgique* (Free Belgium) – an illegal journal of the Belgian Labour Party, Brussels (1915–18).

Draft Theses on National and Colonial Questions for the Second Congress of the Communist International (1920)

1 Written: 5 June 1920. First Published: Published in June 1920; Published according to the manuscript and checked against the text of the proof-sheet, as amended by V. I. Lenin. Source: Lenin's *Collected Works*, 2nd English Edition, Progress Publishers: Moscow, 1965, Volume 31, pp. 144–51. Translated: Julius Katzer.

2 As a result of the revolution which commenced in Finland on 27 January 1918, the bourgeois government of Svinhufvud was overthrown and the working class assumed power. On 29 January, the revolutionary government of Finland, the Council of People's Representatives was formed by Edvard Gylling, Yrjö Sirola, Otto Kuusinen, A. Taimi and others. The following were among the most important measures taken by the workers' government: the law on the transfer to landless peasants, without indemnification, of the land they actually tilled; tax-exemption for the poorest sections of the population; the expropriation of enterprises whose owners had fled the country; the establishment of state control over private banks (their functions being assumed by the State Bank).

On 1 March 1918, a treaty between the Finnish Socialist Workers' Republic and the RSFSR was signed in Petrograd. Based on the principle of complete equality and respect for the sovereignty of the two sides, this was the first treaty in world history to be signed between two socialist countries.

The proletarian revolution, however, was victorious only in the south of Finland. The Svinhufvud government concentrated all counter-revolutionary forces in the north of the country, and appealed to the German Kaiser's government for help. As a result of German armed intervention, the Finnish revolution was put down in May 1918, after a desperate civil war. White terror reigned in the country, tens of thousands of revolutionary workers and peasants were executed or tortured to death in the prisons.

3   As a result of mass action by the Lettish proletariat and peasantry against the German invaders and the counter-revolutionary government of Ulmanis, a provisional Soviet government was established in Latvia on 17 December 1918, which issued a Manifesto on the assumption of state power by the Soviets. Soviet Russia gave fraternal help to the Lettish people in their struggle to establish Soviet rule and strengthen the Latvian Soviet Socialist Republic.

Under the leadership of the Latvian Communist Party and the Latvian Soviet Government, a Red Army was formed, the landed estates were confiscated, the banks and big commercial and industrial enterprises were nationalised, social insurance and an eight-hour working day were introduced, and a system of public catering for working people was organised.

In March 1919, German troops and the white guards, armed and equipped by the U.S. and the Entente imperialists, attacked Soviet Latvia. In May they captured Riga, the capital of Soviet Latvia. After fierce fighting the entire territory of Latvia had been overrun by the interventionists by the beginning of 1920. The counter-revolutionary bourgeoisie established a regime of bloody terror, thousands of revolutionary workers and peasants being killed or thrown into prison.

Memo Combatting Dominant Nation Chauvinism (1922)

1   Written: 6 October 1922. First Published: *Pravda* No. 21 on 21 January 1937; Published according to the manuscript. Source: Lenin's *Collected Works*, 2nd English Edition, Progress Publishers: Moscow, 1965, Volume 33, p. 372. Translated: David Skvirsky and George Hanna.

The Question of Nationalities or 'Autonomisation' (1922)

1   Stalin criticised the minority nations for not being 'internationalist' because they did want to unite with Russia. – *Lenin*